Plugin House

Plugin House

MODERN PRE-FAB ARCHITECTURE

PEOPLE'S ARCHITECTURE OFFICE

WITH 480 ILLUSTRATIONS

CONTENTS

INTRODUCTION

In computing, the term "plugin" refers to a component that adds new features to an existing program. Often, these are not created by the original author of the program, but rather its users and different, unsanctioned authors. Applied to architecture, it represents the act of plugging into found structural conditions within existing communities, by means of a pre-fabricated building system that can be mass-produced and customized. At the People's Architecture Office (PAO), we have been practicing plugin architecture for over a decade. In this book, we take a deep dive into our work and examine how this type of architectural intervention might go some way to addressing the global housing crisis.

PAO was founded in 2010 by James Shen, He Zhe and Zang Feng, as a multi-disciplinary art and design practice focused on work that fosters social interaction and diverse perspectives. PAO's plugin architecture is inspired by architectural concepts from the 1960s, most notably Archigram's Plug-in City, and embodies the desire for flexibility in what we build and how we practice as architects.

Through the exploration of our Plugin House projects, their unique contexts, and the personal stories surrounding them, we reveal insights into barriers to housing access and potential ways to overcome them. The book does not claim to provide a definitive solution to our housing problems, but rather represents an integral part of innovative efforts involving policymaking, financial tools, and public support.

The projects presented here, located primarily in cities in China and the US, vastly differ in their respective contexts, reflecting very specific conditions. Our aim, however, is to use our Plugin House projects to illustrate some fundamental and common issues underlying the global housing crisis, including accelerating economic inequality and social, geographic, and regulatory fragmentation.

We also hope to bridge the gap between two countries that are perceived today as polar opposites to find commonality in the housing crisis—a universal urban concern that transcends socio-political differences. Many of the Plugin House projects we show here are situated in disadvantaged communities, from Beijing's historic hutongs (narrow alleyways lined with courtyard houses) to homeless encampments in Austin, Texas. Presenting these disparate perspectives will clarify and highlight potentials and possibilities for better housing solutions across the world.

Plugin architecture has allowed us to cultivate our interest in engaging more directly with the people our work affects, and to focus on positive social impact. Through our Plugin House work we have ventured beyond the typical realm of architectural practice to work hands-on with building and manufacturing, embracing diverse perspectives from other disciplines, and diligently empathizing with individuals' unique circumstances.

PAO began as an experiment that questioned how architectural practice can have a positive social impact in today's neoliberal economy. Our experience working in places where change happens at breakneck speed has left us accustomed to relying on instinct. We have little time for processing and contemplation, only room for reaction. The journey of the Plugin House project is the result of being led by our curiosities rather than conscious planning. It is a story of trial and error, marked by questionable successes but considerable new insights. This compendium is a reflection on the experiences we have gathered, and has been created in the hope that our work can further contribute to improving the state of housing today.

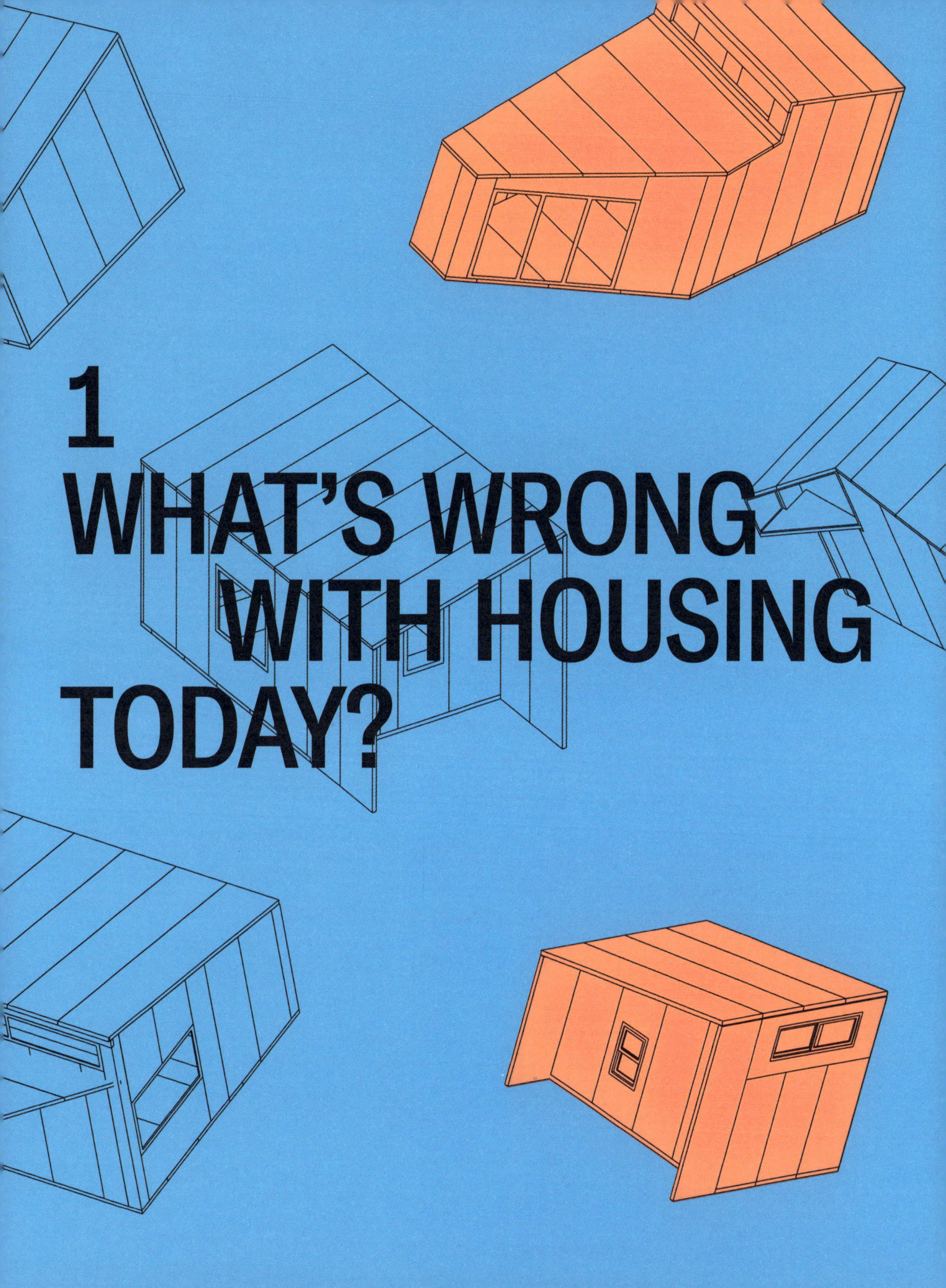

1 WHAT'S WRONG WITH HOUSING TODAY?

Plugin House in Yinlin village, Guangdong province for the Wang family, 2018.

Fundamentally, a house provides shelter and structure for daily life, and yet it embodies so much more than its physical form. It is a canvas of personal identity, reflecting individual tastes and values, and holds memories that connect the past with the present. There is also the social dimension of housing—a house is deeply embedded within communities. Beyond mere shelter, housing represents the concept of "home," a sanctuary of security and aspiration.

However, our perception of housing often overlooks its emotional and symbolic significance, focusing primarily on financial and structural aspects. We must recognize the multifaceted nature of housing, its practicalities and social and cultural dimensions, and the diverse traditions and values it represents to different societies. Unfortunately, while access to housing is a fundamental need at individual, community, national, and global levels, it remains unmet across each of these levels.

Whether housing is discussed from a personal, local, or global perspective, the crisis of housing affordability is interconnected. The high cost of housing is a pressing challenge and the availability of housing in desirable locations is equally significant. There aren't enough houses where people most want to live, and new housing developments often face intense resistance from existing communities.

On a local level, the housing crisis affects communities in numerous ways. Gentrification drives rising housing costs, displacing long-time residents and reshaping neighborhood dynamics. The inability to construct more housing within pre-existing communities escalates property prices, prompting lower-income households to relocate further from city centers. Low-density urban sprawl increases commuting distances and strains transportation infrastructure. The needs of people spread across vast distances strain limited local resources and can lead to underserved communities and food deserts. Furthermore, housing shortages hinder local economic growth by constraining business expansion and impeding workforce mobility.

At an individual level, the housing crisis manifests as challenges in securing an affordable and suitable place to live. Many struggle to pay rent or mortgages, leading to housing instability or even homelessness. This has profound effects on individuals and families, causing stress, insecurity, and physical and mental health issues. Through the personal experiences of PAO's three partners, we provide examples of the incredible change in housing access during our own lifetimes, all in very different contexts.

In the US, homeownership holds deep importance in the American identity [7]. It is seen as an indicator of one's ability to achieve upward mobility through hard work—a core

SHEN FAMILY HOMES AND USAGE OF SPACE OVER TIME

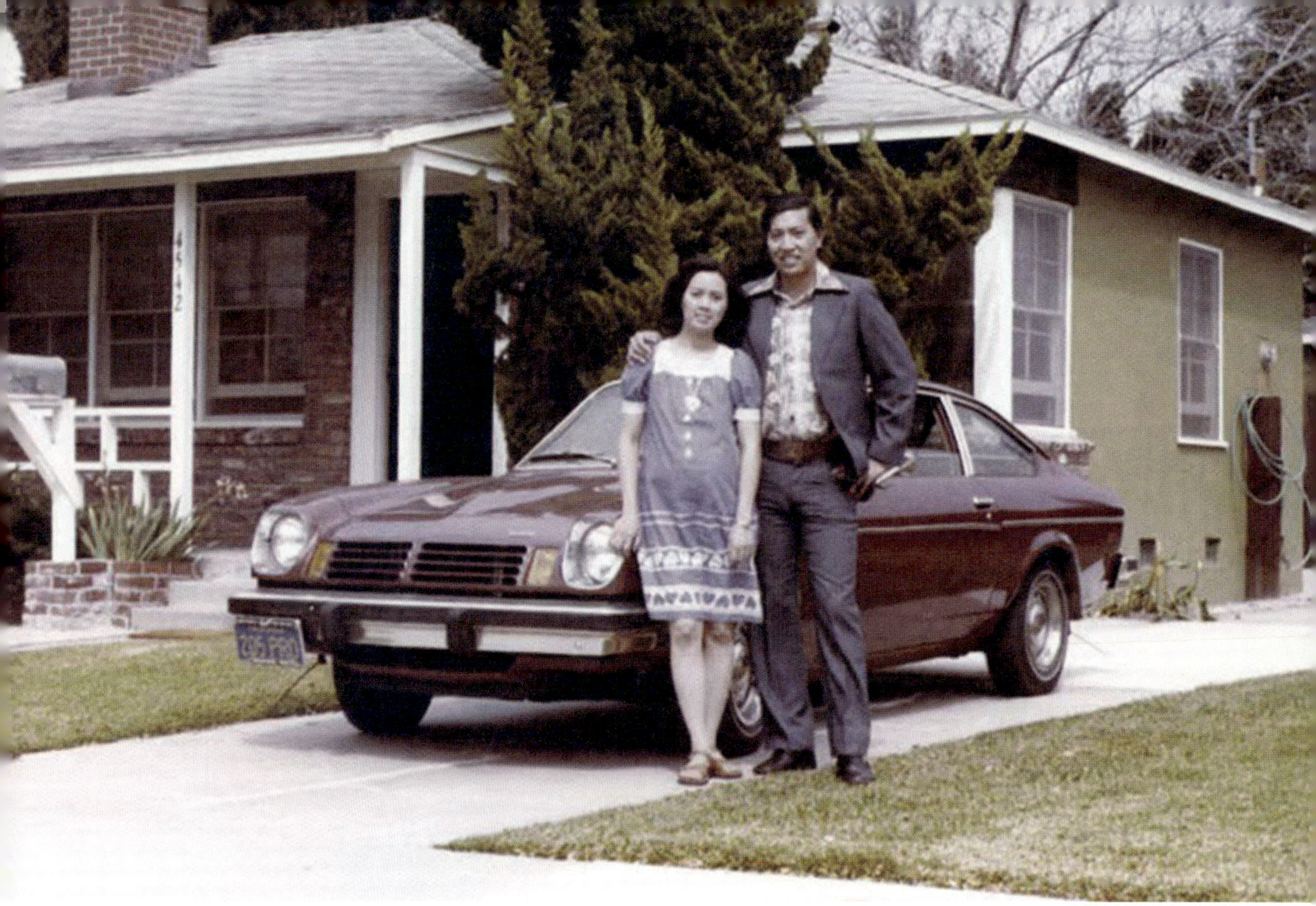

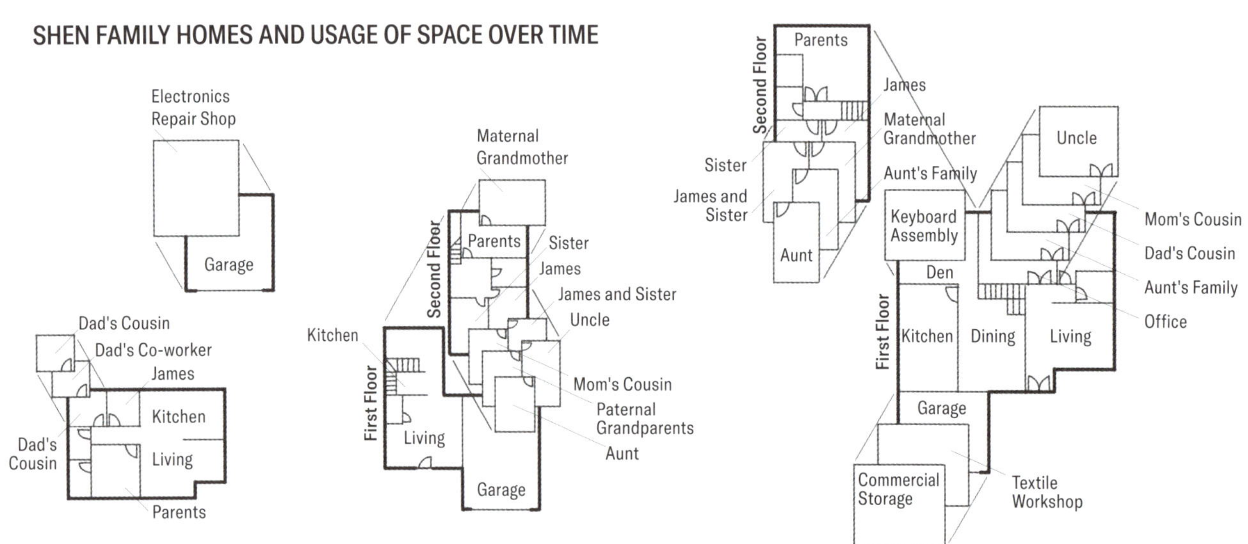

FIRST HOUSE 1977–1986
3 bed 2 bath 106m² (1097.9ft²)

SECOND HOUSE 1981–1988
3 bed 2 bath 108m² (1162.5ft²)

THIRD HOUSE 1983–
3 bed 2 bath 234m² (2518.8ft²)

Mr. and Mrs. Shen pictured in front of their first family home in Long Beach, California in 1977.
Plans of the first, second and current Shen family homes.
Zang Feng in front of his family home in Lanzhou.

notion of the American Dream. This sentiment is exemplified by immigrant families like James Shen's, whose parents emigrated from China to Los Angeles, California in the mid-1970s. Despite their lack of higher education and professional skills, James's parents diligently saved money from a factory wage of $2 per hour while living in a rented studio converted from a garage. Eventually, they managed to purchase their first home in Long Beach—a 120-square-meter (1,292-square-foot) three-bedroom, two-bath house—for $40,000, borrowing $2,000 for half of the 10% down payment.

To supplement their income, James's parents rented out one of the bedrooms. Within six years, they owned three houses and two cars, and had begun their own business. These houses didn't function only as their home, but also the halfway houses of many immigrant friends and families. Different people would come and go and the uses of different rooms would shift to accommodate new visitors who would live with the family, sometimes for up to a year. These homes provided security and stability for James's immediate family and also for many others.

At the same time on the other side of the world in China, housing was readily available. Zang Feng grew up in the city of Lanzhou, Gansu province in government housing, while He Zhe grew up in the countryside near Jinghua, Zhejiang province in a house that had been in his family for generations. Their first homes were humble. Zang Feng's family first home was a thirty-five-square-meter (377-square-foot), two-room apartment in a single-story dormitory with bathrooms shared with other residents. He Zhe's home was a seventy-square-meter (753-square-foot), single-story Chinese farmhouse. His family lived in one room and his grandmother lived in the other, the two separated by a common area. The kitchen and bathroom were located in a separate building on the farm.

Like most city dwellers, Zang Feng's family lived in Danwei communities in social housing compounds. The Chinese concept of "danwei" (单位) refers to a work unit or social organization that was central to people's lives, providing employment, housing, and social services. It replaced the family as the primary social unit in a period when private enterprises and housing did not exist. When Zang Feng was in college his family had the opportunity to put money towards a ninety-square-meter (969-square-foot) apartment in a building constructed by their Danwei worker's commune. Apartments like these were built in locations that experienced a steep increase in value during the 1990s, a period of rapid urban development. Eventually Zang Feng's parents were able to sell this apartment

A view of Lanzhou city in the early 20th century.
A view of Lanzhou city in 2012.

and upgrade to a 130-square-meter (1,399-square-foot), three-bedroom, two-bath apartment further from the city center. The subsequent rise in property values in China's booming cities allowed their families to accumulate equity and enhance their standard of living.

In contrast, He Zhe's parents never moved. They did, however, build a new two-story house in front of their first house when He Zhe was in elementary school. His parents, He Zhe and his sister lived on the ground floor, which had a shared bedroom and a living room. As they grew older, they partitioned the ground floor into three spaces and made use of the upper level. While some rural areas experienced drastic increases in land value during the 1990s, He Zhe's village was not one of them. Since there was and still is little development and economic activity nearby, property prices have not risen like they have in Chinese cities. In fact, the buying and selling of rural property and land must remain within the village; technically, there is no private ownership of land in China. Urban land is typically leased for forty to seventy years, while rural land is owned collectively by the village. Many families in similar rural locations have been excluded from the urban economic boom.

Today's economic landscape in places as diverse as the US and China presents a sharp contrast in housing access. From about 1910 until the 1970s, the US experienced a period of economic prosperity and relatively low economic inequality. Homeownership through hard work was possible

He family home in Jinghua, Zhejiang province, China.
Edward Burtynsky, *Urban Renewal #5 City Overview from Top of Military Hospital*, Shanghai, China, 2004.
Edward Burtynsky, *Suburbs #1,* North Las Vegas, Nevada, USA, 2007.

and strengthened the myth of the American Dream. However, since the 1970s, inequality has increased at an incredible pace to almost unprecedented levels [7].

The changes in China since the 1970s have been even more drastic than those in the US. Economic reforms in the late 1970s led to a substantial increase in the privatization of housing, benefiting families like Zang Feng's. In 1979, 50% of the housing stock was privately owned, compared to 95% in 2015. China had very low levels of inequality in the 1970s; today, however, it approaches US levels of inequality, which are among the highest in the world [18]. Additionally, the income gap between urban and rural households increased significantly, as has been felt by families like He Zhe's [10].

Wages have failed to keep pace with inflation, and soaring house prices have led to increasing disparity in cities like Los Angeles where James lives, and Beijing, where Zang Feng and He Zhe reside. Even individuals like ourselves, equipped with excellent educations, multiple university degrees, advanced skills, and self-employment, find the prospect of homeownership in Los Angeles or Beijing extremely challenging. Those growing up in rural China like He Zhe experience even greater barriers to access, due to the concentration of resources and opportunities in cities. Achieving homeownership through mere hard work and savings is very difficult in the current environment.

"...the consequences of high housing cost burdens for the lowest-income households are significant, reducing spending on food and healthcare and increasing housing instability. The growing obstacles to buying a home also lock out millions of renters from the benefits of homeownership, including protection from rising housing costs and the opportunity to build wealth.

In fact, housing affordability has been worsening for decades. Consider that in 1960, 24% of renters experienced housing cost burdens, but affordability has consistently deteriorated over the intervening decades so that by 2023 the share had more than doubled to 50%. The rise in unaffordability is the result of simple cruel math. Between 1960 and 2021 median rents in the US increased by 73% even after accounting for inflation,

Housing compound in northern China, from the series "Trip to the North (2021–)" by Sun Haiting.

Apartment building facade in Beijing, from the series "Building of Background (2019–2021)" by Sun Haiting.

but over the same period median renter incomes only rose 14%. The situation was no better for homeowners as the median home price increased 167% while owner incomes went up only 54%.

While no part of the US has been shielded from rising housing costs, coastal markets face particularly severe conditions. For many years housing values in most markets in the US were roughly three times median incomes. But as of 2024 it was not uncommon for markets in California to have home prices more than ten times incomes and on the east coast this ratio now often exceeds six times income.

The widening gulf between housing costs and incomes is by no means limited to the US. A recent report examining house price to income ratios in 94 markets around the globe found that none qualified as affordable, while nearly half were severely or impossibly unaffordable." [6]

Chris Herbert, Managing Director Joint Center for Housing Studies of Harvard University

The growing housing affordability crisis is not confined to specific regions. Globally, house prices have risen faster than incomes. As of 2024, 1.6 billion people around the world do not have access to adequate housing and this number is projected to rise to 3 billion by 2030 [1].

Economic disparities, speculative real estate investment, and inadequate housing policies worsen the global housing crisis. Climate change and natural disasters are exacerbating housing instability further, displacing populations and underscoring the urgency for sustainable and resilient housing solutions. In turn, outward urban expansion into natural habitats accelerates the effects of climate change. The housing supply in many cities worldwide is unable to meet rising demand. Concurrently, cities are struggling with an excess of vacant properties of poor quality or buildings that are energy inefficient and so no longer adequate as housing [4].

It is critical to develop architectural solutions to the housing crisis within this context of accelerating socioeconomic and environmental change. While housing issues are complex and specific to local contexts, they are a shared global phenomenon. We hope that taking a close look into PAO's Plugin House projects will help illuminate some of

Bird's eye view of the Dashilar hutong area in Beijing.
Example of informal construction in the Dashilar hutong.

these challenges and possibilities. With an emphasis on adaptability, we address housing needs through revitalizing aging properties and increasing housing supply for middle- to low-income populations in desirable locations.

Plugin House's origins are rooted in tackling housing issues in Beijing's historic Dashilar neighborhood, characterized by hutongs (narrow alleyways lined with courtyard houses). Dashilar presents an extreme example of how the housing crisis affects people on many scales, while the use of Plugin Houses highlights a path towards addressing these problems.

This neighborhood of traditional courtyard houses sits in the heart of Beijing. Its history and location next to Tiananmen Square give it unique value. Unfortunately, decades of continued disinvestment and degradation have led to slum-like conditions and overcrowding. Homes are over a century old, built with methods from a bygone era. They are poorly insulated and leaky, and there is no underground sewage system for them to connect to. Families often live in houses as small as ten square meters (108 square feet) and nearly half of the properties in Dashilar are vacant as the population has dwindled over time.

Residents live in constant uncertainty and therefore have no choice but to find ways to adapt. Without knowing whether they could be relocated and their neighborhood redeveloped at a moment's notice, locals have taken it upon themselves to improve their conditions.

Informal constructions by residents have a certain amount of inventiveness. They are flexible and address urgent concerns. Built as additions or replacements of existing parts, these structures do not encompass the whole of the home. Since informally built structures are not officially recognized by local authorities, they are technically not permanent. Often, authorities turn a blind eye, recognizing the need for informally built structures; however, this is typically handled on a case-by-case basis and there are times when authorities decide that these structures need to be taken down. Residents accept that their situations continue to change. These are "band-aid" solutions that require low investment. And because many informal constructions are built with repurposed materials, they can also be repurposed in a different form in the future.

These grassroots interventions arise from a gap in official policy, which struggles to adapt swiftly to evolving needs. Policy decisions, with their far-reaching consequences, tend to prioritize fixed, long-term solutions. Within such regulatory frameworks, professional architects conceive buildings with a similar permanence.

Additions and renovations do not follow building regulations and are not sanctioned by any approval process. Instead, interventions are negotiated between neighbors and new additions are erected quickly with guerrilla-like transformations occurring overnight. Local authorities have little time to react and often turn a blind eye. In this way tacit approval is given when projects are minor and no one complains. Sometimes new structures are deemed too extreme and are taken down by local authorities, but residents accept these risks at the start of the project.

For this reason, ad hoc interventions are moderate in scale and are introduced incrementally. Techniques are developed through a collective process of trial and error as residents learn from each other's mistakes over time. Extensions, additions, and subdivisions of all shapes and sizes are sprinkled through the neighborhood. They are incorporated with what has come before, in a piecemeal way. Very few buildings remain in their original form, as they have adapted through the ages under shifting uses, different inhabitants, and even transforming political systems. The entire district of Dashilar is an agglomeration of spaces built to meet different challenges over time.

Dashilar is a study of a residential community that has weathered profound transformation and continually struggles to adapt. The famed courtyard houses, built during imperial rule, have been adapted to different uses through the modernization of China and today's expanding economy. While these historic courtyards have undergone conversions to suit contemporary needs, their original structures, some dating back centuries, endure.

However, as these courtyards have been subdivided into smaller units over the years, intricate property ownership arrangements have emerged, posing formidable hurdles for renovation efforts, as is the case in so many parts of the world. Given that different units coexist within the same structure, renovations necessitate unanimous resident agreement. Consequently, inhabitants occupy fragmented sections of the courtyards, while other areas lie dormant or in disrepair, resulting in a mosaic of diverse living circumstances throughout the district.

An aerial view of Dashilar highlighted on the left in comparison with the redeveloped area of Qianmen highlighted on the right.

Many of the newly developed streets of Qianmen remain empty.

Informal construction in the Dashilar neighborhood.

Cestbon

Original Condition of Courtyard 72
Original Condition of Courtyard 72

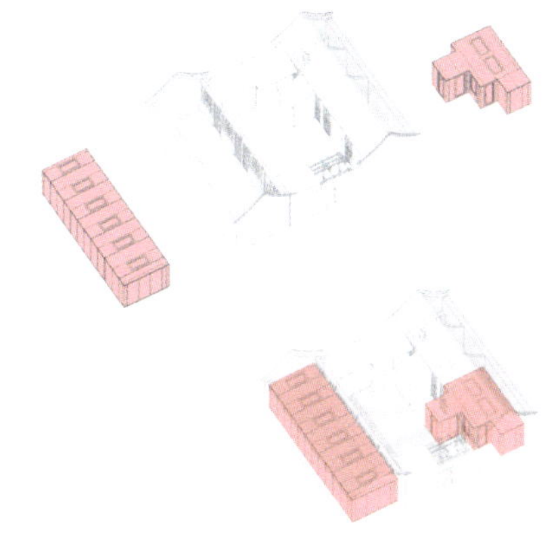

"Dashilar's architectural and cultural history is woven into the sedimental bricolage of its often ad hoc and increasingly dilapidated residential and commercial buildings. Unlike many of the other historic neighborhoods of Beijing, Dashilar was neither blessed nor cursed with an idealized late-Qing dynasty form and had, until recently, developed in tandem with successive systems, governments and economies. Less effective in exercising its mark on Dashilar was the rapid evolution of Beijing's speculative property market of the 1990s and 2000s, leaving it relatively untouched during these recent market reforms. The neighborhood became known as an 'Urban Corner,' retaining its urban fabric and historical authenticity but losing its stature and standard of living. Despite this, Dashilar still houses and hosts a populous community of residents, tourists, and passersby, as it has for much of its history. This is where the contradiction of preservation becomes apparent: the historic architecture and traditional urban fabric are endangered through aged infrastructure and lack of investment. But so too is the neighborhood's way of life, traditional businesses,

1700s
Qing Dynasty
Single-family courtyard.

1965
Mao Era
Private ownership of land is abolished. Original family forces to leave. Courtyard is subdivided into housing for at least 8 families.

1977
Post-Mao Era
Building restrictions relaxed in the aftermath of the Tangshan earthquake. Each family builds illegal additions.

2010
Six households sell to government. Two households remain and correlating illegal additions and sub-divisions are removed.

2014
The Plugin revitalizes the vacant spaces by modernizing living conditions. By leaving the original structure intact, installing the Plugin does not affect existing residents.

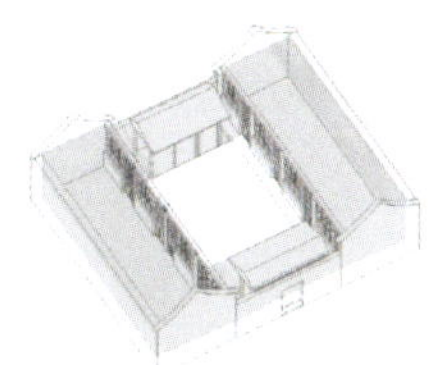

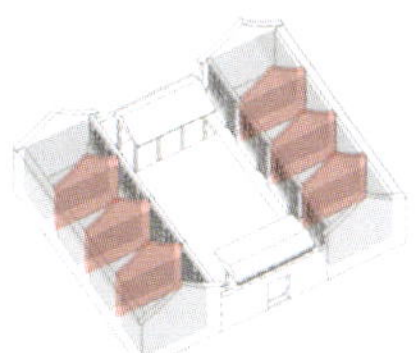

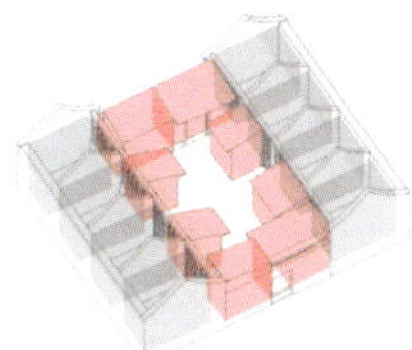

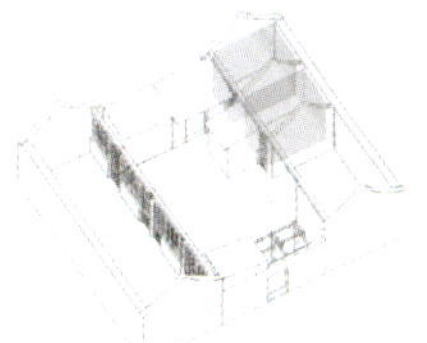

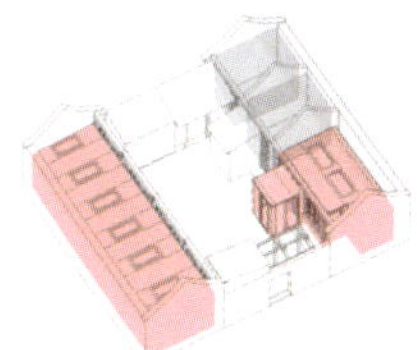

Original artist's impression of the first PAO proposal for the Plugin House concept, south house view.

Original artist's impression of the first PAO proposal for the Plugin House concept, north house view.

Diagram demonstrating the plugin approach of building a house within a house.

Diagram illustrating the evolution of Dashilar's Courtyard 72.

and local craftspeople through changing commercial markets and mass tourism. Must preservation lock down a dynamic built form, and can it only come at the expense of community and authenticity?" [13]

Neill Mclean Gaddes and Yijing Xu, Strategic Planners and Urban Curators, Dashilar Project (2010–2016), SANS (三思)

Dashilar has generally been left untouched by authorities and developers, partially due to the failure of an adjacent district called Qianmen. A large effort to redevelop this area to the east of Dashilar was completed in time for the opening of the 2008 Olympic Games in Beijing, to much fanfare. The historic and mostly residential area was entirely rebuilt as a retail development in a faux historic style. It required the large-scale relocation of residents as well as immense capital investment. With many properties still vacant after more than a decade, the project is seen as a financial failure.

Construction of the first Plugin House demonstration home in Dashilar.

Construction of the office of the Dashilar local government, Beijing Dashilar Investment Ltd., part of the Plugin House pilot.

Front view of the Beijing Dashilar Investment Ltd. office space.

View of Courtyard 72 with the first Plugin House demonstration units: an office and a demonstration home.

Installation of plumbing for the Plugin House demonstration home.
Plugin House demonstration home, part of the Plugin House pilot.
Interior view of the Beijing Dashilar Investment Ltd. office space.

Officials recognized the growing need for improvement in Dashilar but hesitated to take an approach similar to Qianmen. Renovating each courtyard house would be too expensive and disruptive to residents; residents would be concerned about being able to move back in after the renovations. Rebuilding would also mean the destruction of historically valuable structures. There was an urgency and desire to do something different, but no viable alternatives.

In 2013, PAO received an invitation to propose an approach to urban regeneration that avoided relocating residents and demolishing existing buildings. This led to the development of the Courtyard House Plugin, a pioneering method for urban regeneration. The Courtyard House Plugin involved inserting a new building into an existing structure in Courtyard 72 in Dashilar, leaving the original intact and unaltered.

We delved into how local residents informally improved their living conditions through a vernacular architecture, developed without the involvement of architects. By adopting a flexible architecture that incorporates pre-existing buildings, the house-in-house method shares the similar, informal approach used by locals. However, it also offers scalability and a broader spectrum of possibilities. The method was conceived to tackle various facets of urban renewal, and so can be replicated in any crumbling urban center.

The need to install new sanitation systems is often reason enough to raze a neighborhood. We proposed small septic tanks and composting toilets to avoid the need for extensive excavation and demolition. Private bathrooms would mean residents would no longer have to rely on shared public bathrooms. There had been stories of elderly residents suffering while walking to open-air public restrooms in the dead of winter. The Plugin structure itself would be pre-fabricated, provide high-quality insulation and be paired with energy efficient mini-split HVAC units. Efficient heating and cooling would replace age-old equipment.

The proposal was well received and Dashilar's local authorities agreed to move forward with two demonstration units in Courtyard 72. This courtyard was built in the Qing dynasty and was over a century old. After the Chinese Revolution, the residence, belonging to several generations of one family, was subdivided into four properties. By the time we visited the property, one unit was occupied by a renter, another by the owner Mrs. Dong, and the final two were vacant. The Plugin Houses were built inside the two vacant units.

Bedroom exterior and interior after the renovation of Courtyard 72.
View of the bathroom in the Plugin House demonstration home.

One Plugin House became the office of Dashilar staff who focused on work within the community. The other unit became a demonstration home that was opened to the public to visit. The Courtyard House Plugin was very popular and led to much international interest. We were able to show how cost-effective, fast, and practical our Plugin House approach could be. More importantly, it gained support from local residents. These two small Plugin Houses immediately opened up opportunities for PAO to further develop and expand the plugin approach.

Visitors to Courtyard 72 admired how the Plugin Houses were inserted into these old structures in juxtaposition to the courtyard's historic and informally built features. When we first visited the property, it was in very poor condition. The original wood structure was barely visible, buried under mismatched parts built from different materials from various renovations over time. There were patched up areas constructed of found objects and spare parts. Over a century of ground movement left nothing in the building straight. We undertook repairs to existing structures when it was a safety or maintenance concern, including reinforcing structural beams and replacing waterproofing, but otherwise left them as is.

Much of Dashilar's rich and tumultuous past is undocumented and survives as traces found within aggregations of architecture built over time. Each layer of building has its own story as if they are geological strata. Conversations with residents uncovered oral histories that deciphered meaning behind supposedly insignificant architectural features. The Plugin Houses did not reinterpret, sanitize, or erase these features, but were designed to be sensitive to this context and to coexist with the past, becoming part of the local vernacular.

As for the mismatch between the windows of the original wood structure and the modern windows of the Courtyard House Plugin, there was no concern for achieving a single harmonious system. Rather it is the heterogeneity and openness of multiple systems coexisting together that is desirable. This sort of mismatch of architectural style already exists in most cities the world over—indeed, architects often strive to create buildings that contrast with those around them. Just look at the many different styles and scales of architecture rubbing up against each other on the streets of London in the UK.

While the house-in-house approach is valid for many pragmatic reasons, there is also an important socio-cultural element. The layers of history from different periods and informally built constructions are usually seen as incongruous

Interior view of the Beijing Dashilar Investment Ltd. office space.
Details of various layers of construction at Courtyard 72.

and unsightly, but people renovating homes all over the world regularly adapt and add to them. There are lofts, extensions, add-ons and annexes everywhere you look. The ability to give new life to a property while leaving the pre-existing structure intact, in any housing project the world over, invites people to recognize the value of remnants of the recent and historic past and the memories these may hold.

Juxtaposition of different door designs after the renovation of Courtyard 72.

THE SECRET DRAWER IN THE CITY

By Cao Fei

Introduction by PAO

San Yuan Li, a collaborative project by Ou Ning, Cao Fei and U-thèque members commissioned for and exhibited at the Venice Biennale of Architecture in 2003, is a case study of the typical "village-amidst-the-city" phenomenon in the process of urbanization in Guangzhou. Cao Fei's vivid depiction of San Yuan Li offers valuable insight into the nature of China's urban villages and historic cores—places where many Plugin Houses are situated. Her essay highlights the complexities of revitalizing these areas and underscores the necessity of doing so to ensure their communities endure. Two decades later, San Yuan Li continues to evolve. To contextualize her work, we revisited the neighborhood, capturing its enduring spirit amid rapid change. By juxtaposing our recent photographs with those from the 2003 project, we explore its layered history, transformation, and continuity.

Tucked in among bustling market places in the old quarters of Guangzhou, Guangdong province is the historic settlement of San Yuan Li. Translating as "triple prime back-lane," this quaint village precinct has been likened to a hidden closet within the city. Its dank, seamy sidewalks and dark back lanes appear abstruse, as if reminding the onlooker that it holds age-old secrets known to very few city dwellers of the present day. The village has dissolved into obscurity because few people pause from their buzzing daily preoccupations to contemplate its significance or to savor its cultural heritage. Indeed, many are not even aware of its existence. For just one day, we put on the hat of a temporary denizen and begin a sojourn into this ancient labyrinth shrouded in misty fog. During our walk in the narrow back lanes and tight passages of the village, we sniff the strong aroma of garlic and hot spice soup, and listen to the bellows of stall vendors peddling their wares, accompanied by wailing babies sitting close by. We gape at the scampering rats and sneer at sewage dripping down the sides of the portico walls. Then there is a moment to reflect on the inverse relationship between the availability of discount bargains and the shortage of space, between the galling brazenness of the place and a matching vitality.

We are spellbound. Here is a maze of winding lanes, alleyways, and rustic blind passages, creating the crinkles in a larger tapestry that we call the city, drawing us to come closer, arousing our natural curiosity. We look, and we look on, through the viewfinder of our camcorder. But before we can fully comprehend our desire to capture everything around us, an inexplicable sense of anxiety descends upon us. It is as if we are expectant of a certain event somehow manifesting itself. Then the thought dawns on us that the subjects before us are beyond our control. Innumerable pedestrians and tricycles simply keep on darting about, whipping up trails of dust and smoke in their wakes. It is too easy to pan them in and out of the viewfinder. People look back at the camera lens with distrust in their eyes. We keep a critical distance behind our monitor screen, but we really wish we could have the full confidence of all the subjects of our study. Why? Because we are sincere.

We wander along the streets outside the village. Rather aimlessly, we watch the vehicles speed by, crowds of people parading past, and of course, the airplanes in the sky. One roars past overhead, producing such an enormous sound wave that it threatens to flatten every living thing on the ground. It pierces through our hearts, and then emerges from the surface of our skin before evaporating into the air. On an average day, airplanes take off and land at five-minute intervals at the nearby Baiyun Airport. They have become an inseparable part of daily life in San Yuan Li. The year-round thundering noise from jet engines does not seem to have the slightest effect on the locals, who simply keep on with their normal activities. These people appear to have forgotten the constant rumble and scream from airplanes, or else they must have serious hearing problems. Perhaps the densely packed office buildings and dwellings around the village have sealed up every niche from the ground up, leaving no cracks and crannies for the jet noise to seep down into the heedless crowds below.

Entering the village through a side street, we see houses flanking the main thoroughfare, all with television sets or radios blaring at full blast. This deafening cacophony offers the villagers a main source of entertainment and a window through which to peek at the outside world. Not far from a public toilet, the dilapidated Lis Family Clan's Ancestral Temple is now the sanitation service depot for the whole village. Its portal architrave and pole beams are rotten. The patterned woodwork on the door panel is also badly damaged. The tile roof is overgrown with weed and mildew. Obviously, nobody is paying attention to the old temple in distress and there is little hope of anyone repairing the ravages of time. In the main hall, several sanitation workers are chit-chatting away; a few others are tending potted plants. Outside, a team of welders is making a series of pops and crackles, intermingled with the rumble and roar of airplanes flying high in the sky. The welding guns produce intermittent bursts of ultraviolet flashes with flying sparks and puffs of smoke, sporadically lighting up the inscription plaque adorning the temple entrance.

On a nearby pathway, an abandoned rubbish cart gives off a rotten stench. These assortments of burlesque props conjure a mockery of the village's old family traditions, as well as a foreboding of its inevitable changing fate. The other ancestral temples in the village have been turned into either schools or offices. They no longer bear any traditional significance. When history and reality are set in such stark contrast, it gives rise to an overwhelming sense of cynicism. Long ago, this little hamlet was a most dignified and earnest place. But like so many other places caught up in the rush for economic development, San Yuan Li is now driven by all manners of unchecked intemperance, playing out on its streets in various real-life dramas involving risky behavior and crime. With rounds of strenuous clean-up efforts, the village is trying to change its image from a sleaze den to something more benign. However, attempts to remove the social ills also give the place a sense of forlorn hope and despair. We are curious about the village's crazier days before the clean-up. But it seems that even its craziness has slipped into history, alongside the village's heroic past in the revolutionary eras when its spirited peasants rose and fought against an invading British Expeditionary Force. In order to unveil the true personality of this rather unique hamlet, we attempt to dissect and scrutinize it through our camera lens, then reassemble the fragments into an exposé of San Yuan Li from a fresh perspective.

We continue our walk. The alleyways are dark, strewn with litter, and often packed with crowds. Whenever we get lost in the small alleys, and it happens rather frequently, we pause to examine the many objects and people attracting our attention. It is best not to lapse on your concentration while traversing these intricate passageways, as you frequently have to dodge objects coming from different directions. Wastewater may unexpectedly splash down from above, one of the crowds may trip on your heel from behind, or you may collide with one of the ubiquitous motorcycles coming from the opposite direction. All sorts of mishaps await the unwary. The haphazard manner in which things happen begets an alertness that keeps us on our toes rather than distracting us. What we see here in San Yuan Li village with our own eyes is, by and large, a throwback to the stories we heard before about this place, since we soon bear witness to a succession of cop and robber, sex and lust, crime and money plot-lines, plus many, many other enthralling possibilities.

One couple running a grocery store in San Yuan Li came from Hunan province to start a new life after losing their jobs in a state-owned enterprise. They have many tales of local affairs to tell. They say there was a once glowing red-light district in the village, which now languishes in the doldrums. They tell us how the waves of "crackdowns" have hurt their livelihood by driving away their customers, who are mostly migrant workers from the provinces. Then there is the latecomers' resentment and envy towards the well-established native villagers, who charge exorbitant prices and ostentatiously display their wealth. They say that all San Yuan Li residents, newcomers and natives alike, are doing their part to corrupt the place. This is perhaps a rather sad reflection, but it does not obliterate the village's immense cultural legacy, its accepting attitude towards newcomers, its openness and spontaneity. Though it has been dubbed the "sleaze crease" of Guangzhou, people still savor its dirt and grime in apparent delight, and continue to live up their lives here with zest and relish. The fact that the sky is shielded from view by rows of closely placed houses is no hindrance to people pursuing their fanciful dreams in the darkness. For many, this place is a most gratifying paradise, their human nature stark naked, basking under the intense incandescent streetlights.

To really get to know San Yuan Li, we have to put down our cameras. Everything about the village becomes so much more personal and amicable the moment locals accept us and relax. We begin to really feel this place and blend in with the surroundings. The villagers speak a slightly accented Cantonese typical of the outlying areas of the city. Their mannerisms are a curious mix of down-to-earth country folk and the modern-day city slicker. After losing their land to urban development, these former peasants now live comfortable lifestyles thanks to the rental income from the houses they built around the village. There is a limit to the amount of available land for new buildings. Hungry for more space to increase rental income, the villagers have no choice but to contrive ingenious ways of reaching up to the sky, of digging underground, and stretching out sideways in every conceivable direction. They squeeze the already cramped lanes, take over footpaths and public roadways, or erect illegal structures like rickety tin sheds, wooden huts and so forth on rooftops, creating a host of fire hazards in the process. From the eaves and protruding edges of two adjacent houses a mass of drain pipes, wires and cables of all descriptions, plus thick tangles of cobweb, shoot out across the open space above a narrow lane, bundling the buildings together from the second story up, much like two passionate lovers held in a intimate embrace. Even the household Earth Gods living in miniature shrines are forced to compete for space with humans.

The insatiable craving to expand into more space is responsible for this most grotesque dwelling style. The villagers' apathy for their surroundings only adds to the impoverishment of architectural style in their own backyard. Nevertheless, we manage to unearth one most surprising find. Dispossessed of their agricultural lands, the villagers are now reclaiming their rooftops as a sanctuary to retrace their pastoral past, turning them into concrete gardens, laying down goldfish ponds, growing vegetables and flowers, and using the open space to erect aviaries or to raise chickens. Because all of the houses are in such close proximity with each other, virtually every rooftop veranda in the village is interconnected. This fortuitously transforms the countless rooftops into a San Yuan Li hallmark spectacle, an immense "sky plaza," which also turns out to be extremely useful to thieves, since they can jump from house to house, covering large tracks of area in a short time. In an effort to attract tenants, the peasants-turned-landlords have strategically adopted the method of recruiting grocery shopkeepers as their part-time real estate agents. They also put up sign boards or stick advertising posters to walls and lampposts around the village. These rental ads are out there vying for attention among a seething mass of other posters and bills, peddling anything from STD treatments to electrical appliance repair, private detective work, noodle chef training, and go-go girl services. This contrasting graffiti art exhibits a pageantry of anarchic, freewheeling urban commerce.

Filming San Yuan Li village during the rainy season puts a heavy strain on the crew. Under a bleak and cloudy sky, the damp air we breathe in becomes unbearably stifling in the already poor air quality of the village. A stinking odor from piles of garbage permeates the passageways. Totally oblivious to people's presence are packs of well-fed rats merrily scurrying back and forth along the gutters and between their various hideouts. Because of the high population density in San Yuan Li, the village residents produce large mounds of rubbish every day. These can be something of a bonanza for certain creatures and often do become sites of mad scrambles between man and animal. Many wandering vagrants from afar make their living by picking through the village residents' throwaways, looking for any bits and ends of value that can be sold to recycling traders. We are amazed at the apparent ease with which the locals attune to even the most extremes of squalid conditions. They seem to have simply accepted the disarray and filth as part of everyday life.

All kinds of strange acoustic effects stimulate our auditory senses as we walk in the back lanes and alleyways in San Yuan Li. The tiniest of sounds created in such claustrophobic surroundings, be that the turn of a key, or the jangle of

bicycle bells, is instantly amplified into tremendous echoes. A motley soufflé of Cantopop or Mandopop music, Korean or Japanese TV soap operas, as well as Chinese Kung Fu movies pour out from each and every household, colliding, whirling, and bouncing around from house to house. This reverberating melee creates a higgledy piggledy kind of theatrical gallimaufry. Strolling into one of the many privately owned telephone kiosks, our ears are instantly bombarded by a semantic and phonetic mélange of provincial accents and back country colloquialisms. Zero distance between houses means the serious erosion of privacy for landlords and tenants alike. For this reason, windows are covered up with curtains or an assortment of decorations is pasted onto the glass panes. This flimsy barrier is the only thing that covers the murmuring, muttering, whispering, groaning, family squabbles, or amorous liaisons inside the dwellings. Glancing through window screens, one can sometimes see a tenant girl putting on makeup in front of the dressing table, or a bare-chested man preparing a meal in the kitchen. The "deluxe" stainless steel security doors are omnipresent armor-plated emblems in San Yuan Li. They encase group after group of village houses. There are doors behind doors, partition after partition. Burglary is the most common petty crime in the village. Longstanding anxiety over security concerns besets the local residents and tenants, straining their trust on one another. However, living in a social melting pot has nurtured a noteworthy quality in the village residents, making them very adept at embracing and tolerating different values. They have learnt to solve the many problems that can arise from their differences. Here in the village, many situations can spin into warfare, with some protagonists in defense, some on the offensive, and others making conciliatory compromises. Everything unfolds amidst a chorus of rowdy clamors, yet life tends to proceed along at a steady pace.

Up close, we come face-to-face with a hairdresser in a garish floral shirt, followed by a trendy local youngster wearing a head of flaming red hair; after that, a woman in a translucent outfit sails past, then a pair of young girls

开心鲜果园

in school uniforms, and further up the path, some elderly folks lazily lounging around or snoozing in the shade. They apparently come and go in the same alley every day, often rubbing shoulders past each other, or peeking across rooftops observing one another. They remain strangers yet they recognize each other. The image they evoke is one of undisciplined overindulgence, yet they brim with self-assurance, their manners eccentric but filled with zest. Some of them belong here, others will perhaps move on, going from job to job. The shabby surroundings and budget living here suit the sojourners particularly well because, for many of them, a place like this is useful for establishing a foothold from which to explore the city. After they have strengthened their relationship with the metropolis, they will forsake this place in search of another route to enter the urban mainstream. They yearn for flying. Like the airplanes taking off and landing over San Yuan Li, they fantasize someday, somehow, they too could take flight.

As we leave San Yuan Li, we step back into our city life. We begin to doubt if San Yuan Li village actually belongs to the metropolitan community we live in. When we show what we have recorded of San Yuan Li to other people, few of them can really appreciate its true character. The village we know now is a place that is completely cut off from the outside world and yet it remains totally open. It inspires us to ponder many questions, such as how to define a city, or what is a village. Our stopover has only provided us with an open conclusion. What we have recorded is an attempt to unravel the subject's hidden message. The ultimate goal of this narrative is no more than just restating that San Yuan Li village really is a physical, social and cultural entity, and that it does exist in our metropolis.

3 May 2003
Translated from Chinese to English by Simon Young, Shenzhen

PLUGIN MANUAL

WHY CHOOSE A PLUGIN HOUSE?

In a world seeking sustainable and innovative housing solutions, the Plugin House represents a significant step forwards. It's not just a house, it's a movement towards reimagining how we live.

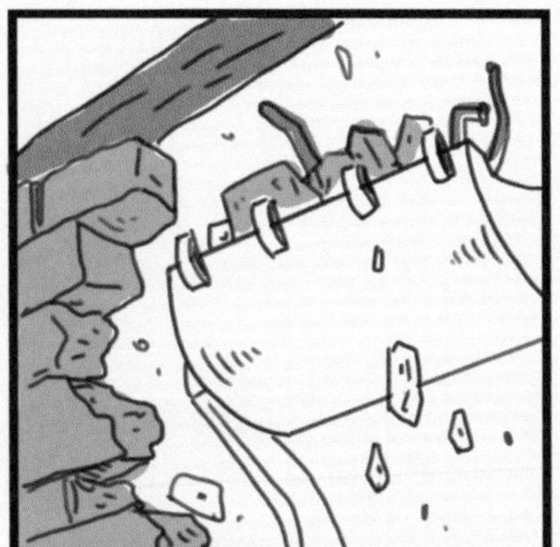

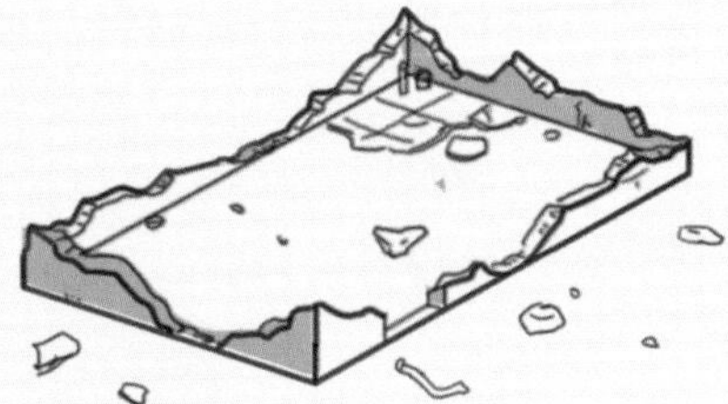

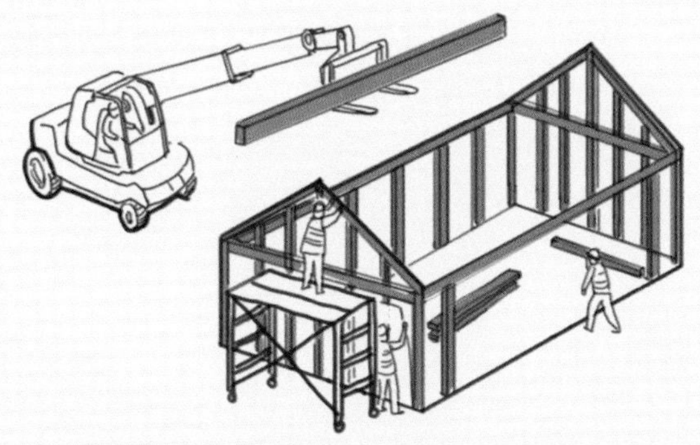

With the Plugin House, you can upgrade your living space without the need for demolition, add housing to your community while minimizing gentrification pressures, and adapt to life's changes without the upheaval of moving.

This approach not only respects the environment by reducing waste, but it also honors the existing fabric of neighborhoods, making it a choice that benefits both individual homeowners and communities at large.

PLUGIN HOUSE

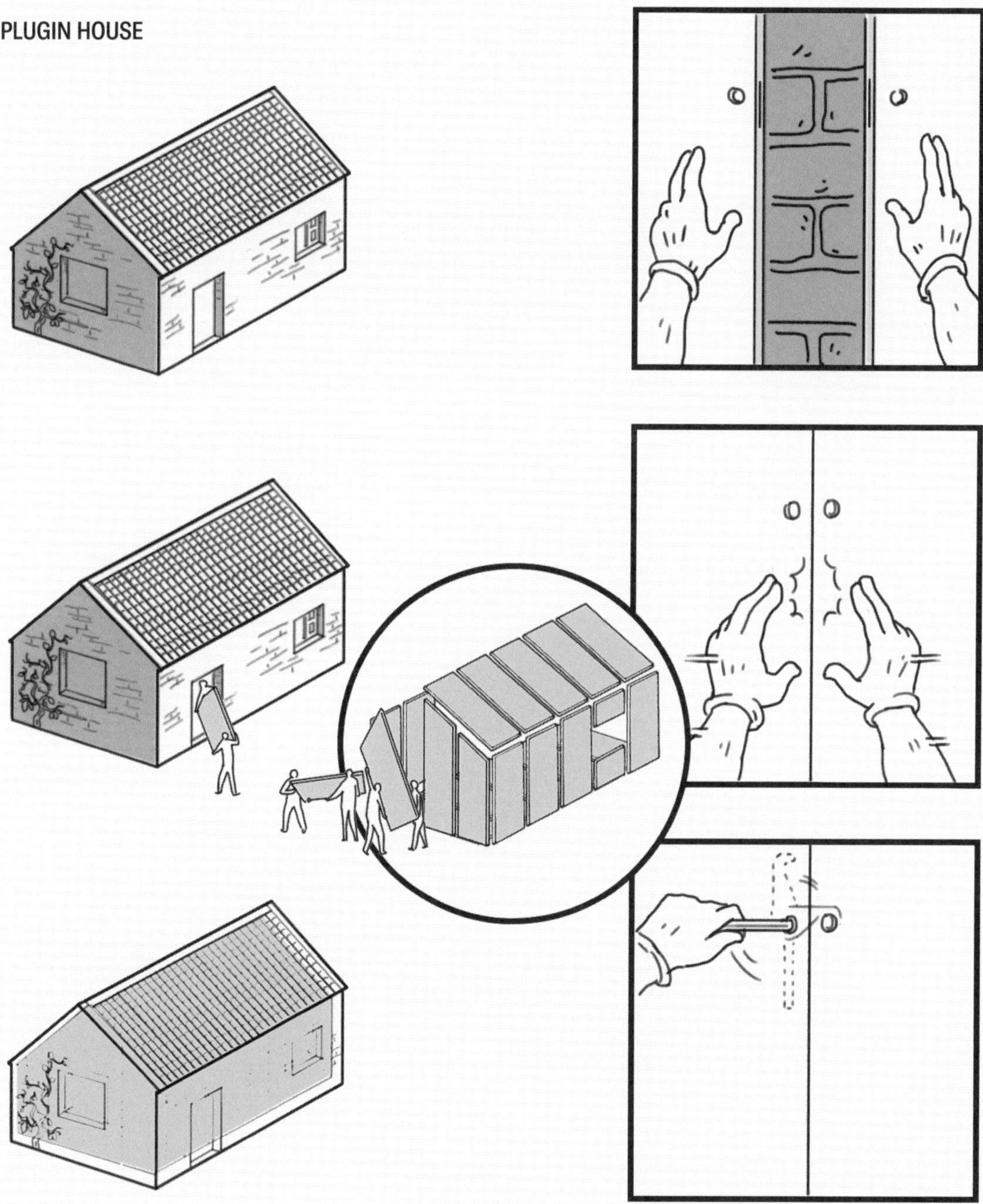

PLUGIN INFILL TO BUILD COMMUNITY

We're excited to move to our new home.

There used to be a lot more kids around here.

SUPER MARKET

Rents keep going up!

This house is too big for us empty nesters!

I'm afraid I can't afford my mortgage!

All these new people moving in are forcing us to relocate.

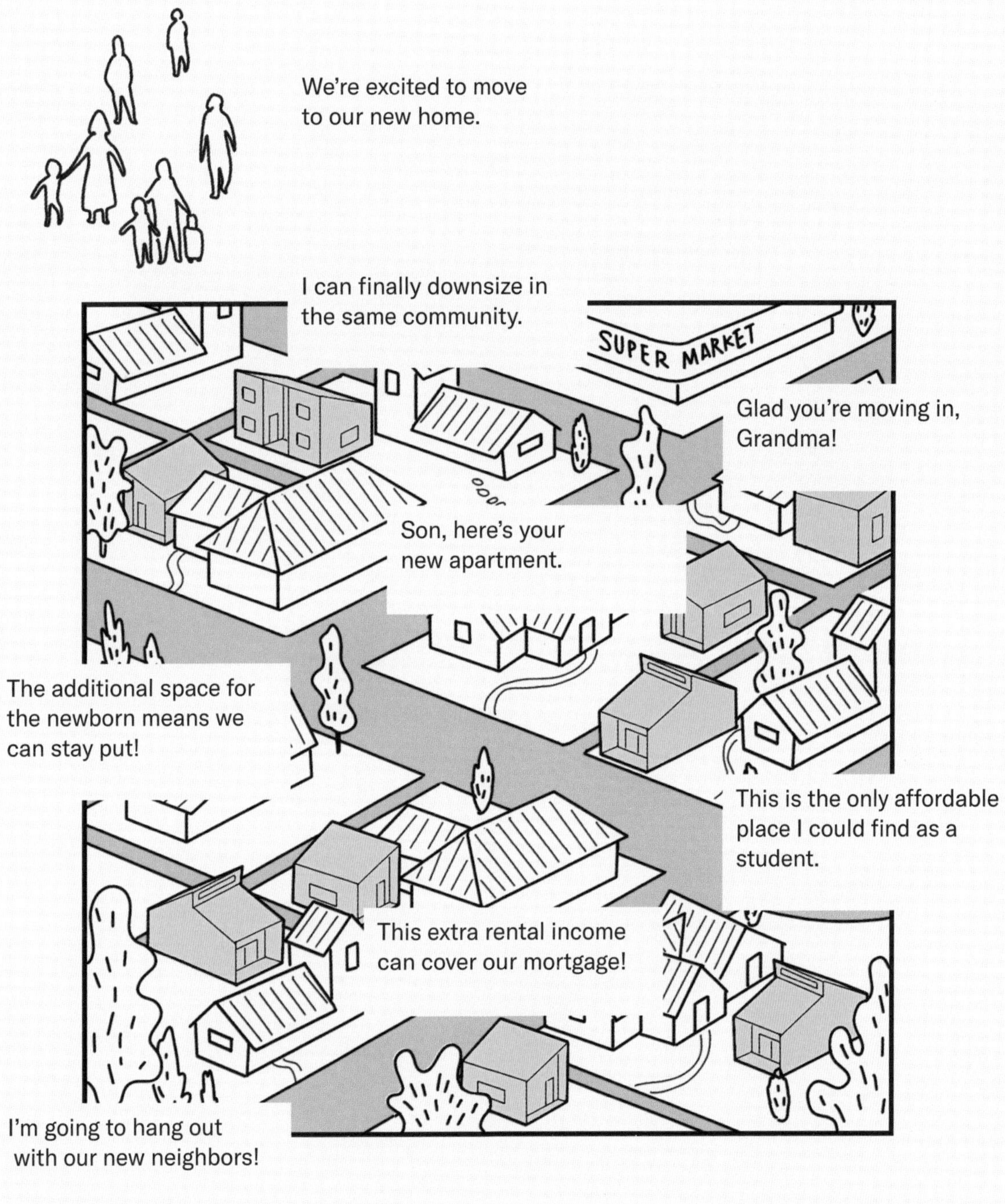
We're excited to move to our new home.
I can finally downsize in the same community.
SUPER MARKET
Glad you're moving in, Grandma!
Son, here's your new apartment.
The additional space for the newborn means we can stay put!
This is the only affordable place I could find as a student.
This extra rental income can cover our mortgage!
I'm going to hang out with our new neighbors!

ACCOMMODATING A LIFETIME OF CHANGE

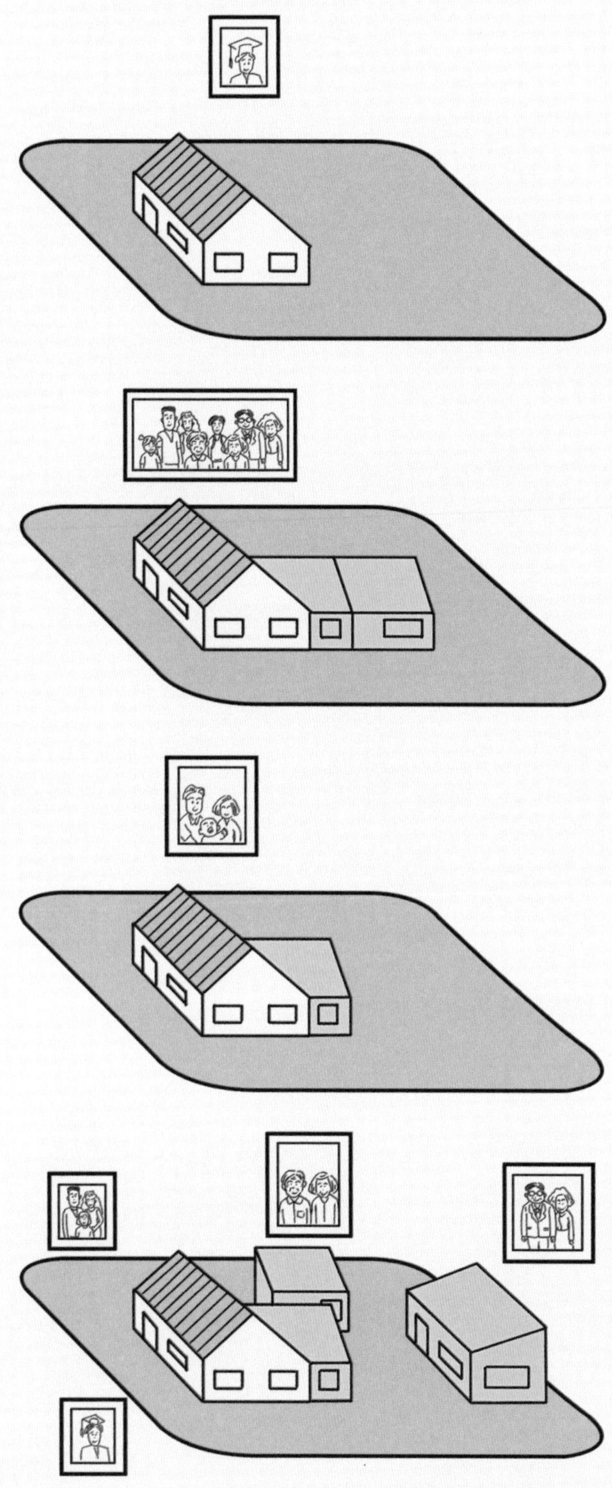

PLUGIN HOUSE BENEFITS

FAST | NO SKILL NECESSARY | ONE TOOL

INEXPENSIVE | ENERGY EFFICIENT

PLUGIN HOUSE DETAILS

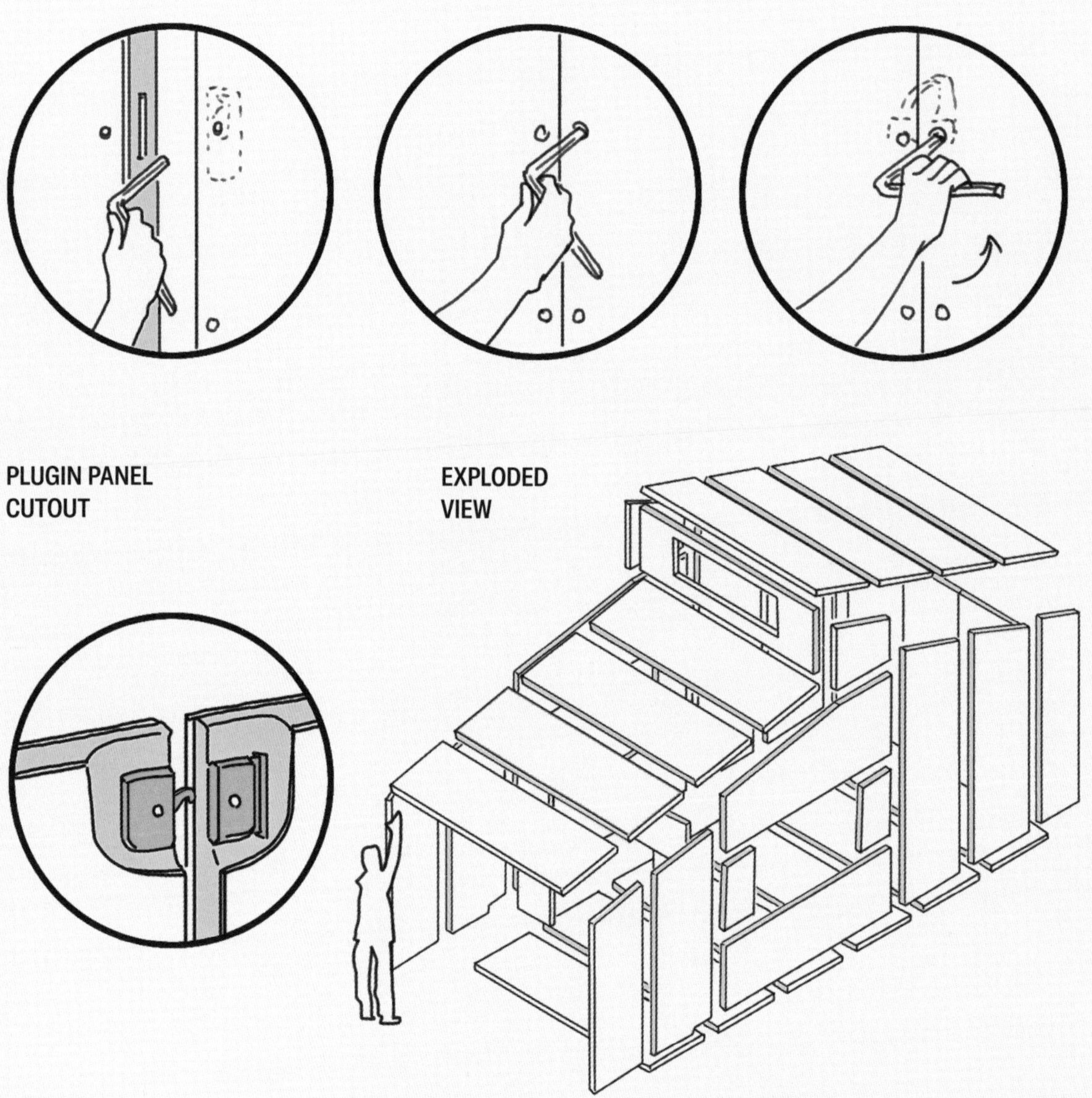

PANEL LAYOUT

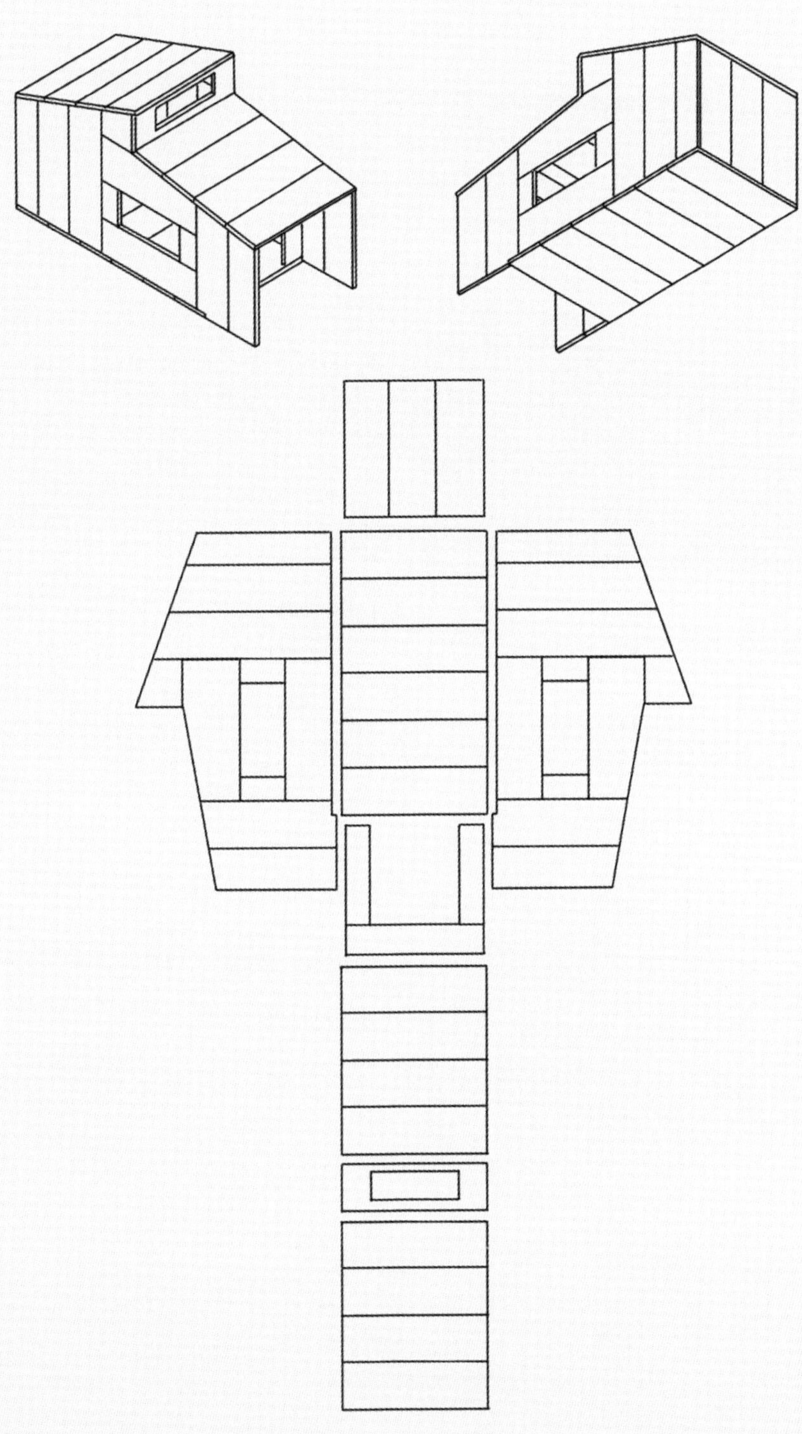

PLUGIN MANUFACTURING PROCESS

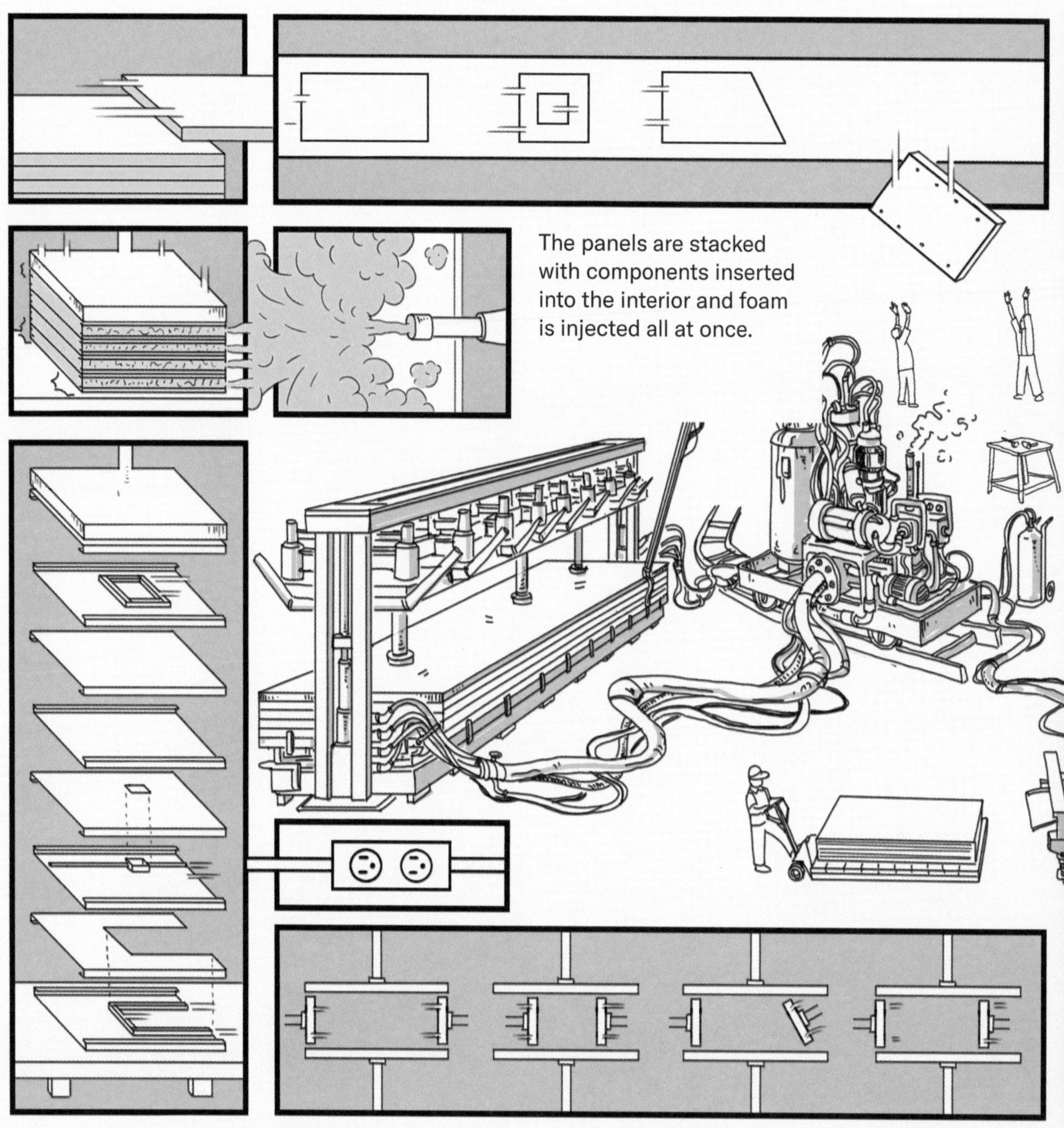

Houses are assembled to test their fit and then disassembled for packing. They are then stacked and shipped out.

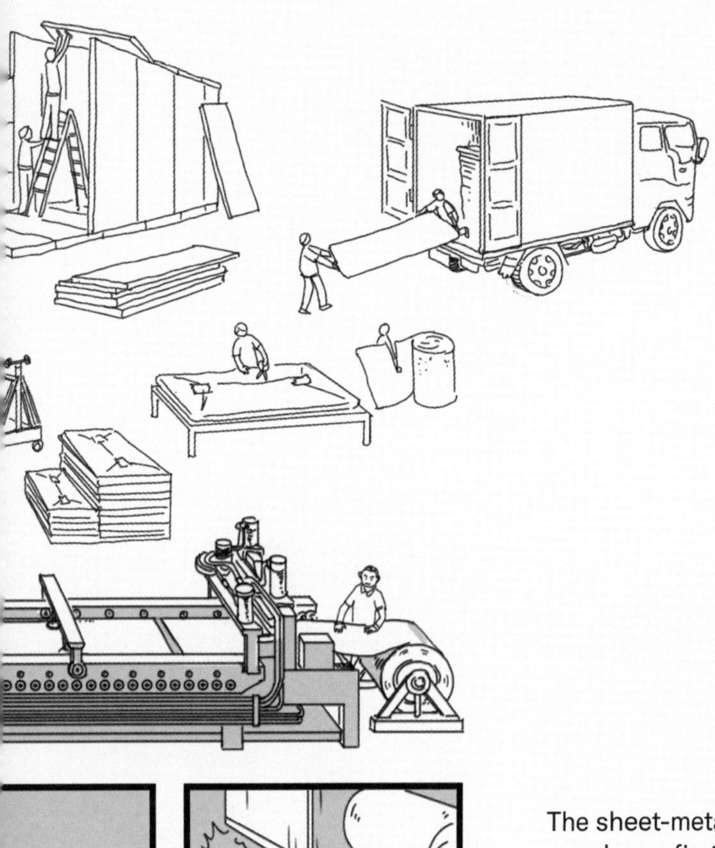

The sheet-metal skin for the Plugin panels are first cut and laid into molds. The panels are manufactured in customized shapes through an adjustable mold.

PLUGIN INSTALLATION PROCESS

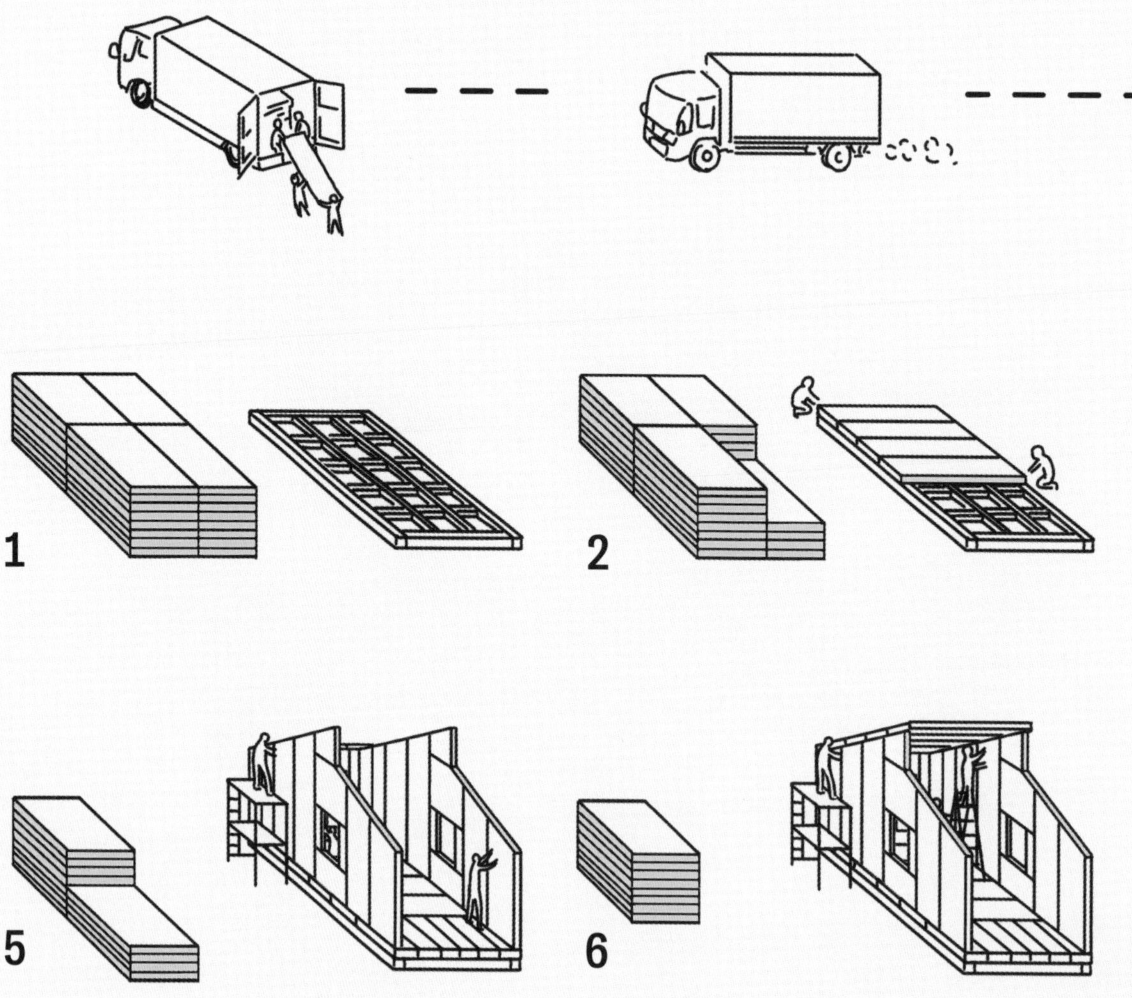

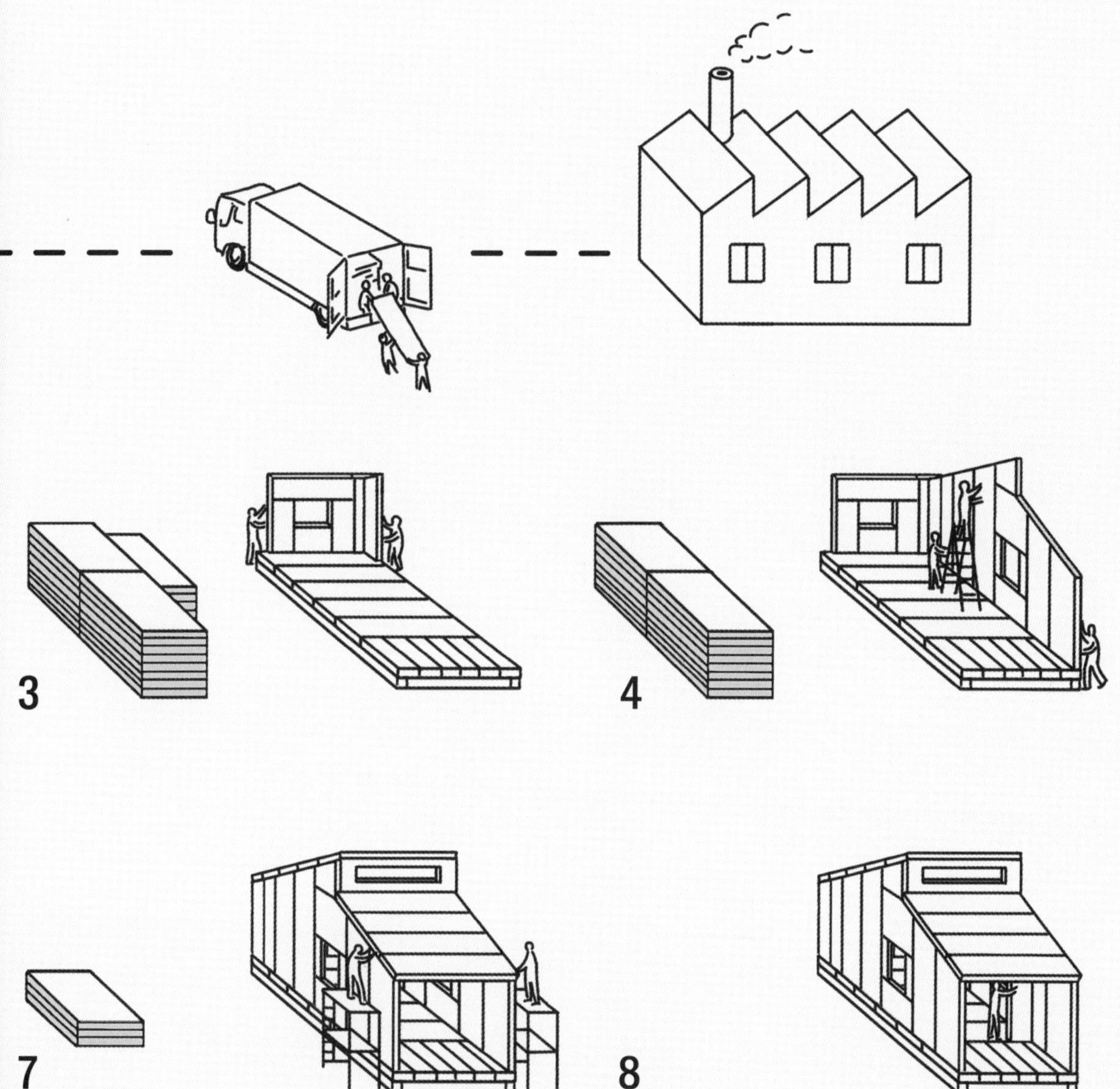
3
4
7
8

PLUGIN HOUSE SPECIAL COMPONENTS

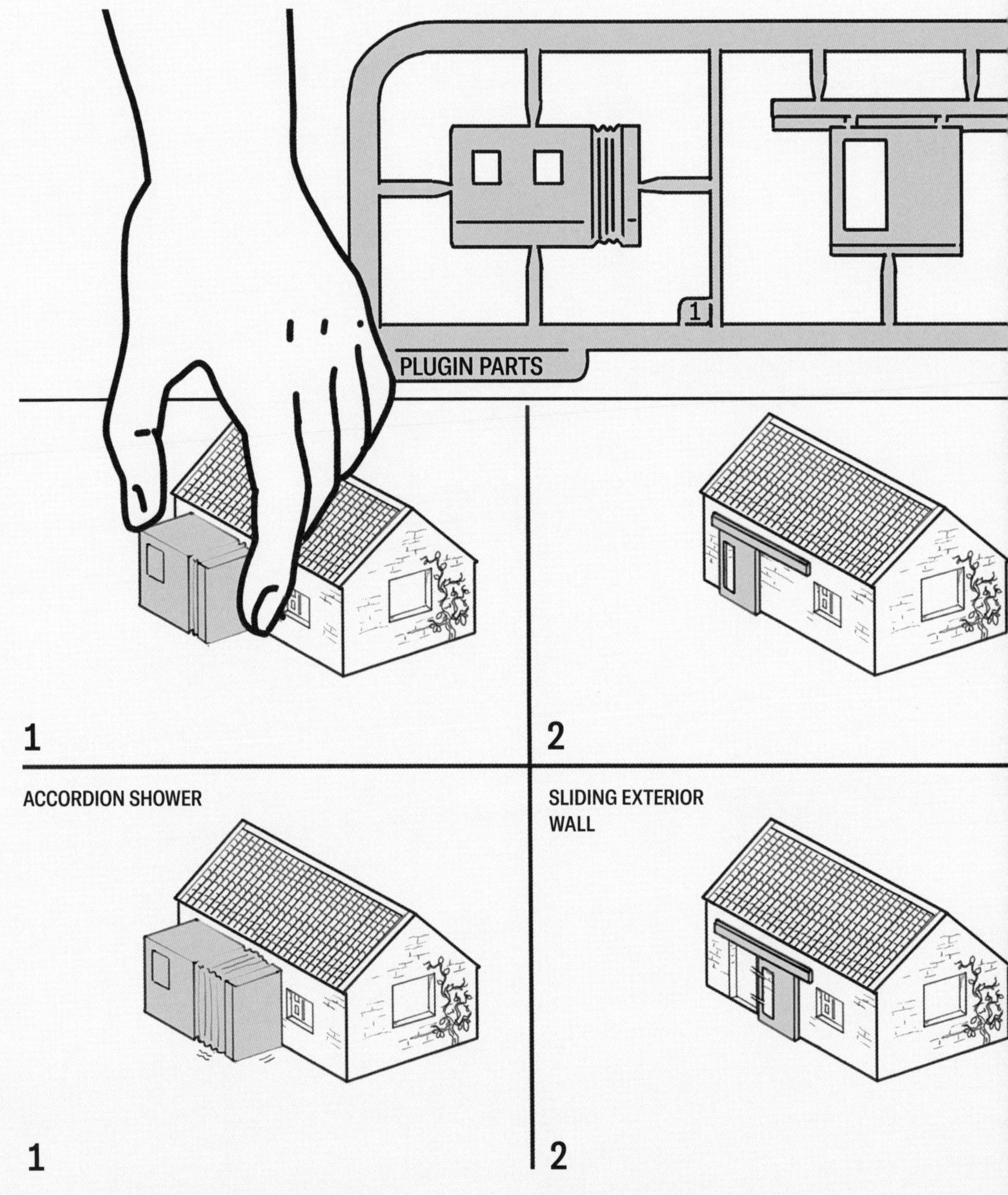

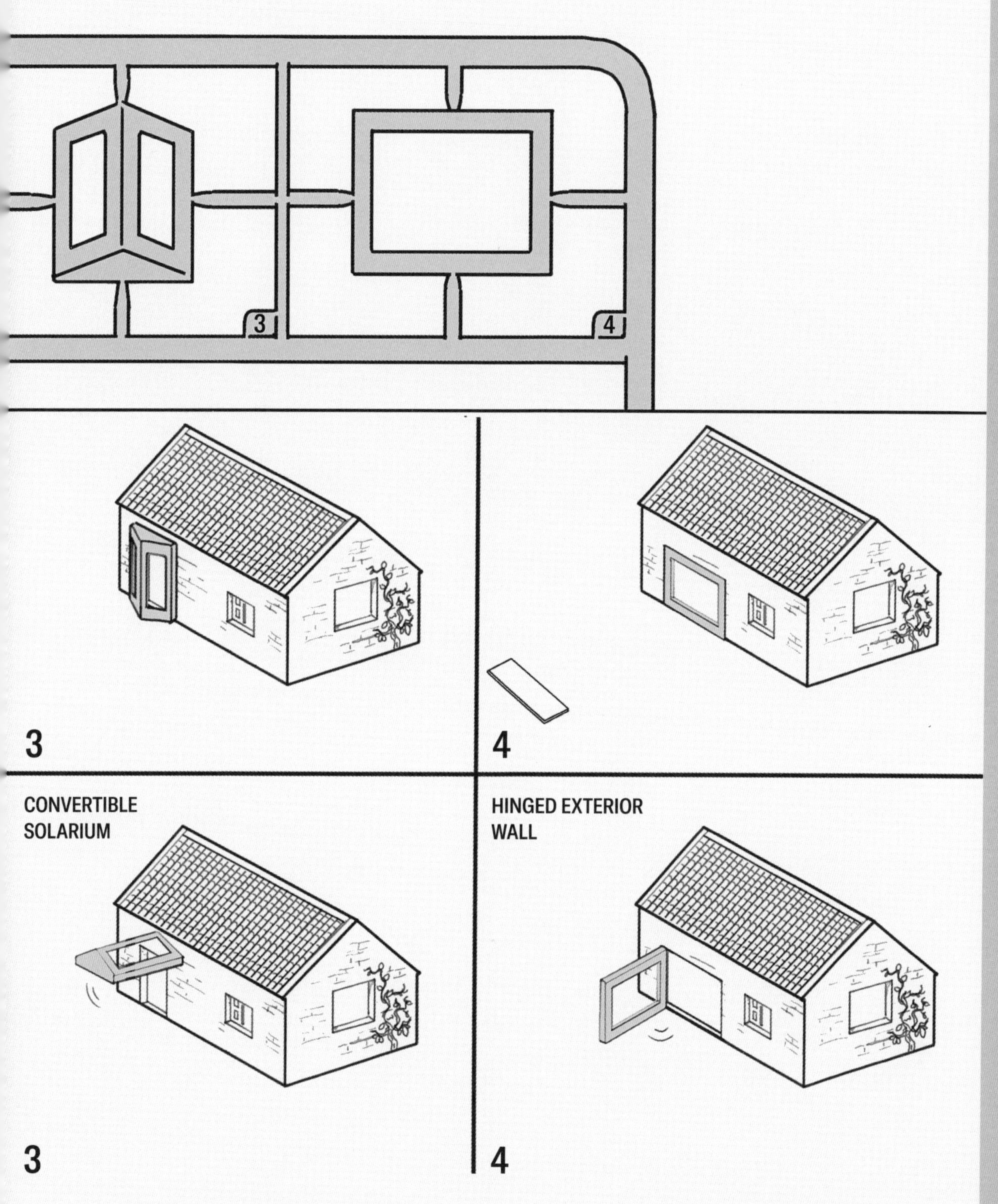
3
4
3
4
CONVERTIBLE
SOLARIUM
HINGED EXTERIOR
WALL
3
4

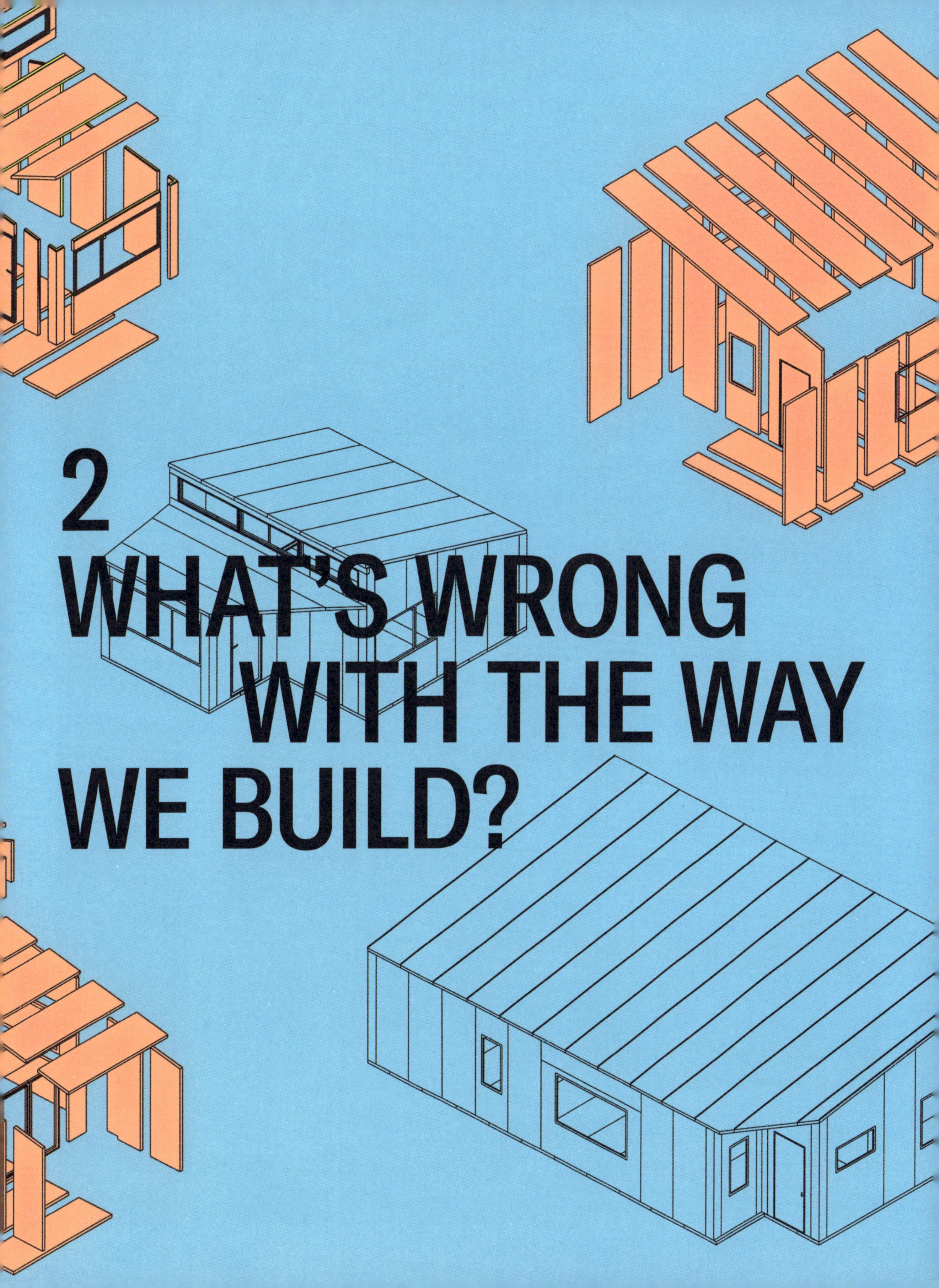

2 WHAT'S WRONG WITH THE WAY WE BUILD?

There have been remarkable advancements in design and building technology and substantial shifts in housing needs in the last century. However, the home construction industry has remained surprisingly stagnant. Using the US as an example, home construction has relied primarily on site-built wood frame construction since the 1930s. There have been incremental improvements in techniques and materials, however the fundamental model of construction has changed very little. This lack of innovation has contributed to the high cost of housing and the slow speed at which it is delivered [3].

This is in stark contrast to other industries; industrialized manufacturing has revolutionized access to affordable quality goods. Often, the manufacturing of products happens in centralized production facilities. Whether cars, shoes, or computers, we do not expect these goods to be made by hand nor fabricated where each customer is located.

The need to conform to the requirements of a site, what is called site specificity, is an aspect that differentiates a house from other products. While a house is in fact a package of many standardized products, the package itself must be customized to suit its context. Site conditions typically start with the particular shape of a site, the characteristics of the soil, and the location of public utility connections. Labor for construction is also distributed and must be brought to each building site. This decentralized mode of production leads to numerous inefficiencies including additional transportation, time, and waste [17].

The specificity of a site also includes requirements dictated by local regulations that often differ from one city to another. This fragmented building and regulatory landscape is one reason why it is difficult to produce housing in large-scale quantities. For a builder, it is difficult to expand beyond their own market if they must make alterations to how they build and the products they use to conform to requirements in new locations.

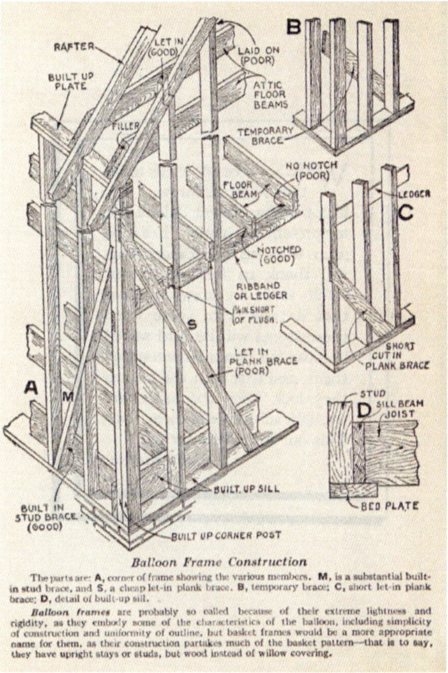
RAFTER
BUILT UP PLATE
LET IN (GOOD)
LAID ON (POOR)
ATTIC FLOOR BEAMS
B
FILLER
TEMPORARY BRACE
NO NOTCH (POOR)
FLOOR BEAM
LEDGER
C
NOTCHED (GOOD)
RIBBAND OR LEDGER
S
LET IN PLANK BRACE (POOR)
SHORT CUT IN PLANK BRACE
A
M
STUD
D
SILL BEAM
JOIST
BUILT. UP SILL
BED PLATE
BUILT IN STUD BRACE (GOOD)
BUILT UP CORNER POST
Balloon Frame Construction
The parts are: A, corner of frame showing the various members. M, is a substantial built-in stud brace, and S, a cheap let-in plank brace. B, temporary brace; C, short let-in plank brace; D, detail of built-up sill.
Balloon frames are probably so called because of their extreme lightness and rigidity, as they embody some of the characteristics of the balloon, including simplicity of construction and uniformity of outline, but basket frames would be a more appropriate name for them, as their construction partakes much of the basket pattern—that is to say, they have upright stays or studs, but wood instead of willow covering.

Construction of a stick-built home, a dominant building technique since the 1930s.

Contemporary construction of a stick-built home, which are still standard in the US today.

Balloon frame construction (axonometric diagram).
St Mary's Church, 1833, Illinois.

Moreover, resistance to change within the building industry hinders the adoption of new technologies and practices that could revolutionize home construction and address the evolving needs of homeowners and communities. Although plenty of alternative approaches to producing housing exist, there is little incentive to adapt new technologies under current conditions. Standard construction relies on manual labor from labor forces that are often rotating or even seasonal. Workers must move from one site to another, making it difficult to train them in new methods, especially if they may be replaced by another person soon after. The result is home construction becomes entrenched in existing methods and products [16].

One of Thomas Edison's single-pour concrete houses being poured in Montclair, New Jersey.

Advertisement for a kit home from the Sears Modern Homes mail order catalog.

Case Study House No. 8, Charles and Ray Eames's home in Los Angeles, California.

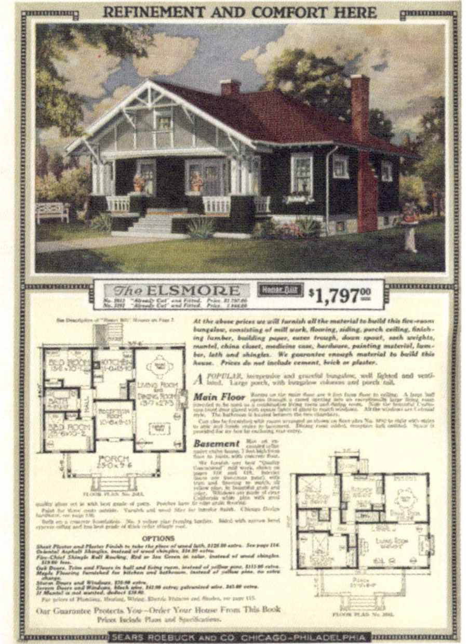

The potential for producing affordable housing for the masses through industrialized manufacturing, also known as pre-fabricated construction, has existed since the industrial revolution. An early example was Thomas Edison's single-pour concrete system, which involved turning a building site into a production line. Each house, with all of its unique features, was cast out of concrete using a continuous mold. Such all-in-one approaches would continue to appear throughout the history of pre-fabrication but with the manufacturing occurring mostly in a factory off site.

One example of a building system that used an opposite approach were the 1908 Sears Modern Homes, which consisted of pre-cut parts that were packaged and shipped disassembled. The on-site construction process was streamlined and efficient because all parts were already available and no additional cutting was necessary. Also known as "kit houses," the Sears Modern Homes were probably the most successful example of pre-fabricated housing in the US: they ceased production in the 1940s after building over 100,000 homes.

By the mid-20th century, pre-fabrication had also captured the attention of leading architects from the US and European Modernist movement [2]. Frank Lloyd Wright, Walter Gropius, Mies van der Rohe, Le Corbusier, Marcel Breuer, and Charles and Ray Eames had all designed pre-fabricated homes in one form or another. Buckminster Fuller and Jean Prouvé, although not trained as architects, were accomplished across multiple disciplines, including architecture, industrial design, and engineering.

Pre-fabricated designs such as Fuller's 1927 Dymaxion House and Prouvé's 1950 Métropole houses were highly influential. Similar to the Sears houses they were also designed to be shipped as pre-fabricated parts and assembled on site. Sears houses relied on traditional wood frame construction and were delivered as loose parts in a wide variety of shapes and sizes. In contrast, Fuller and Prouvé borrowed from the automotive and aerospace industry and designed their houses using a system of repeating modules. They used metal as their primary material, which was more aligned to industrial technologies and could have greater benefit from efficiencies within a factory environment.

Ultimately these examples were too far ahead of their time and only limited numbers of these innovative designs were built. The 1948 Lustron Home was a more successful example of a house developed as an industrial product. It used metal sandwich panel technology and was built entirely out of steel. However, after producing around 2,500 homes the company declared bankruptcy in 1950.

◰ Métropole demountable house by Jean Prouvé in Meudon, France, *c.* 1951.
◫ Packaged House assembly.

◰ Stacked panels of the Packaged House on the construction site.
◳ X-shaped wedge connector of the Packaged House.
◱ Parts for the X-shaped wedge connector of the Packaged House.

FOUR-WAY
THREE-WAY
TWO-WAY
ONE-WAY
POST
CORNER

Panelized systems, similar to kit homes, could be flat packed and efficiently shipped but relied on larger modules and fewer parts that allowed for a quicker assembly process on site. The 1942 Packaged House, developed by Walter Groupius and Konrad Wachsmann, was a prime example of a panelized system. Ten types of panels could be combined and configured to form different designs. The system was particularly notable for its X-shaped wedge connectors that served as the primary fastener for the entire system, simplifying the assembly process. After years of development the venture ended in 1952.

The most common type of pre-fabricated housing in the US today is the manufactured home, also known as mobile homes, which has existed in one form or another since the 1920s. These are entire homes completed in the factory and most often built using wood frame construction. They are shipped to the site with the use of an integrated steel chassis as its base for ease of towing. The wheels on the chassis are removed after the house is installed.

Because manufactured homes are shipped in their complete form, their size is defined by the limitations of roads and highways. The maximum width for pre-fabricated buildings shipped as a whole in the US is 4.9 meters (sixteen feet) but is more commonly four meters (thirteen feet) [14]. Modern manufactured home modules can be placed next to each other and "stitched" together to create larger homes such as "double wides" or "triple wides." Although manufactured homes are widespread, this housing type is seen largely in rural settings and suffers from negative stigmas associated with people of low-income status. This has resulted in its limited use in urban settings where housing demand is high. In cities they are usually relegated to manufactured home communities or mobile home parks.

Modular homes are similar to manufactured homes in that they are also produced in a factory before shipping to the building site. These models do not incorporate a steel chassis and there are versions that can be stacked to form multistory buildings. Manufactured homes and modular homes sometimes incorporate hinged roofs and/or walls that allow for parts of the building to be collapsed for greater efficiency during shipping. Such systems require additional on-site work to cover the hinged areas.

New manufactured homes displayed at a dealership in Austin, Texas.
A range of pre-fabricated housing types and their relationship to shipping.

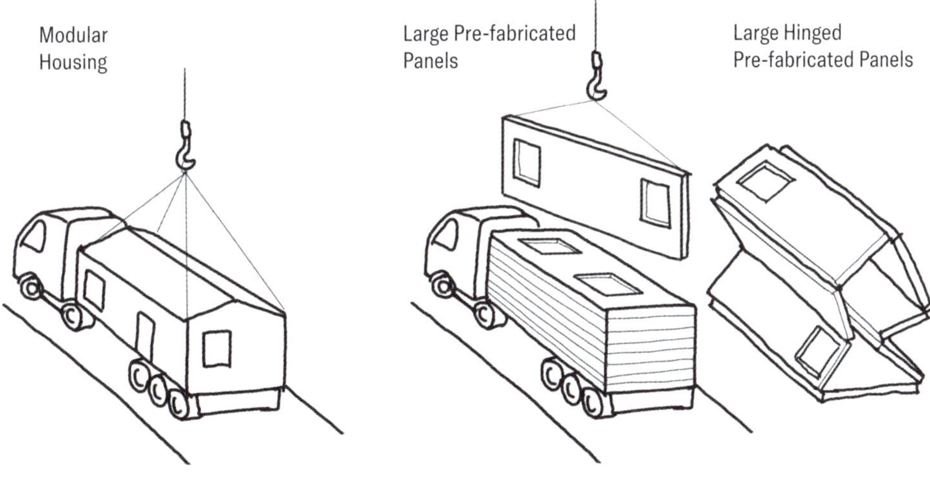

Modular
Housing
Large Pre-fabricated
Panels
Large Hinged
Pre-fabricated Panels

Small Pre-fabricated
Panels

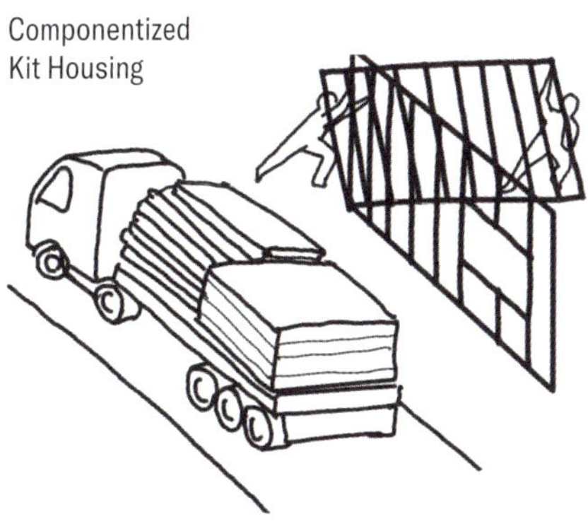

Componentized
Kit Housing

3D printing is a more recent technology that has seen much progress but remains experimental within construction. A 3D printing machine can "print" a concrete structure without the need for formwork. In many ways it is a variation of the Edison single-pour house and shares the idea of placing the industrial manufacturing process in the building site.

The Plugin House system is a panelized system that can be seen as a descendent of the Gropius and Wachsmann Packaged House. Plugin panels are a unique type of structural insulated panel (SIP). The building system consists of sandwich panels produced using an automated injection molding process that incorporates electrical conduit, insulation, interior and exterior finishes into one. Locking mechanisms called cam locks are embedded into the panels as part of the molding process. These cam locks secure panels to one another with a single tool to drastically simplify assembly.

The Plugin House is a pre-fabricated system that sits between a modular or manufactured home that is shipped as a whole and a kit home that is shipped in parts. The cost and limitations associated with shipping from a factory to different sites have substantial implications on the prefabricated system. Modular and manufactured housing can be installed with minimal on-site labor. However because they are shipped in their complete form, shipping efficiency is lost due to the empty space within the homes. The Plugin House, when disassembled, consists of stacked panels and is shipped flat-packed. Systems with parts that can be packed flat lead to much greater shipping efficiency. One shipment can contain multiple homes rather than a singular home.

Details of the cam lock mechanism in a Plugin House panel.
Plugin House panels manufacturing process.

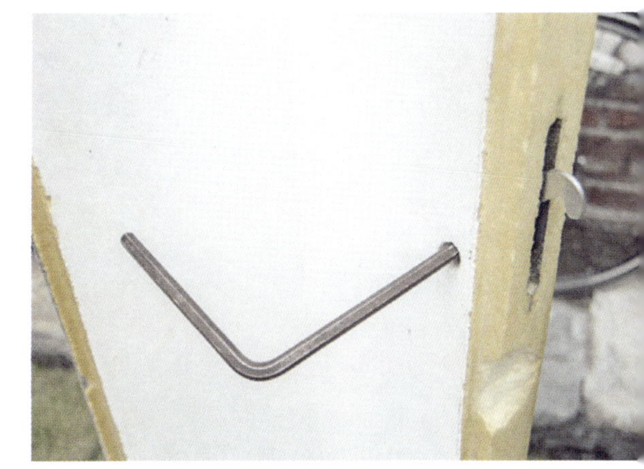

Plugin House panels manufacturing process.

The design of the Plugin House sandwich panel is a departure from the traditional wall assembly of a typical house that includes wood framing as a structure, insulation, wood sheathing, and many layers of finish and weatherproofing materials. By eliminating the need for wood framing, the Plugin panels reduce both the materials used and the complexity of construction, decreasing costs. The panels comprise high-density polyisocyanurate (polyiso) foam core laminated to steel sheet metal on both sides. The materials have multiple purposes. Integrated, they work together as structure, while separately, the polyiso foam functions as high-quality insulation and the sheet metal serves as weatherproofing skin.

Pre-fabricated systems encounter unexpected challenges when applied in real-world scenarios. For instance, in the narrow alleys of Dashilar in Beijing, or the closely populated streets of Rio de Janeiro's favelas in Brazil, it would be impossible to transport a pre-fabricated home built as a whole or to bring in the large cranes necessary for modular pre-fabricated buildings.

The necessity for heavy machinery prevents the delivery of many types of pre-fabricated housing. Even banal elements like electrical wires can make the use of cranes impractical, not to mention the associated costs for specialized labor, scheduling, road closures, and additional fees. In a dense urban location, building a 3D printer to print a house and then to relocate the machinery would encounter significant obstacles and increased costs.

Plugin panels are designed to fit through narrow spaces. Their size and cam lock connections allow panels to be squeezed through narrow alleys, moved into interiors through small doorways, and then assembled from within. The courtyard houses in Dashilar, a protected historic area, must be built using traditional methods, requiring specialized skill that is costly and time consuming. The Plugin House units offer an alternative. Allowing construction in one day and with unskilled labor, Plugin Houses reduce the time and cost of these types of renovation projects.

Plugin panels arriving on truck in the Changchun Jie hutong neighborhood in Beijing.

A Plugin door being carried through a narrow alley into Courtyard 72 in Dashilar, Beijing.

Plugin panel assembly process in the Changchun Jie neighborhood.

Stacked Plugin panels ready for assembly in Courtyard 72 in Dashilar.

A Plugin panel being carried through a narrow doorway in Dashilar.

Aerial view of the PAO office in Dashilar.

◰ Interior view of the PAO office in Dashilar.
◱ Front view of the workshop space in the PAO office in Dashilar.
◲ Construction of Mrs. Dong's Plugin House.
◳ Mrs. Dong lending a hand with the renovation of her Plugin House in Courtyard 72.

Plugin Houses are outfitted with either septic tanks or composting toilets as well as efficient heating and cooling systems. Residents can enjoy modern comforts almost immediately, without suffering the disruption that comes with typical construction practices.

The positive reception to the two Courtyard House Plugins (see page 35) paved the way for additional Plugin projects. Among these was the renovation of Courtyard 37 in Dashilar as a new office for PAO. Relocating our office to the neighborhood meant we were able to embed ourselves in the community where we were working and further familiarize ourselves with local concerns. It was also an opportunity to test the Plugin House system on ourselves before using it for residents.

The project also included two units for interested residents. Mrs. Dong and her son lived in one of the other units in Courtyard 72. At first skeptical, Mrs. Dong became intrigued with the Plugin Houses and approached us after she visited one on a freezing winter day to find it incredibly comfortable and warm. Mr. Sun and his daughter, the second Plugin House customers, lived in a unit that was part of Courtyard 37 and would be PAO's neighbor. There were also four other Plugin Houses that were built as demonstration units in Courtyards 30 and 32.

The Plugin House system now had to accommodate sites with a wider range of shapes and sizes. It was important that the Plugin Houses fit snugly within each of these unique properties without increasing cost. This second phase of the Dashilar pilot gave us the opportunity to demonstrate the incredible customizability of the Plugin system.

◰ Mrs. Dong in front of her completed Plugin House.
◲ The evolution of Courtyard 72 before renovation in 2013, with the first Plugin House demonstration house installed in 2014, and finally with Mrs. Dong's Plugin House in 2015.

Before and after of the interior of Mrs. Dong's Plugin House with her demonstrating her accordion shower.

Before and after of the interior of Mr. Sun's Plugin House with his daughter's new mezzanine sleeping space in Courtyard 37.

⊞ Courtyard 30 East House.
◳ Manufactured home community in Austin, Texas.

The customizability and agility of the Plugin House system is a core attribute and has significant implications on where the system is used and its cost. As one of many in a long history of pre-fabricated systems, it is important to examine the reasons why previous systems have ended in limited use or commercial failure. Today, pre-fabricated buildings make up only a small percentage of housing built in the US. In 2021, manufactured housing consisted of a little over 10% of all new homes built, the largest portion of pre-fabricated housing [6]. Another 3% of housing is modular or panelized [15]. Of all types of pre-fabricated housing, only manufactured homes have generally shown to be lower cost as compared to site-built wood frame construction [6].

While manufactured homes show how pre-fabrication can result in housing that is more affordable than site-built homes, the difficulty of having them placed in urban settings has greatly limited their availability as a housing solution. The negative stigmas attached to this type of housing is entirely cultural. While manufactured homes were once produced at a lower quality than that of traditional site-built homes, that is no longer the case. Generally, it's possible to achieve a higher building quality in factories.

Negative stigmas are linked to the aesthetic features of manufactured housing that relate to their affordability. These include a raised foundation, low pitch roofs, and minimal architectural features. Perhaps the most important characteristic attached to negative stigma is the narrow and long rectangular box shape that dominates manufactured home aesthetics. The different models of manufactured homes can appear repetitive with only superficial differences.

In recognition of the importance of aesthetics, US government agencies such as Fannie Mae (the Federal National Mortgage Association) and Freddie Mac (the Federal Home Loan Mortgage Corporation) require certain architectural features to qualify for federal funding. And many manufacturers are working diligently to provide models such as CrossMods that more closely resemble site-built homes [5]. Modular and panelized systems are the next most common and do offer more customizability. However, they are generally more expensive than site-built homes.

The relationship between the flexibility of a system and cost have plagued the history of pre-fabricated buildings. Previous systems such as the single-pour concrete house and Packaged House failed for a variety of reasons, but a common thread was the difficulty for the systems to be manipulated. As unforeseen needs arise over time, homeowners have found many pre-fabricated systems restrictive. Common changes such as adding an extension to the home or adding another room can be much more cumbersome than with a wood frame construction. In addition, because many systems used proprietary parts, a recurring issue has been the difficulty of making repairs as homes age [14]. For example, parts may have only been available from the original manufacturer or have to be custom ordered. Wood frame construction remains the dominant structural system for all housing in the US, including pre-fabricated homes [14]. For this reason, the majority of parts and services are standardized to integrate with wood frame construction.

The Plugin House is not based on wood frame construction, but the system is designed to be compatible with standard site-built construction methods and home products. Plugin Houses can also be easily modified or adjusted. For example, an individual panel can be unlocked and replaced without affecting other areas of the house. Adding an extra bedroom could be as simple as adding a handful of panels to extend the original house. Alternatively, a new bedroom could be built using wood frame construction that interfaces with the Plugin House system.

Pre-fabricated buildings seldom deviate from four to five-meter- (thirteen to sixteen-foot-) wide rectangular modules, limiting design possibilities to the dimensions of these modules and restricting the shapes that can be created. These constraints render such systems impractical for the irregular and unique properties found in neighborhoods like Dashilar. Take a look around you wherever you live and consider how pre-fabricated buildings might fit into your neighborhood, and what the various obstacles might be. Is there street furniture such as street lamps, bins or bollards that might get in the way? Would electricity pylons and the electrical wires attached to them make accessing sites impossible? Are the spaces between buildings simply too small?

An aerial view of the *pichoneras* suburban housing in Mexico; Jorge Taboada, ALTADEN99, from the series "Alta Densidad," Mexico, 2012.

In contrast to most pre-fabricated buildings, the manufacturing of a Plugin House employs what is called mass customization, where products are mass-produced at scale but also allow for a degree of customizability. The panels are crafted using adjustable molds that can adapt to a variety of shapes, leveraging the speed of the automated injection-molding process. The panelization of a Plugin House system allows for the use of a limited number of panel shapes, which can be assembled in different configurations to create a diverse array of unique designs. The adaptability of the Plugin House manufacturing process and the panelized system make it feasible to produce low-cost customized homes.

The ability to manufacture panels of unique shapes and produce unique designs through different combinations of panels ensures a high degree of flexibility in the design of Plugin Houses. Negative stigmas attached to the repetitive shape and form of manufactured housing can be more easily avoided.

The ability to tailor homes to site-specific conditions affordably is crucial to tackling the housing crisis. In Dashilar, the house-in-house method necessitates a close fit to each site, yet many housing projects in similar contexts avoid specificity in order to reduce costs. Whether constructed manually on site or pre-fabricated, the aim of housing is often to replicate as much as possible. The most favorable condition for this approach is a blank slate site, rather than an intricate urban landscape and pre-existing properties that demand customization. Areas where sites are uniform and conducive to replication tend to be found in underdeveloped locations situated further from city centers and public services.

The efficiencies of sameness and replication play significant roles in the push for outward urban expansion, exacerbating the impacts of suburban sprawl and often leading to disastrous outcomes like the *pichoneras*, or birdcages, in Mexico. This suburban typology built as affordable housing comprises relentless rows of inexpensive pre-fabricated concrete units built in areas with few amenities.

As the development of the Plugin House progressed, we received more interest in applications beyond the house-in-house approach. Could we, for example, use Plugin Houses as urban infill housing? In subsequent chapters we demonstrate how low-cost pre-fabricated housing used as infill may be a better approach to addressing housing needs.

RURAL STORIES

By Andrew Freear

My story

I was lucky to grow up in post-Second World War England at a time when I had access to a free, quality public education. I came from a working-class rural background, but a strong welfare state allowed me the flexibility to navigate setbacks, like failing university classes, without the pressure of immediately finding a job. I could rely on housing support and income assistance, which made it possible to build a life. But things have changed. I lament not just the loss of that system, but also the loss of the belief that good housing is a right for everyone, regardless of whether they are rich or poor.

I was in architecture school just after the time of Archigram, when Peter Cook and his team had already made a significant impact, though the world had started to move on. The images they produced were slightly otherworldly, but what I appreciated most was their utopian attitude toward the world. That really resonated with me, and I enjoyed the sentiment they brought to the architectural conversation. It was at about that time I started to dream about what could be.

When I moved from Leicester to London for architecture school, I fell in with a group that included Eldred Evans and David Shalev, who sponsored me to attend the AA (Architectural Association) in London. Their idea was that I could work for them on weekends and evenings while attending the AA. It might sound like a grueling arrangement, but it worked out fine, at the beginning. Shortly after I started, though, Margaret Thatcher took over British politics, and Eldred and David lost most of their work because they only pursued public projects—schools, hospitals, and housing. As an architect today, it's interesting to reflect on that. Evans and Shalev lost their work, and I lost my sponsor, though the AA took pity on me and employed me in their exhibit building department.

Eldred and David introduced me to David Gray, who ultimately became my AA professor for four years. Gray was part of Lyons Israel Ellis Gray, a renowned architectural practice in London at the time. The firm often collaborated with Camden Council, which was full of young post-Second World War idealists dreaming of a better world. Camden was building low-rise, high-density housing, a response to the growing disillusionment with tower blocks, which had disconnected people from the ground and lacked the community infrastructure they needed. Their mantra was better housing, healthcare, welfare, and education for everyone—not a bad desire to have for a society.

This group of young architects at Camden was led by Neave Brown, who designed the Alexandra Road Estate—a famous housing development that was perceived as brutal and often decried in the press and on punk record albums. At the AA, I wrote my thesis on the project (titled "Alexandra Road: The last great social housing project," which was published in *AA Files 30*, a great honor for a student). While completing my thesis, I met not only the architects and engineers but also the client and many residents, who loved the building, from when it was first constructed to two-to-three decades earlier.

Alexandra Road was designed as low-rise, high-density housing. It's a remarkable scheme with a beautiful park in between, embodying a return to the idea of great utopian green; the stepped section was inspired by the work of Atelier 5 in Switzerland. It is now run by a housing cooperative of residents who

are actively engaged with and committed to their community. The spaces are stunning—truly exceptional. I found that aspirational work to be extraordinary.

Neave Brown also wrote a treatise titled "The Form of Housing," in which he described housing as "background stuff." It was his dream to create modern-day Georgian terraces—good, robust housing that could withstand the test of time. His ideal was homes that are strong, durable, and adaptable, offering flexibility for changing needs.

The Rural Studio story

Today, I pursue these ideas in Alabama in the US, as Director of Rural Studio, a program within Auburn University's School of Architecture, Design and Planning that began in the early 1990s. Its mission is to take students away from the "ivory tower" of academia and immerse them in real-world projects. Students live and work in Hale County, a rural west Alabama county of 15,000 people, in a little town with about 135 residents, essentially in the middle of nowhere. The area has a deep, complex history, particularly concerning civil rights. Just two weeks before Martin Luther King Jr's assassination, he hid from the Ku Klux Klan in a house we later renovated as the Black History Museum. Here they design and build projects that meet community needs, whether it's housing, parks, or community centers. Their education isn't about sitting across from a professor and engaging in theoretical exercises. Our students learn to collaborate, design, and construct their projects, a hands-on experience that differs from most architecture programs.

We started as a housing-first organization, but over time, we expanded into community projects—from small chapels to ball fields. We never said, "No, we can't do this." We figured out how to make it happen. The program has been in the same location for more than thirty years, and students have completed over 220 projects. The community now sees us as both a resource and a neighbor. We make sure all our ideas come from within the community. If we build a library or a firehouse, it's because they asked for help with it. We never impose anything.

The question of adaptability is particularly interesting in our current work. In rural settings, homes aren't seen as wealth generators: they are long-term family assets. Here, people don't buy a house expecting its value to increase so they can then sell it for a profit. Land is relatively cheap, and families tend to move around infrequently. Families maintain a nucleus—a home that remains central to their lives, even if they move away. Their "dream home" is adaptable, durable, and suitable for the local climate and terrain.

To accommodate this tradition of long-term ownership, we're designing multi-generational homes that can evolve over time and suit varying needs. For example, we completed a home for a client named Patriece where part of her house could function as a granny flat, rental unit, or even a home business, like a hair salon.

We've been working on building homes that are self-contained yet adaptable for different family structures. A home might serve a single mother with children or accommodate a multi-generational household, with kids and a grandparent living together. Homes can be inherited and become one of the family's most valuable assets. If we can create something robust and internally adaptable, those homes can truly serve the evolving needs of these families for generations.

In one project we completed, for a client named Reggie, we experimented with a concept called the "pole barn." We built a large roof and slab foundation with two buildings that can serve as starter spaces. This design offers flexibility, allowing the client to expand over time by building new spaces, all while staying under the protection of the big roof. By investing upfront in the roof, columns, and slab, the structure provides immediate shelter and long-term potential for growth.

Rural Studio students assisting with the construction of one of their designs.

Akron Boys & Girls Club 2, a club building designed by Rural Studio in northern Hale County, west Alabama.

This strategy emerged from observing countless homes in the area that were built one room at a time. People often expand incrementally, adding onto their homes as they can afford. With each addition, the rooflines lower, and over time, a new piece of the building on a different foundation may shift, leading to roof damage and leaks—ultimately causing the structure to deteriorate. Our design offers families the opportunity to expand their homes while benefiting from the protection of a large roof and durable slab.

The structures we built underneath Reggie's Home don't touch the roof, allowing the homeowner the potential to extend the buildings over time. During the building process, students learned about Reggie, who grew up on the property. They helped him demolish his old house, which was in poor condition, and built him a new bedroom, kitchen, and dining space in one of the starter spaces. The second volume is what we call the "bonus room," prepped for plumbing and electrical. If he extends these two structures and combines them, it could create a home with up to five bedrooms—all under the protection of the big roof.

Our work on the evolving needs of rural homeowners got us thinking about other adaptable home needs. Rural Studio has had discussions with the Federal Emergency Management Agency (FEMA) about their temporary trailers for disaster victims, which often become permanent homes. Could we instead provide something more sustainable, like a large shed on a slab foundation, that serves as infrastructure for people to rebuild their lives over time?

The need for spaces to be adaptable in the future isn't limited to homes. I'm reminded of a project that was a storefront building for Hale Empowerment & Revitalization Organization (HERO), a nonprofit organization that operated on two- to three-year grant cycles. Initially, students designed the space by filling it with drywall cubicles. One of our friends visited for a review, and he got very angry, saying, "How can you do this? You've got an organization here surviving on grant cycles that doesn't know how it's going to survive and put food on the table in a couple of years. How can you so strongly predict how the space will be used in two to three years?" Thankfully, the team listened. They cleaned out the building and organized the space using chairs, furniture, and self-supporting partitions, making it much more flexible.

Unfortunately, the organization did eventually go into receivership and left the space. But, the space has been rented out to a woman who opened a cafe. If the building had been filled with drywall partitions, this opportunity would never have been possible. Every time I go in there, I think about how the building would have just sat empty. The students had a strong desire to create a lot of architecture in that space; they wanted to build a lot with drywall and showcase their designs. In the end, the simpler design looked like a New York loft: cool, hip, and trendy. It's now a crackerjack of a cafe—and a social center of the town.

Sharing our story with others

Since 2004, we've approached housing as an iterative model. We build houses for individual clients, learning from each previous project, observing

Celebrating the completion of Patriece's Home
Reggie's Home.
Project team for Reggie's Home, from left to right: Addie Harchelroad, Becca Wiggs, George Slaughter, (Reggie) and Paul Fallin.

how people live in them, and then improving with the next house. We started to establish a catalog of housing prototypes. Five years ago, Fannie Mae (the Federal National Mortgage Association) approached us, asking if we had any rural housing models because they had none for their rural mortgages. At first, we thought they were joking: was there really no one else working in this field? Since then, they've sponsored the Studio's Front Porch Initiative (FP). Now, we're working with fourteen housing providers across seven states, helping nonprofits and community organizations build the models that we developed in Hale County. Currently the FP has twenty-two completed homes, six homes currently under construction, and twenty homes in development across the Southeast.

Today, we're focused on designing homes that are relevant and replicable, ensuring our ideas can be applied in other places. We've come to realize that unless the state funds the design and development, no architect, developer, or client

in this country is going to invest the millions of hours we spend designing such 83 to 102-square-meter (900 to 1,100-square-foot) houses down to the finest detail. It feels like a moral responsibility for us to do this work because no one else can or will take it on.

This design gap has been eye-opening for me, especially considering the historical politics that deliberately created such inequalities in the rural South. Through FP, we're working to address these challenges. We use our housing models, making sure they meet local codes, and Fannie Mae covers the costs. Our team works with nonprofit developers and builders, helping them choose the appropriate model, conduct site planning, and make smart decisions up front. There's very little money in these projects, so they need to be built quickly and efficiently. But, it's not just about building a home that is affordable: it's about creating homes that are high performing, energy efficient, and extremely robust—homes with predictable (and low) energy costs, allowing housing partners to invest in efficiency upfront to lower usage costs later.

Ironically, our rural housing models are now being used in cities like Nashville and New Orleans. Smaller houses with flexible footprints are helping in areas where topography makes development difficult, and our work has added value to sites that were previously considered worthless. There's also growing interest in Accessory Dwelling Units (ADUs), and our prototypes are helping with that too.

Regarding rural America, some might say, "Why does it matter in a place seemingly with so few people?" Although population density in rural communities is low, 20% of our nation lives in these areas. Folks in these places grow and raise our food, providing the backbone of our food systems. Off the small roads of rural counties across the nation you'll find a number of non-agricultural industries. Rural communities also provide the raw materials for everything from manufacturing to housing. We owe this fifth of our population a higher quality of life.

Rural housing problems may be more hidden than those in cities, where issues are more visible, but rural needs are no less significant. Beyond housing, rural communities suffer from myriad other challenges. Many rural communities are food deserts. Many struggle with the basics of community infrastructure as well. Sewage systems are an ongoing challenge. Access to broadband, which is nearly non-existent, would make rural life more attractive and reduce the sense of isolation that contributes to political divides. Rural Studio is tackling some of these obstacles, producing much of our own food on site at the Rural Studio Farm and collaborating on a pilot project that will improve wastewater treatment.

In places like the rural South, civic life, connectivity, housing, and poverty are both intertwined and less obvious to the rest of the country. I dream of the potential for these overlooked communities. Though fulfillment of that dream is slow and elusive, we hope that our work makes incremental strides to improve the lives of our west Alabama neighbors.

◰ Regions, Rural Studio Front Porch Initiative, and Chipola Area Habitat for Humanity teamed up to build homes in Marianna, Florida to aid in recovery efforts after Hurricane Michael.

◱ Joanne's Home, part of the 20K Project that would later become the Front Porch Initiative.

3 HOW DO GOVERNMENTS GET HOUSING WRONG?

In cities grappling with rapid population growth, the challenge of keeping pace with change is compounded by outdated regulatory processes. Policy innovation is vital for cities to adapt to evolving conditions like the housing crisis. However, regulation, governing, planning, and building are frequently characterized by rigidity and bureaucracy, significantly impacting housing access.

Governments inherently operate with multiple layers of bureaucracy to ensure stability, but this also leads to sluggish processes that are not conducive to innovative solutions. How does policy innovation happen within governing structures that are not built for experimentation and risk taking? It's crucial to delve into existing solutions that haven't been sufficiently explored or implemented. This entails examining successful strategies from diverse contexts—for example, small-scale pilots or temporary interventions tied to events, such as design weeks and design biennales—and evaluating their potential applicability to the current problem.

In addition, it's essential to explore possibilities that haven't been conceived yet by fostering creativity and encouraging out-of-the-box thinking. This might involve conducting pilots, demonstrations, and experimenting with various ways of testing ideas. By integrating research into existing solutions with the exploration of innovative possibilities, policymakers can craft effective strategies to tackle complex challenges such as the housing crisis.

We found ourselves unwittingly engaged in a process of policy innovation when invited to participate in the Dashilar urban regeneration project in Beijing. This area had been earmarked as a pilot zone for testing novel land-use regulations, allowing for the transfer of ownership of individual subdivided properties rather than properties as a whole. Initially, the potential impact of such an approach was uncertain. While fully vacant properties are relatively easy to repurpose, the high renovation costs often necessitate attracting higher-income residents. However, in Dashilar, most properties are only partially vacant, lacking a clear plan for utilization. Partial occupancy often deters new occupants, as existing residents tend to have a lower economic status. The new policy encouraging the renovation and reuse of these partially vacant properties was untested and lacked a validated approach.

The introduction of the Plugin house-in-house approach served as an experiment within this new policy framework. By renovating properties without making major changes to the existing buildings, we managed to keep costs low and minimize disruption to current residents. Economically, the modest costs ensured that new uses didn't have to cater exclusively to higher-income brackets. Through this pilot, we not only demonstrated the feasibility of a novel renovation approach but also validated the efficacy of the new policy.

Not only were local authorities delighted with the Plugin Houses, but local residents, too. The house-in-house approach helped policymakers and residents recognize the potential of partially occupied properties. The enthusiasm from residents wasn't surprising, given that the idea originated from the residents themselves. It was through conversations with residents and observing their informal property improvements that the house-in-house concept emerged, rooted in neighborhood lessons.

One house-in-house example in Dashilar is the historic Zhongyuan Bank building. Built in 1907, the building housed the first Beijing stock exchange. After the founding of the People's Republic of China in 1949 the building was converted to dormitories. Visitors to the building today would find the ground floor of the double-height central atrium filled with small house-like structures built as extensions of the subdivided units on either side.

The prior adoption of the house-in-house strategy underscores the importance of exploring pre-existing community solutions, even if they're bespoke and not formalized. Dashilar represents a reservoir of grassroots ideas that authorities should seriously consider as valid methods of urban regeneration. It's akin to crowdsourcing ideas from those most affected and with the most at stake on a day-to-day basis.

Nevertheless, it's essential not to romanticize or blindly embrace informality. The prevalence of informality signals a lack of regulation and policy failure, and reflects authorities' struggles to devise effective policies for change. Safety concerns, such as fire hazards and compromised structures, must be addressed. However, rather than dismissing existing solutions, they should be carefully considered alongside any proposed new orders.

Interior view of the former Beijing stock exchange building in Dashilar featuring multiple informal constructions.

"I once believed that my planning expertise could improve urban villages [dense, informally developed communities built incrementally outside official planning systems]. But after years of comparing them with newly planned districts, I've developed a deep respect for the collective intelligence embedded in these self-built environments—communities that emerged without the guidance of professional

Map of informal construction in Dashilar, 2014.
Mrs. Dong with all her belongings placed in the yard of Courtyard 72 as she awaits the completion of the construction of her Plugin House.

planners. They have become a powerful source of inspiration. At the same time, I've grown increasingly critical of the narrow, short-sighted perspectives that often shape planner-led developments, frequently driven by elite interests. What I once saw as flaws in urban villages—irregular plot patterns, limited infrastructure, and fire safety concerns—now seem minor when weighed against their extraordinary value as models of autonomy, self-sufficiency, low-carbon living, and socially cohesive urbanism. In 2003, I provocatively claimed that 'urban villages don't need reform; the real problem is planning.' Years later, I stand by that statement more than ever: it is urban villages that offer essential lessons for how we might reform planning itself."

Huang Weiwen is a Shenzhen-based urban planner and public intellectual. He was the former Deputy Chief Planner of the Shenzhen Urban Planning Bureau. A Loeb Fellow at Harvard Graduate School of Design, Huang is also a founding figure of the Shenzhen-Hong Kong Bi-City Biennale of Urbanism/Architecture (UABB), using the platform to promote experimental, participatory approaches to city-making.

The plugin approach didn't introduce a new concept but rather legitimized a pre-existing strategy. Although novel to city officials, this method of property upgrading was familiar to the community. Hence, local residents embraced the idea, signaling to authorities the potential effectiveness of the new policy. The support from local authorities was partially due to its endorsement by residents.

Although the plugin approach was accepted, there remained a sense of risk for both residents and local authorities. Government officials initially approached our concept with caution. Implementing a pre-fabricated system to construct a house within a house was unprecedented, leading to concerns around potential major issues. However, the speed and ease of installing a Plugin House also meant it could be disassembled and removed just as easily, making it a low-risk proposal due to its flexibility.

For residents, distrust towards the local government had accumulated over time, acting as a barrier to past regeneration efforts in Dashilar. Residents were wary of their properties being taken away, hearing stories of forced relocations, people being barred from returning to renovated properties, and receiving unfair compensation. As a neutral third party, PAO played a crucial role in providing a balanced perspective on the approach. Additionally, the quick installation process of a Plugin House allowed residents to witness the entire process within a single day, further contributing to their acceptance and understanding of the initiative.

Support for our work also extended far beyond the community of Dashilar. The Dashilar urban regeneration pilot was notable for its openness to the public and the result was generous support. To initiate a public exchange of ideas and discussion, the work in Dashilar was promoted during Beijing Design Week, an annual celebration of art and design. Dashilar policy initiatives were matched with placemaking activities, community events, exhibitions, and workshops open to the public. Open calls to artists and designers invited the creative community locally and globally to generate ideas and activities to help engage the public in the reimagining of Dashilar. For a one-week period the entire district was transformed into what Dashilar could be. These annual events increased awareness of Dashilar initiatives, helped sway higher authorities, and generated momentum for the ongoing long-term pilot projects there.

Beijing Design Week in a hutong neighborhood in 2019.

A neighborhood gathering organized by Dashila(b), a community-led development organization, for Beijing Design Week 2012.

Pop-up Habitats used to exhibit the concept of the Plugin House at Beijing Design Week 2013.

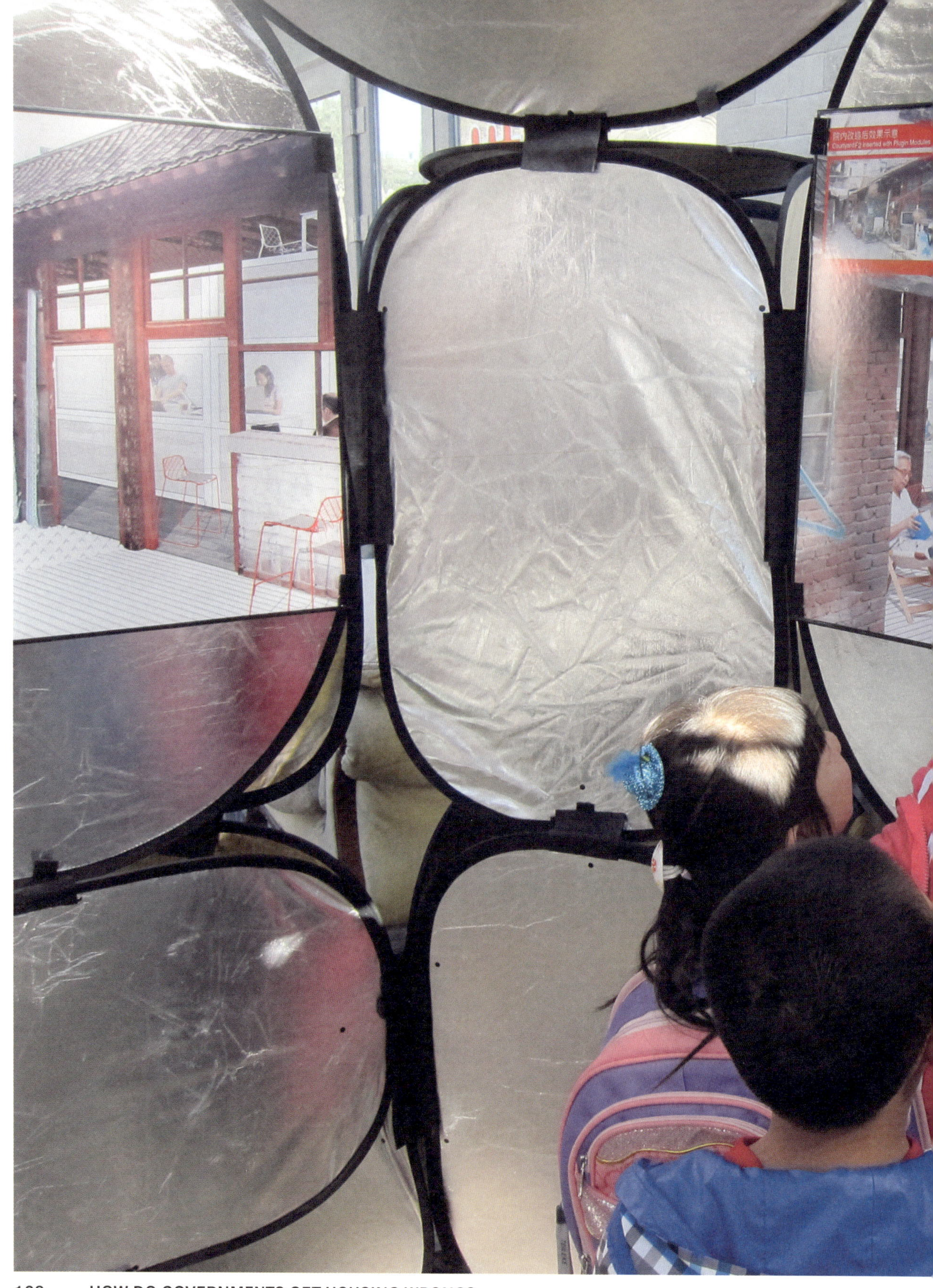

Pop-up Habitats exhibited on a hutong rooftop during Beijing Design Week 2013.

PAO's pop-up Tricycle Shops used as vendor stalls during Beijing Design Week 2015.

Pop-up Habitats installed as a canopy inside a courtyard at Beijing Design Week 2013.

Pop-up Habitats installed as part of an exhibit at Beijing Design Week 2013.

ROUGH
TRADE
WEST
ROUGHTRADE.COM

PAO first participated in the 2013 Beijing Design Week by creating temporary installations in two courtyard houses with what we called our Pop-Up Habitats. We utilized lightweight shade structures to span the courtyards, demonstrating our ability to enhance these properties through minimal interventions. Furthermore, we displayed renderings and drawings of our house-in-house proposal, which caught the attention of organizers and was subsequently chosen as a pilot project.

The exchange of these ideas facilitated notable advancements in the Plugin House system each year, with progress showcased to the public during subsequent Beijing Design Weeks. This platform provided the public with opportunities to visit and learn about our Plugin House projects. Many Plugin units served as venues for exhibitions, workshops, and events during this period.

Our Plugin House work, combined with urban pilots integrated into art and design festivals, generated significant interest. This led to various opportunities and applications in other cities. The Bi-City Biennale of Urbanism/Architecture in Shenzhen is one of China's longest running design festivals and is attached to the instigation of many successful urban regeneration projects. Shenzhen itself was founded as an experimental city and continues to be a center for urban innovation to this day. The biennale presented several opportunities between 2017 and 2018 to build Plugin Houses in urban villages in Shenzhen to demonstrate the applicability of our approach in different contexts.

Urban villages are villages built on land originally designated for agriculture that have, as a result of urban expansion, been encompassed by urban developments. Many urban villages are left in a state of limbo, left out of the benefits of urbanization. Because these properties can't be sold to people outside of the village (due to government policy), many are left abandoned by owners who move to the city. For regulatory reasons many abandoned properties in this location cannot be torn down and rebuilt. In this case, instead of building inside a courtyard house we were invited by local authorities in Shangwei urban village in Shenzhen to build Plugin Houses inside the ruins of old farmhouses. Plugin Houses were used to repurpose these properties until the future of these communities became more clear.

Exhibition of the Plugin House demonstration unit at Beijing Design Week 2014.

Exhibition of the Plugin House at Beijing Design Week 2014.

Neighbors inquire about the Plugin House at Beijing Design Week, 2015.

Bird's-eye view of the Fang Family Plugin House in Shangwei.
View of the Fang Family Plugin House in Shangwei village.
Aerial view of the Fang Family Plugin House in Shangwei.

Overview of abandoned houses and Plugin Houses in Shangwei urban village, Shenzhen, 2018.
Aerial view of the Huang Family Plugin House in Shangwei.
Bird's-eye view of the Huang Family Plugin House in Shangwei.

View of the Fang Family Plugin House in Shangwei.
Interior views of the Huang Family Plugin House in Shangwei.

As the Plugin House expanded to other cities, we were approached by many private individuals who lived near Dashilar who were also interested in the Plugin House system. We found that residents had less of a need for our house-in-house approach and were more enthusiastic about the Plugin House as an addition to a property.

Strict interpretations of land use requirements prevent any additions. In these cases, the projects would have to be built informally. As previously mentioned, additions abound in Dashilar without a formal permitting process. However, in our house-in-house projects we had in fact incorporated some extensions into the designs; in government-funded projects, additions were tolerated.

Mrs. Fan's Plugin House was the first of these accessory structures. Her Plugin House replaced an existing extension that was built as a kitchen. Within this footprint we integrated the kitchen area with the living area in the rear and added a private bathroom. The height of the structure was maximized to increase natural light in the deep and narrow property, and a roof deck was added to expand her recreational space.

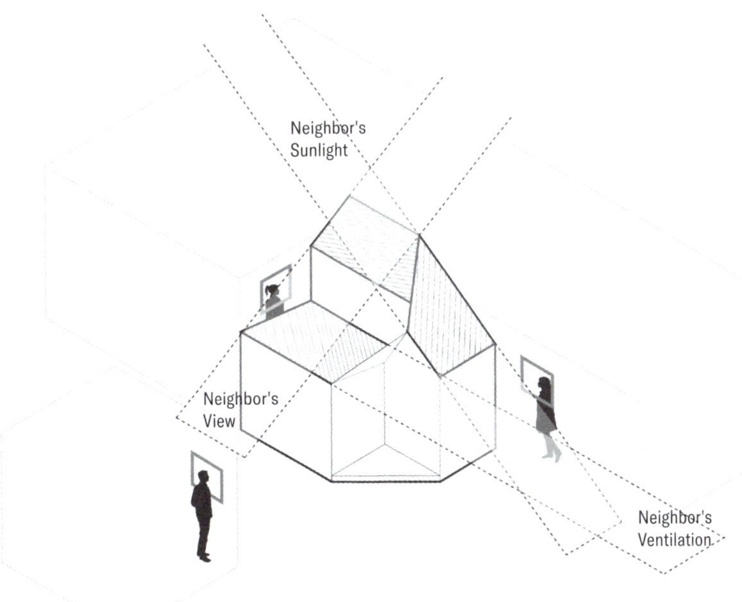

Mrs. Fan in front of her completed Plugin House.

Mrs. Fan discussing her ideas and requirements with the PAO team at the PAO office.

Drawing showing the design constraints as expressed by Mrs. Fan's neighbors.

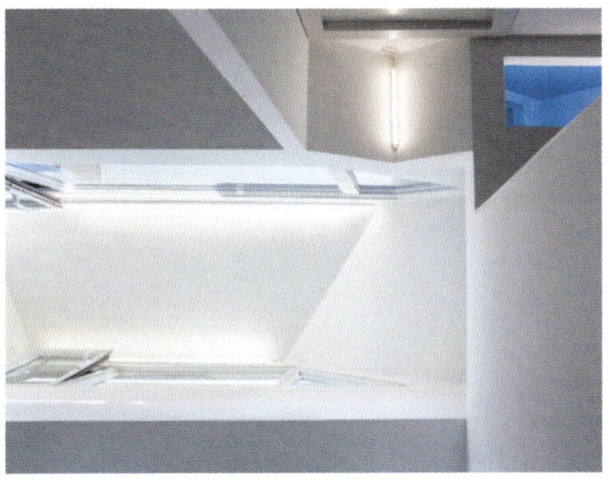

Bird's-eye view of Mrs. Fan's Plugin House.
View of the entrance of Mrs. Fan's Plugin House.
View of Mrs. Fan's roof terrace.
Interior view with Mrs. Fan inside her completed Plugin House.
View of the clerestory windows and elevated ceiling inside Mrs. Fan's Plugin House.

◰ Mr. and Mrs. Wang in front of their Plugin House in Yinlin village, Guangdong province.
◱ View of Mr. Li's Plugin House, constructed inside his backyard.
◲ Mr. Zhao in front of his Plugin House in Dashilar.
◳ View from above the entrance, stairs, and terrace of Mr. Zhao's Plugin House.

We continued to build other accessory structures; some were extensions of homes such as Mr. Zhao's Plugin House and others were independent structures such as Mr. Li's Plugin House, which was built in his backyard. We found, in general, opportunities for the use of such small residential structures in China was limited. While the need was there, the informal conditions of such projects made it difficult to expand this type of work. In general, the predominant residential typology in China consists of high-rise towers rather than one-story, single-family homes.

While small structures built as additions to existing properties were mostly built informally in China, on the other side of the world, we found a growing interest in the US to promote such structures, known as Accessory Dwelling Units (ADUs). Historically, ADUs in the US were informally built structures, too. Today there are strong efforts towards making better use of land and densifying cities through encouraging the building of ADUs. Many American cities aim to relieve their housing crisis by encouraging homeowners to build ADUs in their backyards.

While many city governments and communities see the potential of ADUs, there is also much opposition from local residents. The barriers to ADUs are indicative of those experienced by many housing initiatives and among these is the "not-in-my-backyard" ideology or NIMBYism. NIMBY notions include the fear of negative impacts on an existing community due to development. Concerns range from the impact on traffic and parking spaces from increased housing, to lower property values due to the introduction of lower-income residents. The response is often to prevent new construction through a variety of means which include resistance to regulatory changes that would make the building of ADUs easier.

In the US, we found opportunities to promote ADU legislation and engage the public in housing policy discussions through the use of the Plugin House as a temporary event installation. We combined our experience with art and design festivals with the unique ability to quickly install and dismantle the Plugin House. In 2017, PAO proposed erecting a Plugin House demonstration unit in front of Boston City Hall to the Mayor's Housing Innovation Lab (iLab) in Boston, Massachusetts. The work of the iLab was policy innovation and supported initiatives that engaged the public, policymakers, and building professionals.

"In 2015, Boston established the iLab to fundamentally rethink how we develop, design, and fund housing. Faced with the shortcomings of traditional building approaches and escalating construction costs, we are exploring innovative materials, methods, and designs to drive down housing costs. Recognizing that current methods are inadequate to meet residents' evolving needs—smaller households, diverse family structures, and new ways of living and working—we are experimenting with innovative models to create housing that reflects contemporary life. This work, exemplified by our collaboration with James Shen on the Plugin House demonstration, sparked public discussion about novel approaches to meeting Boston's evolving housing needs".

Marcy Ostberg, Deputy Director, Mayor's Office of New Urban Mechanics in Boston and former Director of the Housing Innovation Lab, Mayor's Office of New Urban Mechanics in Boston.

Volunteers assembling the Plugin House demonstration unit at Boston City Hall.

The Plugin House demonstration at Boston City Hall.

Visitors viewing the exhibition inside the Plugin House demonstration unit at Boston City Hall.

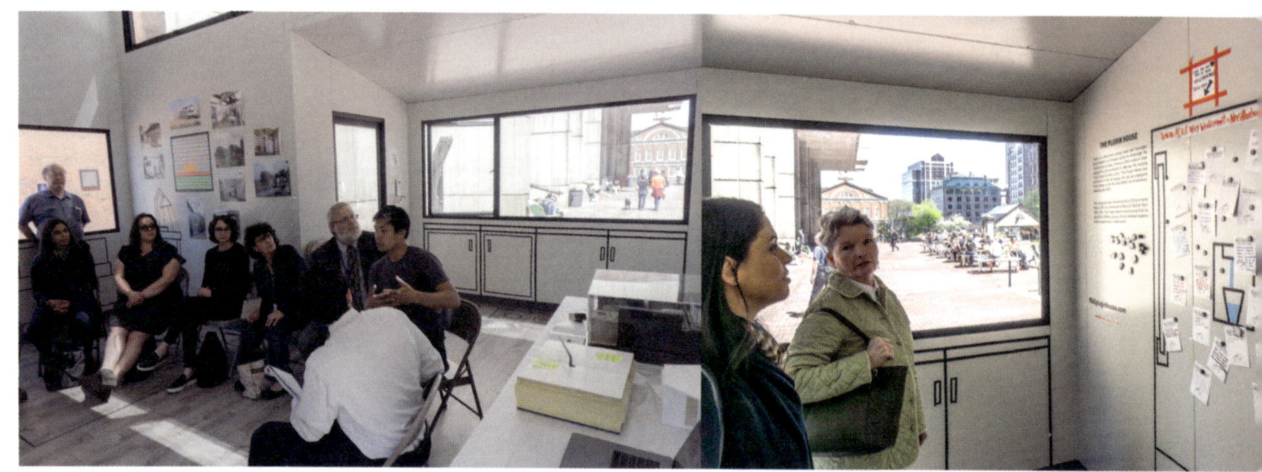

The Boston City Hall Plugin Demo was set up with a small exhibition inside and was used as a venue for public events that addressed housing issues. Visitors were invited to tour the house, ask city staff questions, discuss new policy ideas and leave comments. Roundtable discussions were held among community leaders and policymakers. It was a learning experience for all those involved. The feedback was displayed on the walls of the Plugin House and documented for later reference. This data helped policymakers craft a new ADU policy that was passed later that year.

Discussing ADU policy inside the Plugin House allowed participants to experience the size and scale of the type of housing that was the subject of conversation. People would walk into the house and exclaim: "Wow, it's much larger than I expected!" or "I can totally imagine this in my backyard." Seeing an ADU in person in this context helped bridge the gap between abstract policy concepts and personal experience. Immediately, people thought of benefits to having an ADU, such as an extra living unit for their college-age kids or for their aging parents. Much of policy work is to communicate complex relationships to the general public. But this is often with the use of limited tools such as papers and presentations. Through direct experience, the demonstration unit made it possible for people to achieve a sophisticated understanding of cutting-edge housing policy. They were able to come up with their own ideas and conclusions that would have otherwise been much more difficult.

View of roundtable discussion with policymakers on new Accessible Dwelling Units (ADU) policy inside the Plugin House.

Visitors view the message board inside the Plugin House.

View of questions and comments on housing issues collected from visitors inside the Plugin House.

Student volunteers building the Plugin House at Harvard Yard as part of Harvard University's ARTS FIRST festival.

The ability to quickly erect and disassemble the Boston City Hall Plugin Demo lowered the barrier of acceptance for something new and different. The suggestion of building a fully fledged house in front of city hall would typically bring up all sorts of red flags and permitting concerns from authorities. But visitors were not visiting a model of a house, but the actual thing itself. That said, the project was also clearly presented as a temporary design installation that left the site unchanged after the event.

The installation and removal of the Plugin House was accomplished by volunteers with no previous experience in construction. These activities became events in and of themselves. We were able to show some of the advantages of the Plugin House system without much explanation. And the volunteers, having first-hand experience at the ease in using the system, became natural advocates.

Moreover, the Plugin House has served as a valuable pedagogical tool in academic contexts, offering students hands-on experience in building a house. At Harvard University in Massachusetts, students installed the Plugin House in Harvard Yard for the university's annual ARTS FIRST festival, where it served as a pop-up arts venue for a week, showcasing

THE NORTH FACE

The Plugin House demonstration unit in Harvard Yard.
Student volunteers building the Plugin House at Harvard.
A DJ set at the Plugin House.
A concert at the Plugin House.
Visitors view the exhibition at the Plugin House.
A performance from a student dance troupe at the Plugin House.
Kids and parents gather at the Plugin House.

performances of spoken word, dance, and music to the public. Similarly, students at Auburn University's Rural Studio in Alabama built a Plugin House as part of their curriculum, where it remains permanently to support research comparing other innovative building technologies. These educational initiatives highlight the adaptability and accessibility of the Plugin House concept, furthering its impact beyond community development projects.

We've discussed ways of innovating with land use regulation and how to engage the public in the process. Equally important is the regulatory environment that governs building technology innovation. The challenge of bringing new building methods and technologies to market is often not the technology itself but rather the navigating of the complexities of building regulation. The process of approval for new technologies can be murky. Building construction is predominantly guided by prescriptive building codes, dictating every detail of construction, from wood stud spacing to drywall screw placement. Deviations require performance data, raising complexities when introducing new materials or structural systems not prescribed in the code.

Plugin Houses undergo extensive testing to meet regulatory requirements, including inspections of the production process in the factory. However, the fragmented regulatory landscape poses challenges, with certifications obtained in one jurisdiction not always recognized in others. Encouraging standardized testing and certification processes could mitigate some of these obstacles [11].

The Plugin House at the Rural Studio in Newbern, Alabama.
Students at the Rural Studio construct a Plugin House.

The path to regulatory approval remains unclear, especially for smaller companies or startups. The testing and certification process, while essential, demands substantial financial resources, often limiting access to larger corporations. Streamlining testing and certification procedures and providing clearer pathways to regulatory approval are essential to fostering innovation in building regulation.

The development of testing regimes that keep pace with technological advances is also extremely challenging. By the time a new testing method is adopted, building technology may have progressed beyond its relevance. Until such barriers are overcome, the role of new technology in reducing housing costs will be highly limited [3].

Structural testing of the Plugin panels.
Full-scale fire test of the Plugin panels.
Fire test of the Plugin panels.

DESIGNING FOR CHANGE

By Marina Tabassum

Bangladesh has experienced incredible changes within my lifetime. I witnessed the birth of our nation in the 1970s, and from that point onward, it has faced numerous challenges. The Bangladesh Liberation War in 1971 resulted in the killing of hundreds of intellectuals. After the war ended, the country experienced internal power struggles for two decades; Bangladesh endured periods of autocratic rule, and economic development progressed slowly. It wasn't until the late 1990s that the country began to transition towards democracy.

Bangladesh had been an agricultural economy for many years, but as the open market economy took hold, we experienced a boom in the garment industry. Villagers were attracted to cities with stories of success, leading to extensive urban migration from the countryside that continues to this day. From what I've seen, this has not led to any improvement in human living conditions. Industrial development has only intensified socio-economic inequalities.

Marina Tabassum, Khudi Bari, Bangladesh, 2020–present.
Marina Tabassum, Museum of Independence, Bangladesh, 2015.

Khudi Bari homes are built in areas susceptible to flooding.
Marina Tabassum, Women Led Community Center, Rohingya Refugee Camp, Camp 8W, Kutupalong, Ukhiya, 2022.

In addition to socio-economic challenges, the country also faces significant environmental threats due to its geographic location in the world's largest and most populous delta. The effects of climate change on its hydrological system have caused massive displacement, which is exacerbated by people's lack of land rights.

Informal settlements in Bangladesh highlight the systemic failures in urban planning and governance around these complex dynamics. These settlements underscore the urgent need for innovative architectural responses. Blaming residents of informal settlements for building them illegally overlooks the underlying causes—a lack of viable housing options and inadequate urban infrastructure. Architects can play a pivotal role in advocating for inclusive urban development strategies that prioritize the needs of marginalized communities.

These are difficult but crucial issues for architects to engage with. Architecture itself is a relatively young profession in Bangladesh. The first school of architecture was only established in the 1960s. Now, after several decades, architects can claim they have established a foundation for the profession. Today, architects mainly serve a limited portion of the population with traditional services, such as designing private homes, interiors, and renovations. At the same time, the economic landscape is marked by widening disparities both within cities and in peripheral areas. Architects must adapt their role and innovate to address broader societal challenges.

The limited role of architects has troubled me from the moment I began practicing. Architects must take on roles that are more proactive and visionary. They need to be keen observers and critical thinkers, understanding the broader socio-economic and environmental contexts in which they operate. It is not sufficient to wait for clients to pursue architects with dream projects; architects must engage proactively with communities and stakeholders, offering their knowledge and services to improve living environments and promote inclusive design.

Innovation in architectural practice is crucial. It goes beyond creating aesthetically pleasing structures; it involves offering solutions that address pressing societal needs. This shift demands architects envision projects that serve the greater good, ensuring people's right to good design and a good living environment.

Architects need to expand their roles to encompass work beyond traditional practice. To address the pressing challenges of our time, research plays a pivotal role. It allows us to delve into issues overlooked in conventional architecture, providing a deep understanding of local demographics and needs. Being on the ground and engaging directly with communities enhances our ability to respond effectively and precisely.

I teach a global housing studio at the Delft University of Technology in the Netherlands focusing on low-income housing, often looking into informal sectors in Bangladesh. Our work has been about finding a balance and creating a more inclusive approach to housing, rather than viewing informality as a separate entity. Bangladesh's capital Dhaka is dominated by real estate speculation. Its development is based on a plot-based system, with small plots of individual land ownership. Due to inheritance laws, landowners often can't divide their land further and must build upwards, requiring investment many can't afford. This has led to agreements between developers and landowners, where developers supply the capital to develop a site in return for a percentage of the completed apartments. This model has become the norm in Dhaka and has resulted mostly in developments that cater to high-end and upper-middle-income families. Consequently, there is a significant lack of housing for lower-income and middle-income families. While recently there has been more attention paid to middle-income housing, the lower-income sector remains largely neglected.

In response, we advocate for the integration of lower-income housing within new developments to make them more inclusive. Working with policymakers is crucial and our research aims to influence policy so that a certain percentage of housing is designated for lower-income families. People in the informal sector, ironically, pay the highest rents in the city. A single room rents at $80 a month, which is a significant burden for families in Bangladesh, considering many earn only around $150 per month. This leaves them with very little to survive on.

To confront these disparities, we are developing new types of projects that involve renting land in locations where high land costs make ownership prohibitive. The idea is to lease a site for ten to twenty years and construct housing there. Eventually, the landowner could choose to purchase the house, or we could negotiate an extended rental agreement when the initial lease period ends. We're exploring various models like this to find solutions that improve living conditions and adapt to the complexities of urban environments. Trying out different financial approaches is crucial in this endeavor.

For us, funding research projects independently and surviving as a practice is very challenging, so we need to collaborate with non-governmental organizations or donor agencies to secure funding. This can come from research

Marina Tabassum, Khudi Bari in Tahirpur, Sunamganj 2020–present.
Khudi Bari under construction in Char Hill, Chadpur 2020–present.

grants or implementation grants. However, raising this funding is also challenging. As architects, we are not trained to write grants or to produce financial and operational reports. This is entirely new territory for us. Nonetheless, it's crucial to navigate these challenges to ensure that our research and ideas have a meaningful impact.

This is why we at Marina Tabassum Architects created the Foundation for Architecture and Community Equity (F.A.C.E), which functions as a completely different entity from the architectural practice. The architecture office is responsible for research and design, while the implementation side of projects is handled by the foundation, a nonprofit through which we apply for grant funding. To implement projects, we partner with other NGOs and work together with them.

How you structure your practice depends on your location, the issues you are dealing with, and the people you are working with. Your target group, the beneficiaries, or those you want to serve all influence the creation of a practice that is much more contextual rather than something generic. We have to innovate new ways of practice, and there is no given formula for that.

The concept of plugin architecture is an interesting and innovative idea that exemplifies this approach. Architects have always been trained to design for permanence. We've been taught to aspire to create enduring buildings, like museums, that remain after we are gone, serving as a testament to our great architecture. However, I think time requires something completely different. A Plugin House may not exist in twenty or thirty years, just as the Khudi Bari (Tiny House) I've designed doesn't have to last for hundreds of years. Both are about the ability to adapt to changing circumstances and addressing pressing and relevant issues of our time.

In this context, the Plugin House is a wonderful idea because it makes it possible for people to remain in their communities while improving their living conditions by accommodating their specific context. This approach doesn't erase their existing way of life but enhances it.

The Khudi Bari is a building system we developed akin to the Plugin House. It is a low-tech system that people can easily build themselves, consisting of a basic structure that uses locally available materials. It was crucial for us that occupiers could construct, dismantle, and relocate it as needed. As a modular system, it can also expand; scaling it up allows it to transform into a school or community space. It resembles a Buckminster Fuller Dome in its space-frame-like form.

In our case, land rights are a significant issue. Where we build, there is often no formal land ownership. Mobility becomes crucial because people might have to move if they cannot remain on the land. This is especially true in certain areas we work in, like the middle of rivers, where people live temporarily on newly formed sand beds. Instead of moving to cities, they're living off the land. These sand beds are only stable for about eight to ten years, so people live there for that period. There's no regulatory structure; it's more about the ecology of the place where they're living and its natural system. After about ten years, the government and policies start to take shape. Because many residents don't have rights, it's challenging for them to remain. Under these conditions people also choose to move from the countryside to the city. The Khudi Bari would allow residents to bring their home with them.

Our construction process is adapted to remote areas where basic infrastructure like electricity and roads is absent. Parts are pre-fabricated on the mainland where access to power tools like saws and drills needed for bamboo cutting and assembly is available. We first assemble the structure on the mainland, then disassemble it for transport by boat to the sand beds. From there, carts pulled by cows or horses transport the parts to the building site. This modular approach also simplifies disassembly for potential relocation. By removing the roof and flooring, it's even possible to lift and move the lightweight structure as a whole, much like moving furniture.

For us it's crucial that our proposals are not imposed on people. From the outset, our concern has been that any project must be embraced by the community. They must willingly accept the idea and be eager to live in it for the project to succeed. Otherwise, it risks becoming just another short-lived experiment that fades away, and that's not our goal. We want this initiative to endure and become a genuine solution to a real problem. We avoid imposing specific materials; instead, the structure is designed to accommodate whatever the homeowners prefer, whether salvaged corrugated metal sheets, bamboo, or other locally available materials. As long as the structure is solid and temporary, homeowners can continuously build upon and extend it, customizing their facades according to their needs and preferences.

We ensure the community is intimately involved through the entire process. This inclusive approach ensures that everyone feels a part of the project, fostering a sense of ownership and commitment. We encourage homeowners to participate in building the Khudi Bari, starting from the foundation, in collaboration with our team.

In many locations, homes are threatened by river-bank erosion. These can be sand beds that are constantly changing in shape and size. The placement of Khudi Bari structures are decided by the community, based on the anticipated direction of land erosion. While our influence is limited, we assist in refining layouts. The two-story Khudi Bari design allows residents to relocate to upper floors during floods, and if necessary, disassemble and move the entire structure to a different location.

When we started with the idea of the Khudi Bari we weren't sure if people would accept it, therefore the process was crucial. We chose locations where NGOs were already present and providing assistance with livelihood related to challenges such as market linkage, farming, crafting, or tourism. These NGOs have established trust within the communities, which gave us a foundation to build upon. We didn't want to start from scratch; we aimed to test our housing concept in places with existing community support. The initial Khudi Baris allowed communities to see the difference between their fragile structures and the sturdiness of our design. This sparked interest and acceptance. Adapting to these demands requires continuous innovation in practice. There's no one-size-fits-all approach; each context and stakeholder group necessitate a tailored approach. By involving the community in every step, from site selection to construction, we ensured a more inclusive and accepted process.

We now know there is a proven need for this housing. People have accepted it, and the houses have survived through two cycles of various weather, including thunderstorms and flooding. Local communities have embraced the houses, making modifications like adding rooms or extending kitchens. Since there is a need, we aim to create an ecosystem where houses can be built without our direct presence. Up until now, we've been in a research phase, keeping the fabrication of our steel components centralized in the city of Dhaka. We work with a few workshops to manufacture parts and send them to building sites. But now, we are considering larger-scale production of this system and how to train local workshops. Our focus is on creating an infrastructure and a network of local suppliers, builders, and communities in the areas where we have already built Khudi Baris.

This approach becomes more like an intervention into the vernacular architecture. The houses blend in with the local style once the structure is covered, looking like regular homes with two levels. The key difference is the robust structural system that can withstand high winds better than traditional vernacular houses.

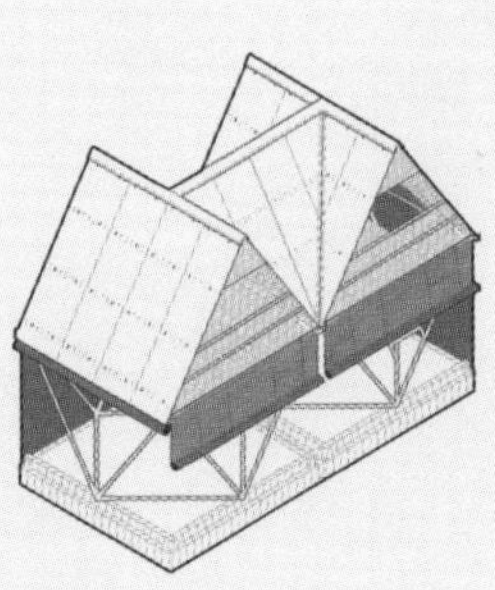

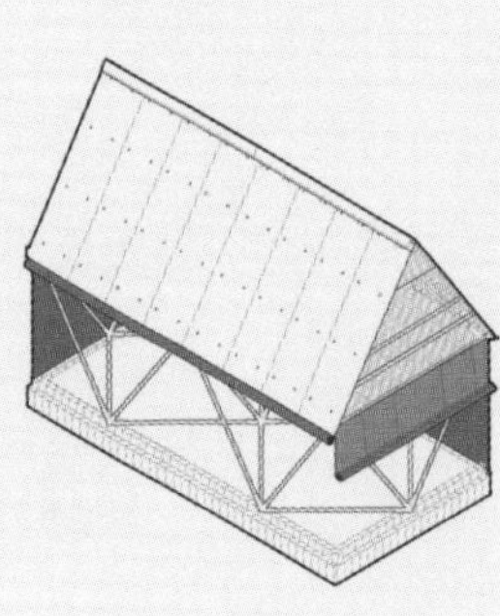

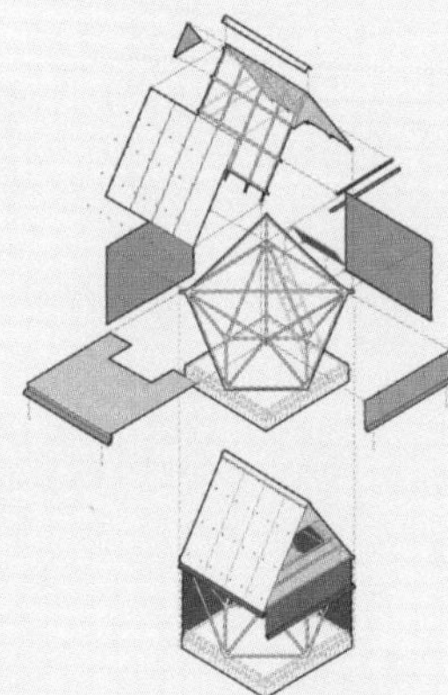

Demonstrating the Khudi Bari housing concept to the community through the use of interactive models.

Khudi Baris with the first levels modified.

Digital diagrams demonstrating different versions of the Khudi Bari module.

Creating an ecology where local suppliers, builders, and steel workshops have the capacity to build and supply these houses locally will also reduce costs. Currently, each house costs about $500, including transportation and on-site support. By localizing production and training builders, we can significantly reduce these costs. The structural system is simple enough that a carpenter can construct it with minimal help from the community.

Building this ecological framework entails more than physical construction; it involves nurturing a network of stakeholders capable of sustaining the initiative independently. This includes local suppliers, builders, and community members who can continue building and modifying houses without our direct involvement. By fostering this ecosystem, we aim to create lasting impact and empower communities to address their housing needs autonomously.

Marina Tabassum, Aggregation Center Khudi Bari, Montoliya and Lomboghona, Teknaf, Cox's Bazar District, 2021–2022.
Marina Tabassum, Khudi Bari, Bangladesh, 2020–present.
Marina Tabassum, Women Led Community Center Khudi Bari, Camp 8E, Kutupalong, Ukhiya, 2022.

PLUGIN

STORIES

COURTYARD 72 PLUGIN HOUSES

I'm Courtyard 72; I'm what you'd call a traditional Chinese courtyard house. All houses in Beijing used to be built like me, but today we're very rare. I was built in Dashilar during the Qing dynasty and I've gone through pretty tumultuous times. It's written all over me.

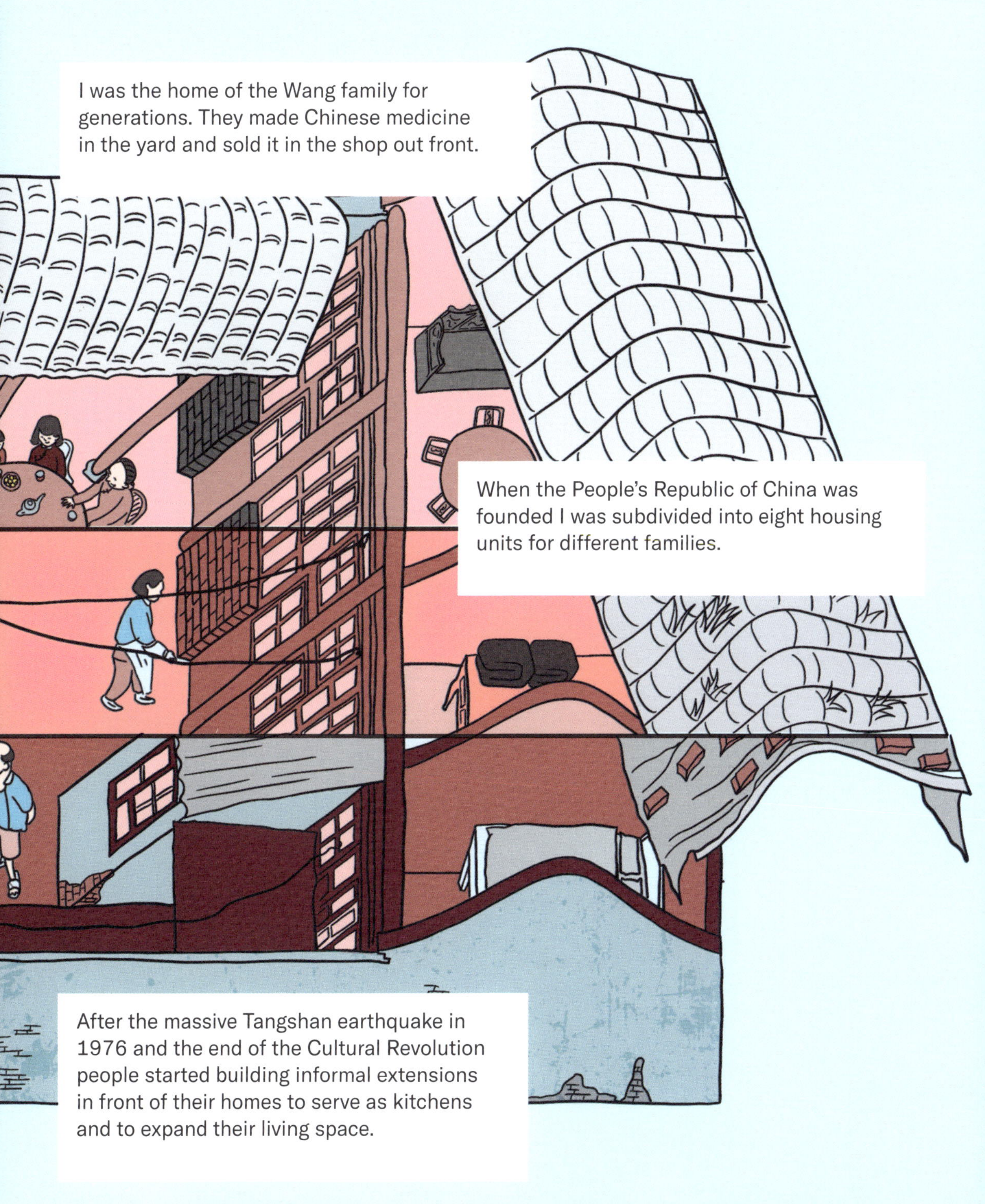
I was the home of the Wang family for generations. They made Chinese medicine in the yard and sold it in the shop out front.
When the People's Republic of China was founded I was subdivided into eight housing units for different families.
After the massive Tangshan earthquake in 1976 and the end of the Cultural Revolution people started building informal extensions in front of their homes to serve as kitchens and to expand their living space.

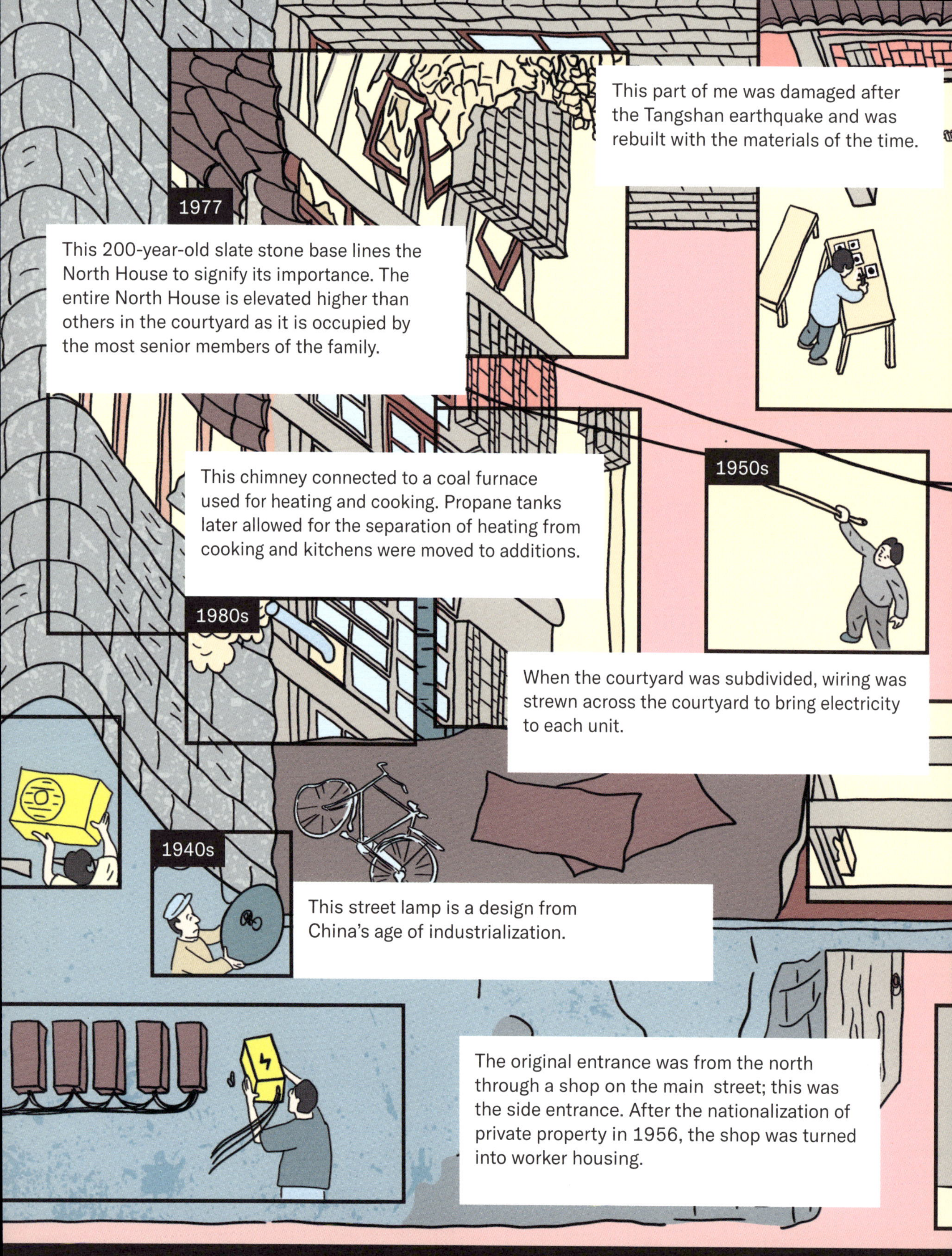
This part of me was damaged after the Tangshan earthquake and was rebuilt with the materials of the time.
1977
This 200-year-old slate stone base lines the North House to signify its importance. The entire North House is elevated higher than others in the courtyard as it is occupied by the most senior members of the family.
This chimney connected to a coal furnace used for heating and cooking. Propane tanks later allowed for the separation of heating from cooking and kitchens were moved to additions.
1950s
1980s
When the courtyard was subdivided, wiring was strewn across the courtyard to bring electricity to each unit.
1940s
This street lamp is a design from China's age of industrialization.
The original entrance was from the north through a shop on the main street; this was the side entrance. After the nationalization of private property in 1956, the shop was turned into worker housing.

These informal additions were built soon after the Tangshan earthquake, as the devastation created an urgent need for housing. There was little oversight and residents took advantage of this opportunity to enlarge their homes.
1980s
All houses in Beijing were originally built with a high-quality gray brick.
I was built by a Muslim family so I was originally painted green, the color of Islam. The rounded shape of my columns show the influence of Western aesthetics during the Qing dynasty.
1700s
These traditional clay roof tiles were originally packed with mud for insulation. The tile's shape and vertical tiling allowed excellent drainage.
1900s
This corner became rounded after over 100 years of things being moved in and out. The accumulation of rubble from construction over centuries has made the ground outside higher.

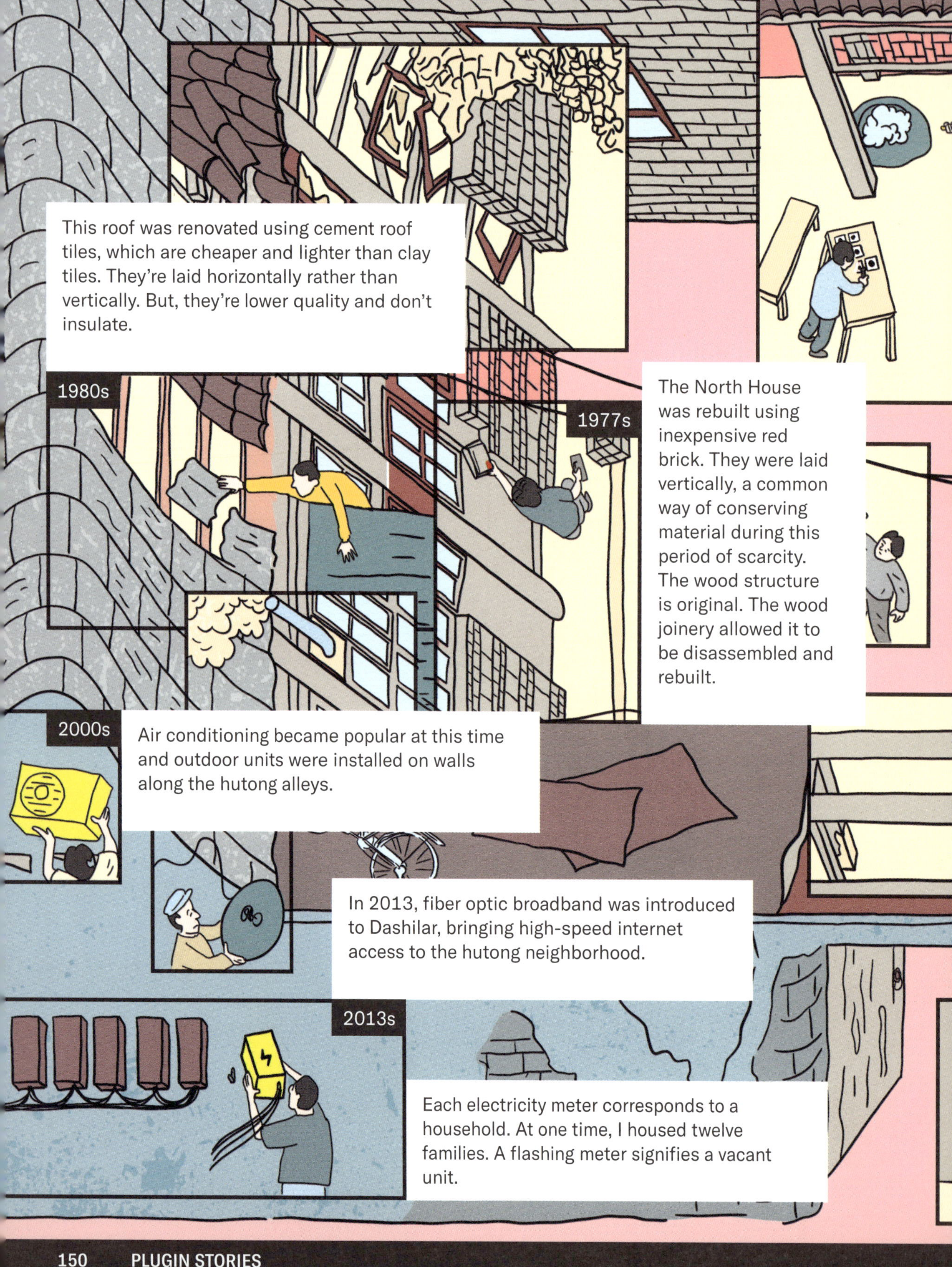
This roof was renovated using cement roof tiles, which are cheaper and lighter than clay tiles. They're laid horizontally rather than vertically. But, they're lower quality and don't insulate.
1980s
1977s
The North House was rebuilt using inexpensive red brick. They were laid vertically, a common way of conserving material during this period of scarcity. The wood structure is original. The wood joinery allowed it to be disassembled and rebuilt.
2000s
Air conditioning became popular at this time and outdoor units were installed on walls along the hutong alleys.
In 2013, fiber optic broadband was introduced to Dashilar, bringing high-speed internet access to the hutong neighborhood.
2013s
Each electricity meter corresponds to a household. At one time, I housed twelve families. A flashing meter signifies a vacant unit.

This neighborhood was known for its Chinese medicine shops. In front of me was a pharmacy and the Wang family lived here and produced medicine in the courtyard.
1950s
1990s
As an inexpensive way to stay waterproof, tarps were draped over my aging roof and held down with unused brick, furniture and other collected artifacts. The tarp needs to be replaced annually.
A common splicing technique was used to replace the degraded bottom portion of my columns which have degraded and become unstable. The covered walkway originally connected the courtyard to the shop in the front. These walkways were later walled up as private additions.
1970s
Repairing brick walls with a fibrous layer was a popular and cost-effective technique.
1970s

By 2013, over half of my space was vacant and I wasn't well maintained at all. PAO gave me new life by inserting two new spaces within my old bones.
The North House became the main office for the Dashilar urban regeneration project.

Mrs. Dong witnessed the entire process of upgrading with skepticism, confusion, and also curiosity.
Part of the South House became a model Plugin House residence. It featured a private bathroom, a rare feature in this area.

Mrs. Dong has lived in a unit in the South House since 1995. She shares her 14-square-meter (150-square-foot) home with her adult son.
When it's warm she can dry her clothes in the courtyard but in the winter she hangs them indoors.
Her kitchen was built as an addition separate from her living area. She needs to walk outdoors to go into her kitchen.
Her kitchen is basic, consisting of a hot plate and a refrigerator. Electrical appliances are connected to outlets in her bedroom.
This outdoor area in front of her bedroom and next to the kitchen can be temporarily converted into a shower. She opens both doors and draws a curtain for privacy and showers with a hose attached to her kitchen sink.

Dirt is constantly falling from the clay tile roof and brick walls so she's covered the interior with fabric to reduce the dust.
She needs to keep her furniture away from the walls to avoid creating more dust, further reducing the interior's usable space.
Every inch of space is used for storage including the undersides of her table and bed, the top of her wardrobe and electric heater, and the ledge of the windowsill.
She's described her living conditions as harsh; the electric heater isn't sufficient for the coldest days of the winter and there is no air conditioning for the hot summers.

MRS. FAN'S PLUGIN HOUSE

Living in a courtyard house is an experience like no other. Here, amidst the labyrinth of hutong alleys, familiar faces are around every corner.

A subtle nod, a brief smile; daily greetings need no more than that, we've always known each other.

Hello, I'm Mrs. Fan.

In my sophomore year of high school my parents bought an apartment on Fushi Road.
Why this longing for the hutongs?
I cherish my childhood memories...
Hoop rolling with friends.
Treating myself to candied hawthorn fruit.
Learning about the world of birds.

Growing up there was pure joy.
I don’t like living in an apartment tower. Even the doorways make neighbors feel cut off from each other.
The thrill of my first bicycle.
Writing couplets for Chinese New Year.

Moving back to the hutong area is hard for parents to understand. But Mrs. Fan's father saw an article on the Plugin House at just the right time.
Oh, look! Here's a group of young architects working on the hutongs.
PAO
PLUGIN HOUSE
Welcome! Our office is also renovated using our Plugin system. How can we help?
Hi! We saw the article about the Plugin House in the newspaper, and we're interested in renovating our hutong home...
I have a limited budget but I'd like to move back into my old courtyard house but with a modern standard of living.
We sat together with the architects to address our concerns.

The renovations were remarkably smooth; quiet, dust-free and swift. My neighbors were astounded!
The shape of the house was designed to maximize space without overshadowing neighbors.
Unfortunately we neglected to speak to one neighbor beforehand.
When the Plugin House was completed, everyone was very impressed. They didn't think something like this was possible in this part of the city.
Mrs. Chen, it's been a long time. I'm glad we can catch up.
It's a shame we haven't spoken for so long. I think the house is fine as long as you don't block the view out of my window.
: Even though we've finished
building, it's no problem.
We can just cut right through our panels to make sure your neighbor has the sunlight she had before.
PAO
PAO
PAO

Life in the hutongs can also be difficult.
People live very closely together.
And because these neighborhoods are centuries old, the building construction and sewage system are also old. We have to share communal bathrooms.
My mother and I are really claustrophobic. We can't stand staying in small spaces. Before renovating, the old house was really dark. With no natural light inside, there was no difference between night and day.

This new roof deck allows me to have my own garden and makes it easy to dry clothes in the summer. Looking at the surrounding environment from here is very pleasant.
Now that the renovation is done the house is bathed in light, making the space appear larger. I love the comfort of sunlight falling down on me.
The composting toilet is off-grid and makes having my own bathroom possible. It's very convenient.

Housing in the city is unaffordable.
TAXI

As a child growing up in hutongs
I have many warm memories.
Living here, I can afford to live in
the city center and close to work.
My commute is reduced and my time
can be spent with my newborn.
I'm really happy with how the house turned
out. I hope others find inspiration in this
fusion of old and new. A life close to roots, yet
with contemporary comforts. I think everyone
should be able to improve their standard of
living and remain close to the communities
they feel connected to.

RURAL PLUGIN HOUSE
Hello, I'm the Rural Plugin House. In 2017 I was transported across dirt roads by tricycle and built by Mr. Wang and his friends in a rural area of Guangzhou in southern China.

Lifted off the ground and easily put together, I'm seen as a "temporary" building. There is a real lack of housing in these areas, so being removable was the only way I was allowed to be here.
It was always Mr. Wang's dream to live in the countryside.

Mr. Wang was tired of his office job and the hustle and bustle of the big city.
广州地铁

Searching for a more balanced life, for both body and mind, he quit his job and sold his apartment and moved with his wife to the countryside to be an organic farmer.
Mr. Wang enjoyed being in the sun and rain tending to his ten acres of land.

At 27 square meters (290 square feet) Mr. Wang called me small but beautiful. I provided him the comfort of modern amenities that he's used to from urban living.
Soon after moving in, Mr. Wang's daughter was born. Instead of plastic toys, junk food and artificial landscapes, she started her life in nature.
Playing under the vast sky, her friends were bees, worms, fireflies, vegetables, fruits and flowers.
Mr. Wang's experiment of working in nature extended to learning from nature.

One year later the Wang family moved to the mountains and I became a hub for locals. Community members, some from the city and others from local villages, would live here, often on weekends.
It was a chance for families to observe nature, for kids to learn in a natural environment, and for people to connect with each other and the local community. I was a bridge between the urban and rural.

CHRIS BAKER'S PLUGIN HOUSES

After college, I worked in a homeless shelter. I really connected with the people there—they were my people. I felt at home.
Today, I run The Other Ones Foundation (TOOF), a nonprofit that manages Esperanza Community, an emergency sheltering site for people experiencing homelessness.

Austin is one of the most expensive cities to live in, and we're in the middle of a massive homelessness crisis. We founded Esperanza in 2020, right after the city banned camping. People had nowhere to go.

The governor designated an unused Department of Transportation lot as a place for people to relocate—but without management, it turned into a kind of post-apocalyptic Burning Man festival.
Nearly 200 people had set up tents on the blacktop and in old truck bays. Residents jostled for a single electrical outlet and a shower they constructed from a cold-water hose surrounded by upturned pallets. Dogs ran loose among the tents and portable toilets, dodging cooking fires.

Esperanza Community is a non-congregate housing community—which means people live in small, private units.

We prefer this model because privacy helps vulnerable people feel safer. It also makes the community easier to manage, with fewer enclosed shared spaces. People like being able to open their front door and step right outside.

In traditional congregate shelters, dozens of people share a single space, often with little privacy or security.
Others live in SROs—old buildings or hotels converted into single-room housing. These often feel unsafe, with shared hallways and minimal separation between units.
If something goes wrong in one room, it can affect the whole building.
207

In 2021, I invited Plugin House to help us expand Esperanza. We've been working together ever since.

What makes TOOF special is how we integrate wrap-around services—case management, food distribution, job training—right into the community. Plugin Houses are a big part of that, used for case officers, food distribution, and job training.

At TOOF, we also offer job training and employment for residents. People from the community helped build the Plugin Houses with minimal training. It gave them a chance to literally build the place they live in.

Since then, we've expanded and worked with Plugin House on masterplanning other sites—and on designing new types of housing and facilities, like a job training center and units with private bathrooms and kitchens.

DRAWING, KNITTING, AND PLUGGING IN:
A conversation with Sir Peter Cook

In thinking about architecture, invention is a crucial factor; it's not just about taking what is available. Throughout all the periods of my career, I have been fundamentally interested in the extension of the architectural vocabulary. It's not necessarily about having the most original plan in mind, but rather about pushing the boundaries and expanding the language of architecture.

The concept of the *Archigram* magazines stemmed from earlier ideas. Plug-in City, based upon some ideas coming out of the Montreal Tower project (intended to form part of the stadium for the 1976 Olympic Games in Canada), aimed to critique traditional system building. It proposed the use of pre-fabricated parts and plugin components that could be arranged in diverse ways, almost like sculpting. This project incorporated innovative ideas such as a hovercraft functioning as a movable building and primitive climate control systems that allowed for adaptable cityscapes. We envisioned a breathing city with inflatable and movable elements. One of my early axonometric drawings encapsulated these embryonic concepts, which evolved into more sophisticated representations that I worked on after my first year of full-time teaching.

Teaching at the age of twenty-seven, after inheriting the fifth year of the Architectural Association (AA) in London due to my boss's sudden departure, was exhausting. Handling students older than myself was a challenging experience. This period of intense intellectual and psychological engagement with students led to a nine-month hiatus from drawing. I was doing a lot of thinking, but no drawing. When I resumed, it felt like an outpouring of bottled-up creativity and critical thought, culminating in a significant section drawing.

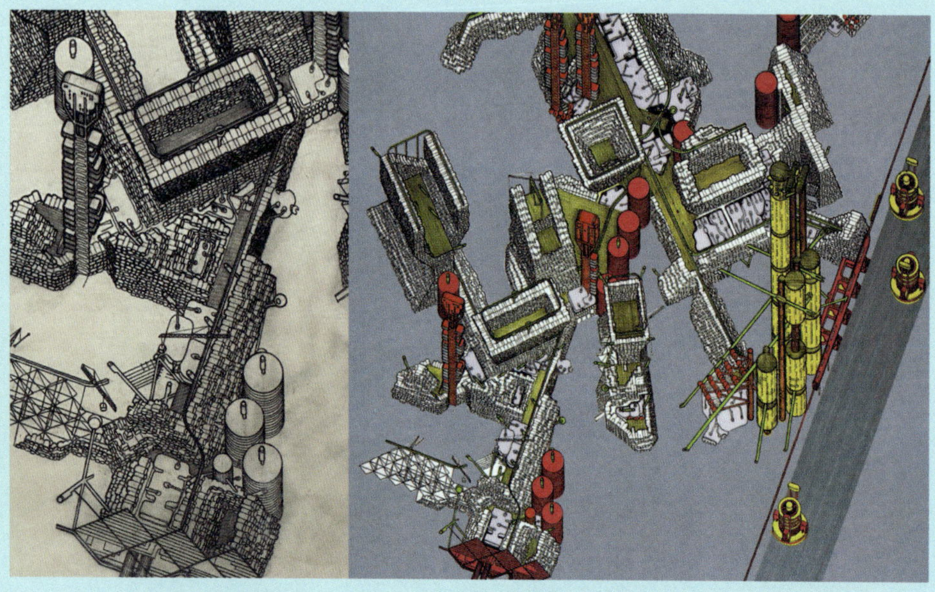

Plug-in City, axonometric overhead views, Peter Cook (Archigram), 1964

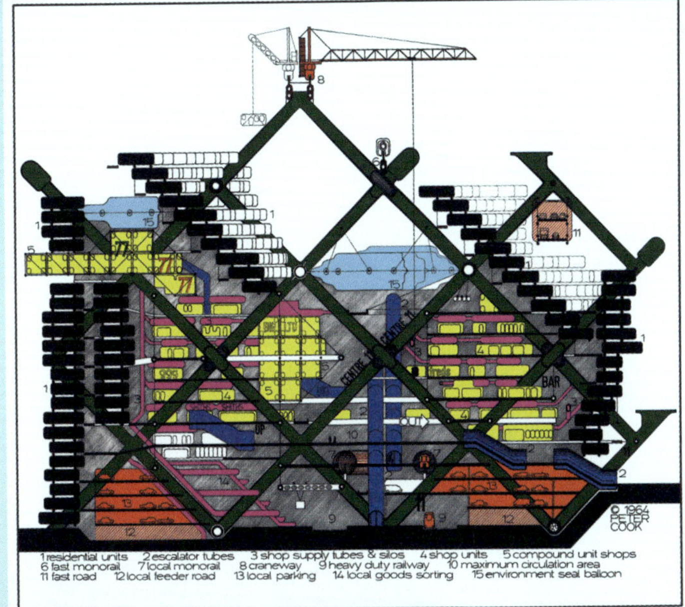

Plug-in City, section, Peter Cook (Archigram), 1964.
The People's Canopy in Leuven, Belgium, 2017.

In Plug-in City, the megastructure concept emerged, embodying the idea that architectural components could grow dynamically. This drawing was intended to convey a vibrant, almost "fruity" quality, reflecting the ever-evolving nature of urban environments. Living in a city, one realizes it's not always bright and shiny; there's a patina that adds character, a theme that resonates in my work.

Drawing, to me, is about envisioning something that doesn't exist. It's a perspective, a way to imagine and create new realities. The advantage of hand-drawn sketches is their freedom from the constraints of correctness. Unlike computer drawings, which demand precision and adherence to rules, hand-drawing allows for any whimsical idea to take shape. With a pen, I can explore endless possibilities, letting my imagination run wild without the computer's restrictions telling me what's incorrect or unfeasible. These creative liberties are essential. When people ask what would happen if I worked on the ground now, I imagine that the computer would make some tasks much quicker. However, the intriguing question is whether this speed would introduce an element of predictability. Take, for example, some of Mike Webb's scenes. They are still so strange, almost ethereal, and defy conventional depiction of position or sequence. You can't quite grasp them fully, and I think this type of drawing is crucial.

Today, many projects are produced using tools that demand accuracy, which can force designs to be overly precise. It's like the joke from the comedy program *Little Britain* where the character says, "The computer says no." It's amusing because, when I'm drawing, nobody tells me "no." Even if my idea seems silly, there's no restriction stopping me. Whether these hand-drawn concepts can be built is another question. However, the process might lead to innovative solutions through entirely different routes. The freedom to explore without immediate constraints is invaluable in the creative process.

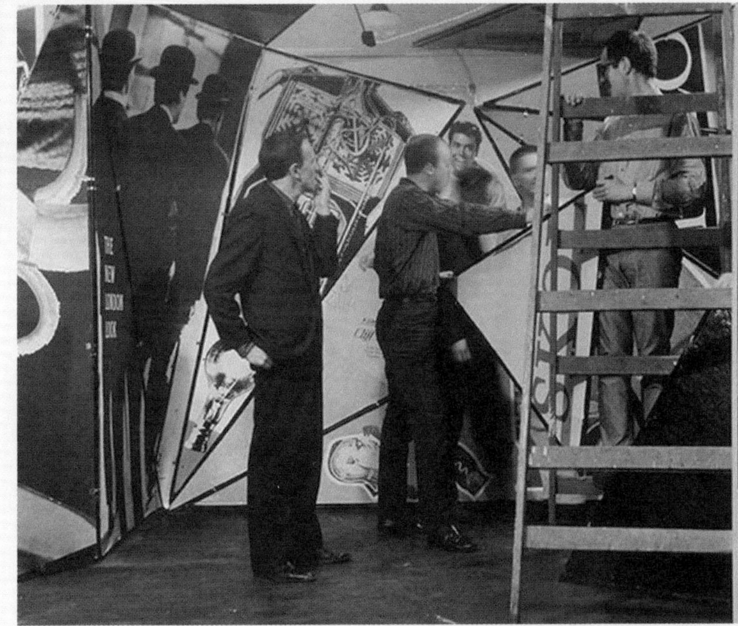

The foundation of the Plug-in City drawings originates from my day job at the time, where we were engaged in system building. While we didn't construct the projects ourselves, our focus was on pre-fabricated housing, various housing projects, and even a railway station. This professional backdrop led to the formation of Archigram, a group assembled by Theo Crosby to work on commercial projects for a large construction company. The group was an eclectic mix, unaware of their collective potential, eventually producing two or three magazines and engaging in academic activities such as lecturing at Cambridge University.

We were the children of Buckminster Fuller—David Green, Mike Webb, and I were deeply influenced by his ideas. Our work was a mix of social housing and pre-fabricated projects. While our day jobs were relevant, we always knew we could push far beyond the conventional boundaries.

I was fortunate to meet Reyner Banham, the architecture critic who lived across the street. By pure chance, he introduced me to Buckminster Fuller, and a host of other designers. We were much younger, but we saw these figures not just as names in books but as real, approachable people. This personal connection was invaluable because it showed us that there was a broader, active community, especially in Europe, where many eccentric characters were experimenting with unique projects. In the north of England, for example, some people were working on fiberglass houses and quirky railway designs. While these projects didn't always succeed, they demonstrated that tangible, innovative work was being done beyond theoretical concepts. This real-world engagement stood in stark contrast to simply seeing things in books.

Fang Family Plugin House in Shangwei urban village, Shenzhen.
"The Living City" exhibition at the Institute of Contemporary Arts in London, 1963.

Our workspace was unique, situated in a site hub behind a railway. It fostered a special camaraderie, as some of us, including Webb, Green, and I, had known each other previously. Meeting the rest of the team added to the dynamic environment. Amidst our daily tasks, the same individual who brought us together secured funding for an exhibition called "Living City." This exhibition was crafted in the same building, in a downstairs shed where we welded metal pieces and engaged in hands-on work. It felt reminiscent of school days, except we were being paid.

During the early Archigram days, before Ron Herron, Warren Chalk, and Dennis Crompton joined, it was just David, Mike, and me. I won a small competition for an old people's housing project, which was never built. This win gave me some money, the first time I ever had such financial freedom. We decided to spend part of it on producing *Archigram 2* and indulged in experimenting with materials.

We bought fiberglass, which turned out to be quite challenging. David purchased it, and we ended up with fiberglass all over our hands—an absolute nightmare. Despite the mess, David created an incredible fiberglass structure. Meanwhile, I was experimenting with making inflatables using a vacuum cleaner and sticky tape, setting up inflatable structures in the garden. These hands-on experiences were formative, giving us a sense of "being there" and physically engaging with the materials.

Today, many people turn to the internet for inspiration. They find intriguing images and concepts online, but they miss the tangible experience of seeing and interacting with these creations in person. Meeting the creators and observing their work up close, even if it looked decrepit or was smaller than expected, provided a depth of understanding that can't be replicated by a digital image. Seeing a project in reality—its thickness, texture, and flaws—gives a true sense of its essence. This tangible experience is crucial. While I'm known for my drawings, my true focus is on the physicality of materials and structures. I'm actually a "stuffist," deeply committed to the material and tangible aspects of architecture.

In recent times, I've completed a few buildings, though not as many as I would like. I am still actively trying to undertake more building projects. However, I have increasingly focused on creating drawings that are independent of any specific buildings or projects. The drawings are sometimes thematically connected to the projects I'm working on, but often they explore entirely different tangents because I allow myself to think freely. Ultimately, they are about extending the vocabulary of architecture. In simple terms, they explore what happens when you bend materials, change their nature, or transition from something soft to something mechanical. They imagine mechanical elements melting into floating structures or armatures sprouting vegetation. This is why I always liked PAO's cycle structure, the People's Canopy, which embodies a similar quality.

James Stirling once wrote about the contrast between the neat, orderly fronts of London streets and the chaotic, interesting backs. I think this idea also resonates with some of the Plugin House iterations. I would call this "knitting" into different sites. The last building I completed during the COVID-19 pandemic exemplifies this philosophy. It was a modest structure on a university campus, built in a ditch. The site was challenging, confined to the size of two portacabins and that ditch. However, by cleverly extending parts of the building, I was able to capture additional space in front of the neighboring building. This involved digging out the ditch and effectively dropping the building into it, transforming a constricted site into a functional and innovative space. This project underscored the importance of engaging with the site's unique conditions, adapting creatively to its limitations and opportunities. It's this kind of hands-on problem solving that I find particularly enjoyable and fulfilling in architecture.

I think I'm still a believer in the belief. It might sound very old-fashioned, but I feel it's incredibly important. How do we deal with these issues? Housing, for instance, is something architects have always been optimistic about. In reality, I've only completed two pieces of social housing. While it's not a large number, these projects are very satisfying. One accommodates about thirty families, and the other has around forty to fifty units. It's not a huge impact on a global scale, but it's significant for those individuals.

In these projects, even small details matter. Placing the bathroom in the right spot or ensuring the occupant gets a good view from the window can make a difference. Adding a quirky staircase is a touch I hope they enjoy. I call this approach "knitting," too. In the past, if a pullover had holes, Granny would mend it rather than throwing it away. Patchwork quilts operate on a similar principle, where various components come together to form a cohesive whole. This concept applies to architectural planning as well.

In a recent competition project, we had a funny corner to work with. I suggested we turn it into a cozy spot where someone could enjoy a cup of tea. Instead of seeing it as a flaw, we saw it as a feature. This is what I mean by "knitting"—integrating odd bits into a site creatively. The building process often involves making the most out of unusual or unexpected elements. Embracing these quirks and weaving them into the design can transform potential issues into unique features.

Vallecas Housing by Crab Studio, Madrid, Spain, 2012.

Peter Cook and Colin Fournier, Kunsthaus Graz, Austria, 2003.

An example is also the Kunsthaus Graz project in Austria, which was constructed on an eccentric site that dictated the shape of the structure. The site required the building to twist and squeeze around existing old houses and historical ironwork, creating a balloon-like form. Despite the logistical challenges—seventeen different subcontractors and a site too tight for a tarp crane, which had to be stationed across the street—it was a highly enjoyable project.

Working with such challenging sites is far more interesting than dealing with flat, bland ones. On flat sites, you have to invent and improvise to create intrigue and engagement. This improvisational aspect of architecture, finding curious ways to arrange things when faced with constraints, is a fascinating test of creativity and resourcefulness.

Considering the state of things today with systems that could actually allow for flexibility and change, I believe it's an important direction. Many people resist this idea, but I do not. It's something we've discussed for a long time, and only now is it gradually being realized in certain areas. However, resistance persists among many architects who might view such flexibility as frivolous, likening it to a toy-town concept suitable for children or amusement parks, but not for serious, substantial city planning. This resistance, I think, stems from insecurity and a desire for cultural and structural stability.

Many people crave stability and the establishment of their culture, which they perceive as fragile. This resistance isn't about the materials themselves. Architecture can be made from paper, rubber, civic codes, or even reused cushion covers. The issue is the perceived fragility of their cultural identity. In some countries, there's a tradition of constructing with flimsy, transferable materials, often sticks. This reflects a mindset that values flexibility and adaptability. On the other hand, some countries have a tradition of building with stone or reinforced concrete, reflecting a "cave-thinking" mentality. These materials symbolize permanence and solidity.

Interestingly, flexibility might seem to contradict sustainability. While a structure might be designed to last a specific number of years, permanence isn't always the goal. Architecture, in my view, should not be built with the notion of eternal permanence because buildings rarely serve their original purpose indefinitely. Most buildings I've worked in were designed for entirely different uses, such as disused church halls, old Jacobean or Georgian houses, or even sheds for trains. The charm lies in repurposing these spaces rather than adhering strictly to their original function.

I've never considered myself popular; I simply pursue my vision. Some people become enthusiastic about my work, while others remain indifferent or perplexed. The appeal of Archigram, for me, is its accessible language, making complex ideas understandable and thus engaging to a broader audience.

4
WHY SHOULD WE PRIORITIZE COMMUNITIES?

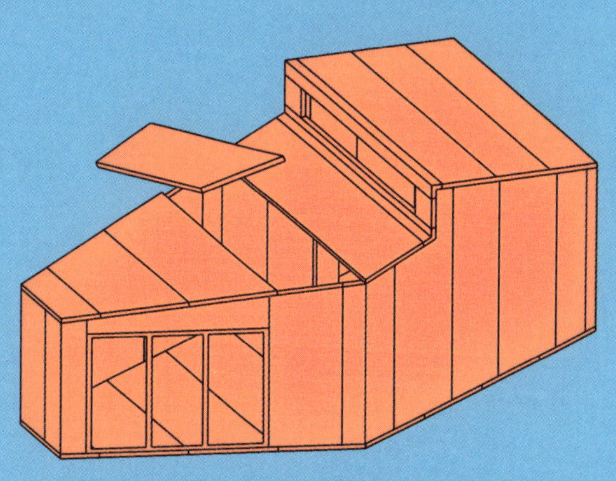

Bird's-eye view of Mrs. Fang's Plugin House.

The Plugin House aims to provide better housing by offering innovative alternatives to conventional urban development. Recognizing the disconnected nature of sprawling cities, it proposes creative solutions for densification without outward expansion. By doing so, it aims to preserve communities and enhance their resilience.

Investing in existing communities holds significant value due to existing infrastructure such as parks, schools, and services. Outward expansion distances people from these resources, increasing reliance on cars and leading to congestion, offsetting any affordability gains from homes farther from city centers. Conventional urban development often brings with it gentrification pressures, too, where rising property values can displace lower-income households. This can lead to existing residents being priced out and again forced to move further away from essential services.

Investments in public amenities should benefit as many members of the community as possible. How can we add more housing within existing communities, increase investment here, and prevent displacement while ensuring a diverse socio-economic mix of residents?

While gentrification is complex, urban development doesn't have to be a zero-sum game. Increasing housing stock and density within a community can accommodate more people without displacing others. However, simply adding more housing is not a panacea for gentrification. It's crucial to consider not only the cost of housing but also its location. Plugin architecture offers examples of urban interventions that increase housing access through infill while maintaining convenient access to city centers, economic opportunities, and social services. By distributing greater density across a larger area, gentrification pressures can be alleviated, fostering a more inclusive and sustainable urban environment.

In our work in Dashilar in Beijing and urban villages in Shenzhen, we encountered unique conditions due to the absence of market pressures, despite these locations being desirable. The age of the properties and infrastructure deterred investment, compounded by the limited market dynamics. Vacant properties were prevalent, partly due to restrictions on buying and selling in an open market.

Dashilar, as a historically protected area, restricted property transactions to local authorities. Private developers were barred from entering the market, curbing speculation significantly. Similarly, urban villages in Shenzhen operated under restricted property markets, with ownership vested in the village collective. Properties couldn't be sold as urban property, preventing speculative activity common in other areas.

In the urban village of Shangwei in Shenzhen, Plugin House projects faced the challenge of renovating abandoned properties with unclear ownership, prohibited from demolition despite their dilapidated state. These regulatory environments created conditions that, while diminishing the attractiveness of these locations, also presented opportunities for alternative uses.

The minimal investment required for renovation using the Plugin House system, coupled with limited market dynamics, mitigated gentrification pressures in these projects. This unique regulatory environment fostered innovative solutions while safeguarding against displacement and speculation.

Bird's-eye view before and after renovation of the Huang Family Plugin House.

Street view before and after renovation of the Huang Family Plugin House.

As the Dashilar project expanded, we devised guidelines for the entire district to ensure the seamless application of the Plugin House system to every property. The objective was to utilize plugin renovations dispersed throughout the neighborhood to elevate the overall quality of the surroundings.

Dashilar's architectural landscape predominantly consists of courtyard houses, characterized by a central square area bordered by buildings on different sides. Given that multiple living units share these communal spaces, improvements to one property inherently benefits others. This philosophy aligns with the concept of "urban acupuncture," as coined by the Spanish architect and urban planner Manuel de Solà, which advocates for enhancing dispersed yet strategically chosen locations to stimulate urban regeneration. This approach stands in contrast to traditional redevelopment strategies, such as blanket redevelopment of entire neighborhoods or concentrated investment in large centers.

To establish guidelines for implementing the plugin approach in Dashilar, we started by conducting a thorough mapping of the entire district, pinpointing all vacant properties. This data enabled us to identify three general types and sizes of properties that would be suitable for the Plugin House system district-wide. We analyzed the range of variation required within each type and size, balancing standardization with the need for customization. Furthermore, we examined the various courtyard configurations, considering properties with multiple courtyards. We assessed the location and accessibility of each space within these courtyards, as well as their capacity to accommodate self-contained sanitation services or the need for composting toilets. This comprehensive analysis provided valuable insights into optimizing the Plugin House system across Dashilar.

Interestingly, the wood construction of traditional courtyard houses in Dashilar lent itself to a systematized approach. With a regular column grid and standardized interlocking parts, this construction method resembled an ancient system of pre-fabricated components. Additionally, traditional Chinese wood joinery is designed for easy disassembly and reassembly, making it particularly suitable for renovations where parts may need replacement. The standardization of components further simplifies the replacement process, contributing to the ease of maintenance and longevity of these structures.

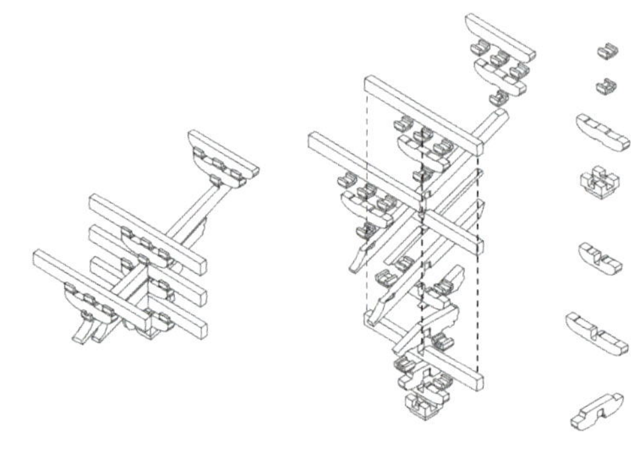

Traditional Courtyard House

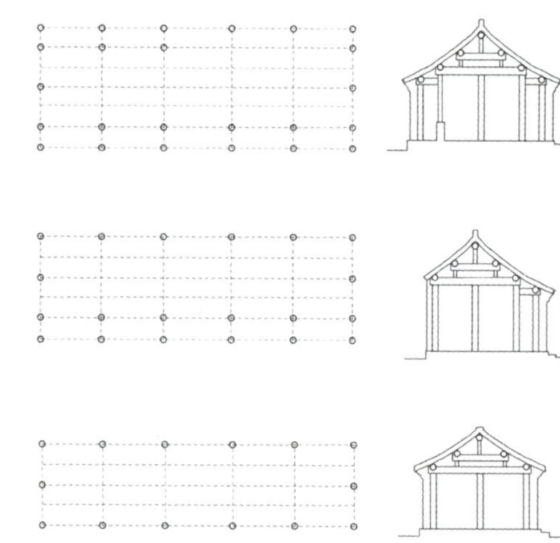

Modular Courtyard System

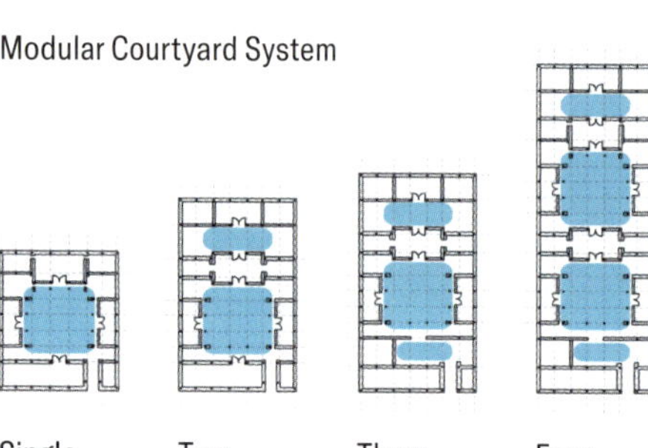

Single Courtyard | Two Courtyards | Three Courtyards | Four Courtyards

Moreover, the standardized layout of the courtyards, reflecting a hierarchical social structure based on cardinal directions, enhances the seamless integration of the Plugin House into these historic structures. This consistency in spatial configurations facilitates the adaptation of modern renovations while respecting the traditional architectural heritage of Dashilar.

Extensive discussions with local residents and in-depth studies of bespoke renovations informed the integration of various spatial strategies within the Plugin House system at the individual unit level. To enhance residents' comfort and foster a closer connection to outdoor space, we designed several types of large openings. For example, entire rooms could lift upwards, providing a seamless transition between the interior and the courtyard. Additionally, we designed exterior walls that could slide to the side or tilt outwards, effectively expanding the interior space into the outdoors. These innovative design features helped ease the difficulty of living in such dense locations.

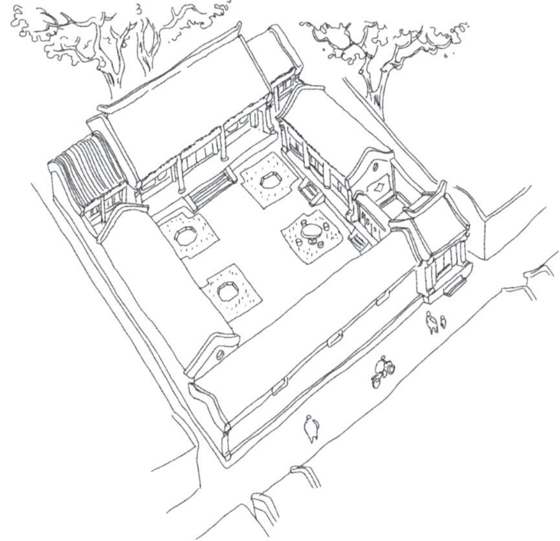

Example of traditional Chinese wood joinery system, exploded view, and modular parts.

Traditional courtyard house modular spatial system.

Traditional courtyard house modular courtyard system.

Example of a common DIY approach to creating temporary additional private space by connecting two open doors.

Example of a temporary additional private space by connecting two open doors.

Mrs. Dong's original shower space created by connecting two open doors.

Traditional Chinese courtyard house.

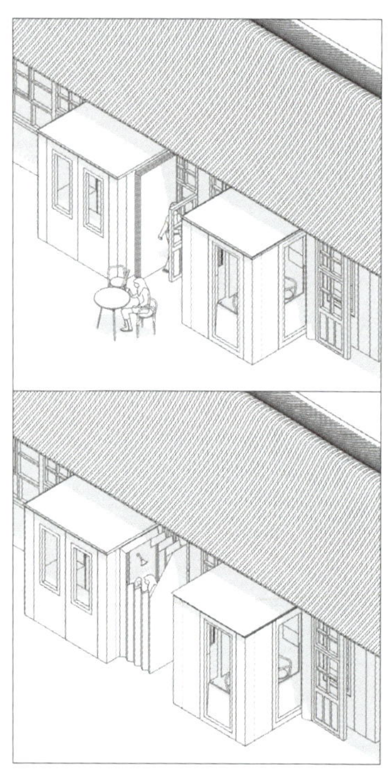

Drawings of the retractable accordion shower for Mrs. Dong's Plugin House.

The retractable accordion shower designed as a replacement for Mrs. Dong's original shower space.

The retractable shower at Mrs. Dong's Plugin House in open position.

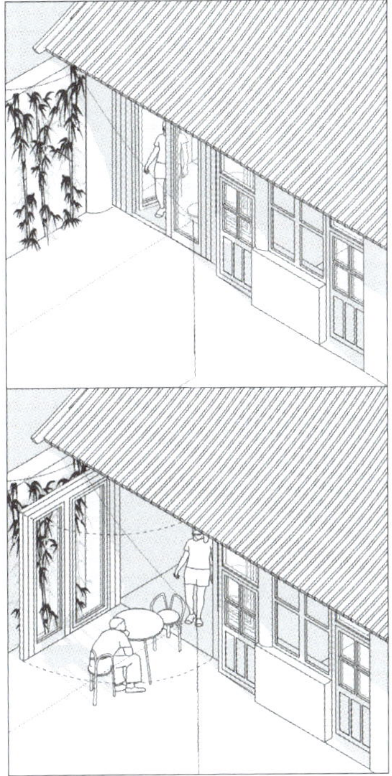

Plugin House with hinged exterior wall feature open in South House of Courtyard 32.

Interior view of South House of Courtyard 32 with hinged exterior wall closed.

Diagrammatic drawings of the Plugin House with hinged exterior wall feature in Courtyard 32.

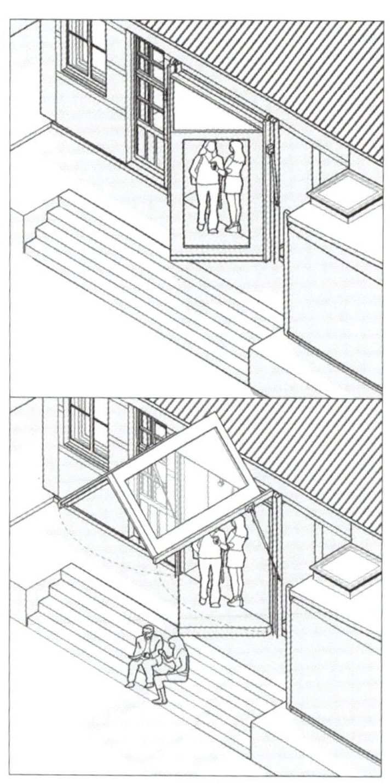

Diagrammatic drawings of the convertible solarium feature in the PAO office.
Convertible solarium feature replaces an informal addition (in open position) in the PAO office in Dashilar.
Convertible solarium feature (in closed position) in the PAO office.

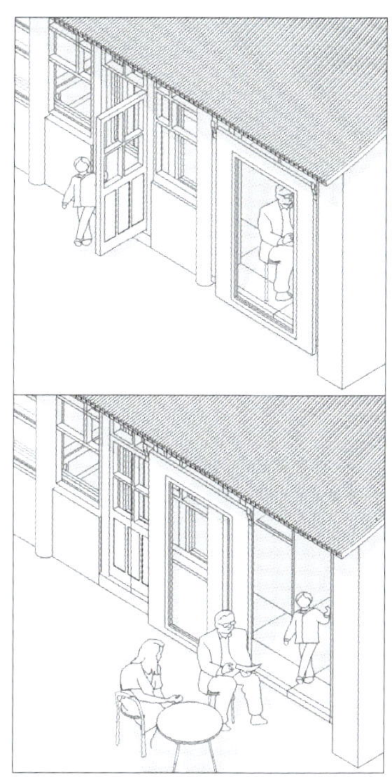

◰ Plugin House with sliding exterior wall feature in Courtyard 30.
◳ Diagrammatic drawings of the Plugin House with sliding exterior wall feature.

Given that many Plugin House residents are elderly single parents sharing living quarters with their grown children, privacy emerged as a top priority in the design process. To address this, Plugin Houses were designed with special consideration for privacy and comfort. Internally, the houses were constructed with insulated ceilings that mirrored the slope of existing pitched roofs, despite most interiors typically being built with horizontal suspended ceilings. This design feature opened up a substantial amount of new usable space under the roof, facilitating the incorporation of mezzanines.

These mezzanine levels offered precious additional living areas, providing parents and children with separate sleeping quarters. This design feature not only enhanced privacy but also promoted comfort and autonomy for all residents. By creating distinct areas for rest and relaxation, Plugin Houses effectively met the unique needs of multigenerational families while fostering a sense of privacy within the shared living space.

In Dashilar, our efforts focused on upgrading numerous properties phased over several years. In contrast, our work in Jingdezhen, Jiangxi province involved the simultaneous renovation of multiple properties. Jingdezhen boasts a prestigious history in porcelain production, spanning over 1,000 years. Once the foremost center of Chinese porcelain production, it supplied imperial porcelain to the emperor and court after direct imperial control was established in the 14th century. However, the shift towards industrialization prompted the relocation of ceramic workshops to large manufacturing facilities, leaving many historic workshops vacant in Jingdezhen's core.

Interior view of Mr. Zhao's Plugin.
Mr. Zhao with his cat inside his new Plugin House.
The location of four courtyard Plugin House renovations in the old town center of Jingdezhen, Jiangxi province, 2021.

Section perspective of Plugin House units in Jingdezhen Courtyard P-58.

Section perspective of Plugin House units in Jingdezhen Courtyard H-20.

Exploded view of Plugin House units in Jingdezhen Courtyard P-58.

Exploded view of Plugin House units in Jingdezhen Courtyard C-34.

Exploded view of Plugin House units in Jingdezhen Yanghua Nong Courtyard.

Exploded view of Plugin House units in Jingdezhen Courtyard H-20.

Individual Jingdezhen Plugin House units.

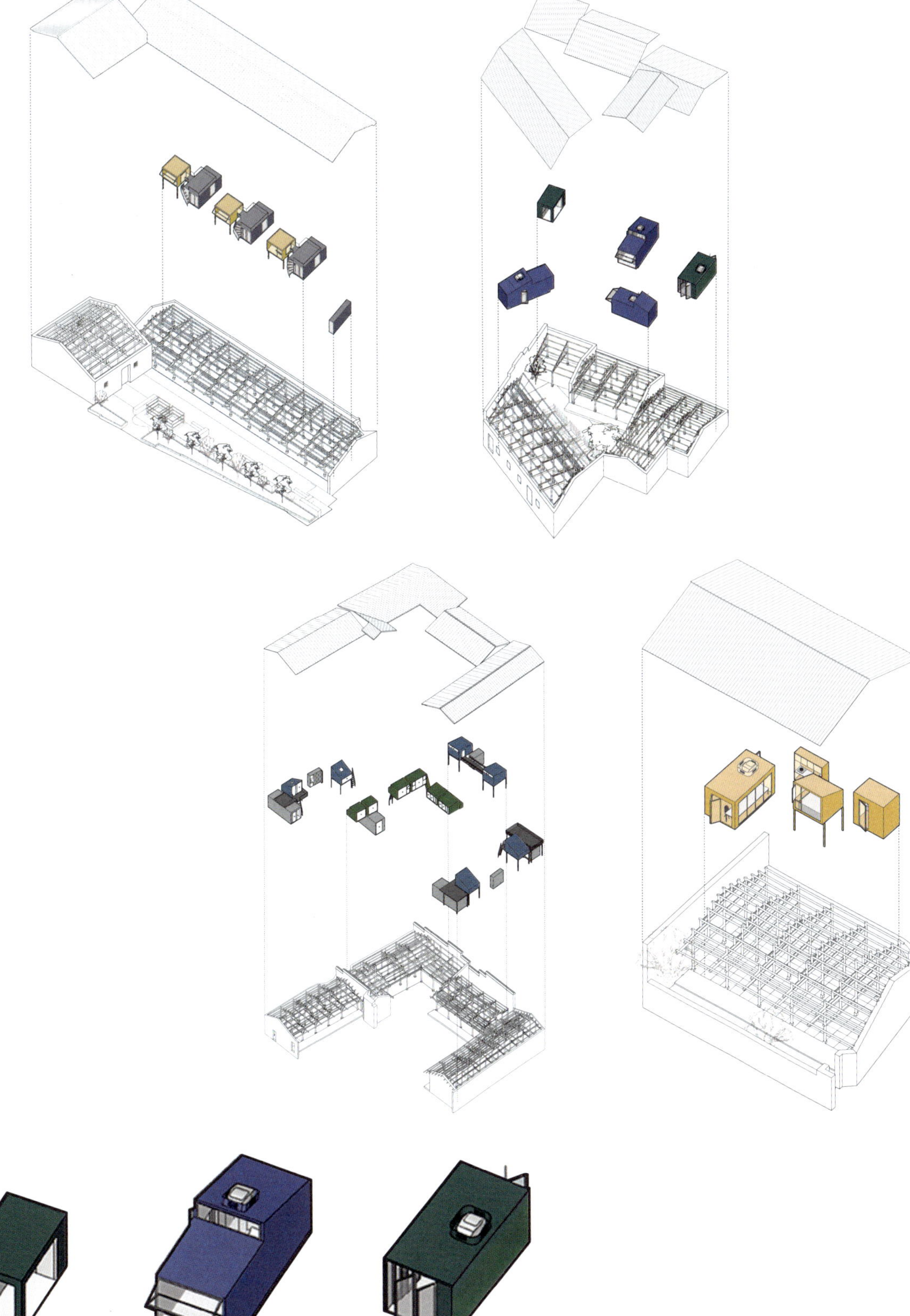

PAO was enlisted by local authorities to renovate a large number of historically protected ceramic workshops into live/work ceramic studios, ensuring the continuation of Jingdezhen's esteemed tradition. Preservation mandates dictated that none of the original structures could be demolished, and any alterations must adhere to traditional materials and methods. However, to entice artists and revitalize the historic center, modern amenities were imperative. The house-in-house approach emerged as a fitting solution, offering flexibility and minimal disruption. Its appeal to the authorities made it an attractive option for renovation, facilitating the integration of contemporary comforts while safeguarding the heritage of Jingdezhen's architectural legacy.

Much like in Dashilar, we devised a systematic approach to courtyard upgrades, employing various models and configurations tailored to the requirements of each property. We introduced bedrooms, bathrooms, kitchens, and two-story structures with mezzanine levels intricately woven within the original wooden framework. The Plugin structures provided air-conditioned space while the remaining interior areas of the original structure were left open-air for use as workshops. Jingdezhen exemplifies how one system could be efficiently customized and implemented across multiple properties, yielding substantial, widespread impact.

Front view of the Jingdezhen P-58 Plugin Houses featuring elevated Plugin bedroom units and ground-floor live/work space with a bathroom facility.

Plugin kitchen unit in the Jingdezhen C-34 Courtyard.

Courtyard view of the Jingdezhen C-34 Plugin Houses featuring the original ceramic drying racks.

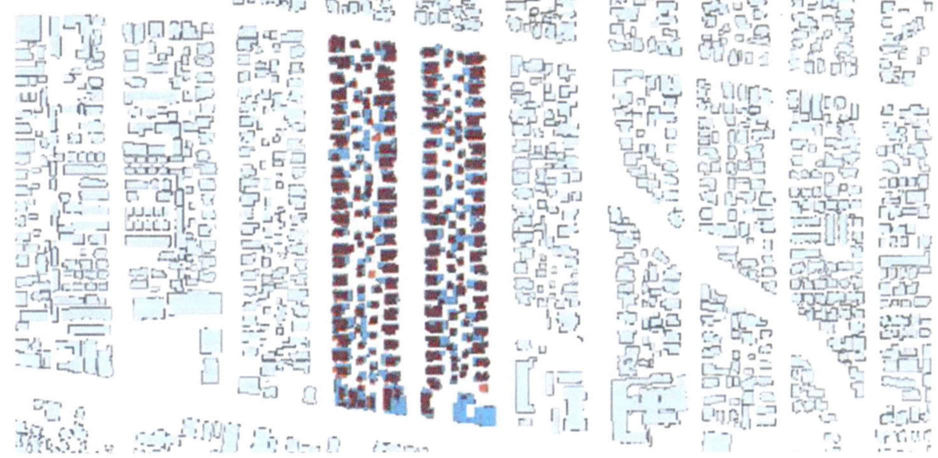

Our work with Accessory Dwelling Units (ADUs) in the US illustrates how existing properties can be optimally utilized on a scale surpassing that of projects like Dashilar and Jingdezhen, which were confined to the size of a neighborhood. In China, where high-density, high-rise apartment buildings dominate the housing landscape, the construction of small single-story housing units is uncommon. Opportunities for Plugin Houses in China were limited to special case scenarios that were hard to come by. However, the prevalence of low-density developments in North America, Europe, and elsewhere in Asia and in Australasia makes the Plugin House concept much more well-suited. Regulation supporting the building of ADUs in the US makes the potential for better utilizing space for housing on a city-wide scale with Plugin Houses more possible. Utilizing the yards of suburban and urban neighborhoods, ADUs hold promise for addressing housing demands, especially in rapidly growing cities.

The existence of ADUs in the US is due in part to widespread suburban development and the prevalence of single-family zoning. Single-family zoning is a planning restriction applied in the US and Canada in the early 1900s that restricted the types of housing that could be built in certain areas, favoring detached, single-family homes. By the time of the post-Second World War housing boom, the greatest expansion of housing in US history, single-family zoning had become firmly established as a dominant feature of urban and suburban development in the US.

◰ Plugin bed and bathroom unit in the Jingdezhen C-34 Courtyard with ceramic workshop in the foreground.

◫ Workshop view with an elevated Plugin unit inside the Yanghua Nong Courtyard in Jingdezhen.

◱ Elevated Plugin bedroom unit inside the H-20 Courtyard in Jingdezhen.

◳ Overlay of building footprints on parcels zoned for single-family residential use from 1966 (red) and 2008 (blue) in the Huntington Park area of Los Angeles.

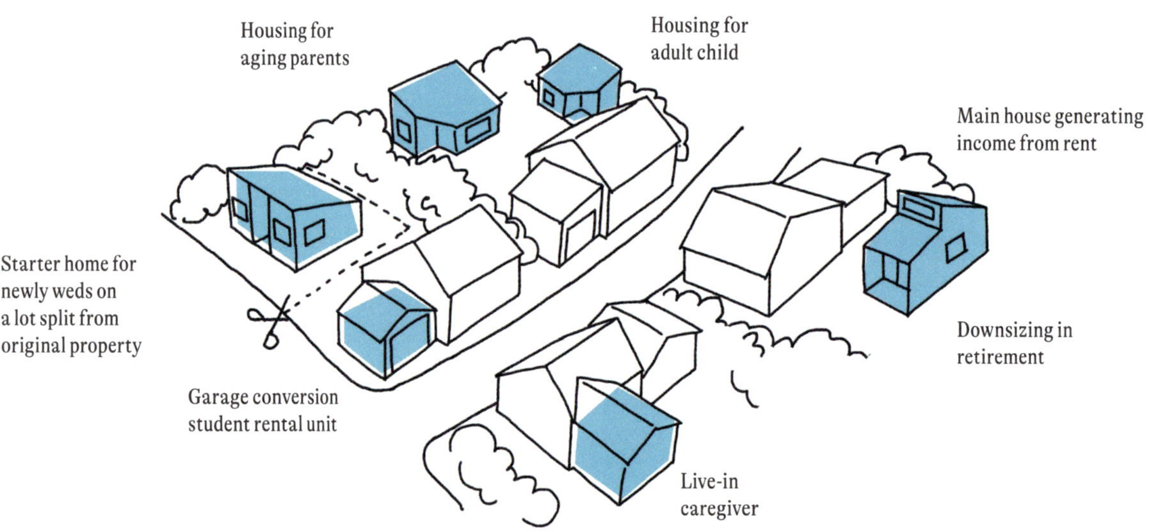
Housing for
aging parents
Housing for
adult child
Main house generating
income from rent
Starter home for
newly weds on
a lot split from
original property
Downsizing in
retirement
Garage conversion
student rental unit
Live-in
caregiver

Before the introduction of single-family zoning, US cities often exhibited greater flexibility in adapting to the demands of their population. The absence of strict single-family zoning regulations meant that developers had more freedom to respond to changing demographic trends, economic conditions, and housing preferences. They could build multi-family dwellings or adapt existing structures to meet evolving needs without being constrained by zoning restrictions.

ADUs address the housing needs of the "missing middle," offering multi-unit buildings and small housing options that cater to various household sizes, incomes, and lifestyles. This term describes the lack of diverse housing choices, bridging the gap between high-rise apartment buildings and single-family homes.

As demographics evolve, so do housing needs. For instance, urban households in the US are shrinking, and there is an increased demand for smaller homes as the population ages. Simultaneously, by the 2010s, many baby boomers had become "empty nesters," finding their homes too large for their needs. However, downsizing while staying within the same community poses challenges due to limited alternative housing options and established social ties.

ADUs provide an opportunity for homeowners to move to a smaller unit in their backyard while renting out their main residence, offering supplemental income—especially beneficial for retirees with limited savings or income sources. Rising housing costs and changing cultural norms have also led to increased multigenerational living. ADUs can accommodate aging parents, earning them the monikers "granny flats" or "in-law units," as well as adult children, promoting close family bonds and shared living arrangements.

The need for more housing and a greater diversity has at times been met by informal building of ADUs. This was the case in south-east Los Angeles, California from the 1980s to 2010s where a surging population with few housing options in single-family zoned areas resulted in a proliferation of un-permitted ADU construction [9].

View of a typical suburban neighborhood development in the US with single-family zoning.

The potential for Plugin House ADUs as backyard homes.

Since the late 20th century numerous countries, including the US, have adopted progressive policies to encourage ADU construction. In many residential neighborhoods, alleyways flanked by rows of houses with large backyards are commonplace. ADUs in this context, often referred to as "alley flats" or "laneway homes," boast convenient access and a separate entrance from the main house, making them highly appealing to renters or buyers.

In such scenarios, a neighborhood's density could potentially double. ADU scenarios vary widely, ranging from carving out space within existing properties to detached structures. While some cities restrict ADUs to rental use, others permit lots to be split and sold. Additionally, certain cities allow for the construction of multiple ADUs on one site, facilitating higher levels of density and providing diverse housing options to meet varied needs.

While ADUs have the potential to address various housing concerns, their ability to significantly increase access to low-cost housing remains uncertain. However, the first Plugin House in the US, located in Austin, Texas, serves as a valuable example of how an ADU indirectly helped increase access to affordable housing. The Alamo Plugin Demo was situated in the backyard of a property owned by a local housing nonprofit called Blackland Community Development Corporation. To raise funds for its initiatives, the site was split, allowing the backyard to be sold. Consequently, the ADU operates independently from the main house, equipped with its own address, electrical, and water meter. This ADU provides much-needed rental housing in a single-family zoned neighborhood, offering units that are more moderately sized than the majority of available housing options. The smaller size helps limit rental costs, ensuring affordability compared to other alternatives in the area.

Because ADUs are mostly one- or two-story structures they cannot be the solution to all housing needs. Cities must include high-density multistory residential buildings to meet housing demand. However communities need a way to transition from low-density single-family communities to high-density neighborhoods populated by multi-family buildings. ADUs can act as an interim solution towards achieving higher density. While the necessity for increased density often dictates greater vertical construction, intermediary steps are crucial to facilitate the transition of communities to higher density development.

Another Plugin House, The Blue House Project, constructed on a vacant site within a planned multi-family housing development in Austin served as a transitional agent, albeit not as a residential unit but rather as an artist studio. This temporary structure was installed to accommodate an

View of the Alamo Plugin Demo after becoming The Blue House Project artist residency space.

Interior view of new artwork in progress by resident artist Elizabeth Lopez.

artist residency while the larger housing project navigated the multi-year process of permitting and rezoning. Rather than leaving the site vacant, the Plugin House served as a valuable asset for artists in a community abundant in creative arts but lacking in artist facilities and resources. Although the Plugin House was temporary, the artist residency it housed would continue in a permanent home within the completed development.

The Plugin House not only provided a space for artists but also facilitated community gatherings and events, fostering social connections to the site while awaiting approval. By introducing activities representative of what was to be expected from the upcoming development, the project garnered significant community support. This program helped expedite the approval process for the housing development, which aimed to increase density and provide a substantial number of affordable housing units. The Plugin House initiative not only addressed immediate needs but also contributed to the broader goals of the housing development, showcasing the potential of creative solutions in urban planning and community engagement.

The widespread issue of homelessness in American cities has become a pressing and visible manifestation of the housing crisis. Recent studies have reaffirmed that exorbitant housing costs are the leading cause of homelessness. The cities with the highest rate of homelessness are also the most expensive. Especially in the wake of the COVID-19 pandemic, there has been a growing interest in non-congregate sheltering as a novel strategy to address homelessness. This approach entails creating communities comprising individual homes, usually averaging around nine to eighteen square meters (100 to 200 square feet) each.

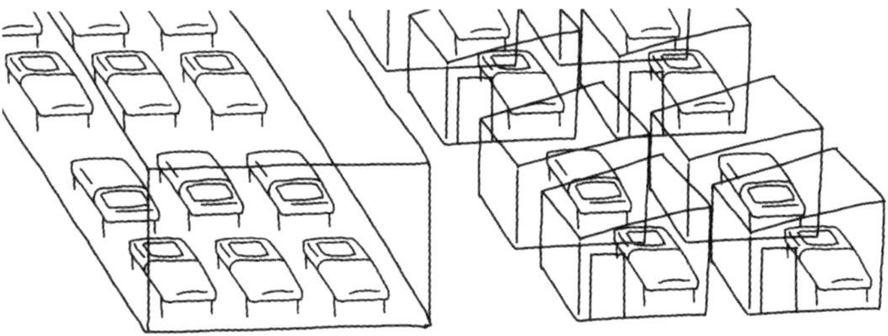

View from the street of the Alamo Plugin Demo.

Resident artist Elizabeth Lopez in the doorway of The Blue House Project studio.

Artist showcase event at The Blue House Project artist residency space.

Transportation of the fully assembled Alamo Plugin Demo to a different lot.

Congregate sheltering versus non-congregate sheltering.

In contrast to congregate sheltering facilities, which include Single Room Occupancy (SRO) multi-tenant residential properties or large homeless shelters housed within expansive buildings like gymnasiums, non-congregate sheltering offers several advantages. Congregate shelters often impose restrictions such as curfews, the separation of couples, and limitations on pets. Moreover, the shared nature of these facilities provides little privacy and limited space for personal belongings. SROs, while providing more privacy than congregate shelters, still present challenges. Communal spaces like corridors can feel unsafe, and multi-unit buildings can be difficult to maintain, often falling into disrepair due to shared utilities.

Non-congregate sheltering, with its emphasis on individual units, helps limit the spread of disease, as each resident has their own private space. Additionally, the privacy and independence afforded by individual units contribute to residents' self-sufficiency and preparation for independent living. This can be particularly important for people who experience discrimination such as the LGBTQ+ community. This approach represents a significant step toward addressing the complex issues surrounding homelessness in urban areas.

The problem of homelessness is extremely complex and burdened by a multitude of barriers with NIMBYs among the most difficult. Therefore the locating of sheltering communities where people experiencing homelessness can stay as they transition to living off the streets is particularly sensitive.

A planned Plugin House community at Puʻuhonua o Waiʻanae, the largest homeless encampment on Oʻahu, Hawaii led by a Native Hawaiian community, offers a rare example of self-determined housing that has successfully navigated opposition. After years of threats of government sweeps, community leader Twinkle Borge negotiated directly with the governor to prevent displacement. In 2020, the community raised funds to purchase twenty acres inland, relocating on their own terms. In Phase 3 of development, Plugin Houses were used to build permanent homes and communal kitchens and bathrooms. Once complete, the agri-village will be home to 250 residents. Community-led and rooted in care, Puʻuhonua o Waiʻanae fosters a safe environment for families and children facing addiction, medical issues, or homelessness.

Artist's impression of the Plugin agri-village at Puʻuhonua o Waiʻanae on Oʻahu, Hawaii.

View of the TOOF Esperanza Community site in Austin in 2020 before renovation.

View of the TOOF Esperanza Community site in Austin in 2025 with renovation in progress.

Plugin House has worked with The Other Ones Foundation (TOOF), another nonprofit servicing the homeless population, for many years to provide buildings to support their work. TOOF manages the 100+ Esperanza Community, a non-congregate emergency shelter complex in east Austin, where numerous Plugin Houses are sited. In the case of Esperanza, the community is built on a state-owned site no longer in use that was originally used by the Texas Department of Transportation. Because it is state-owned it is exempt from city laws such as zoning. This has allowed TOOF to work much faster to build the Esperanza Community.

The needs of the Esperanza Community constantly shift and change, therefore TOOF must remain flexible. For this reason Plugin Houses were also designed with flexibility in mind. The units are designed to be movable with a forklift. Certain units have a removable wall that allows a duplex to be converted into a single unit. And Plugin Houses are designed to support a range of functions and uses that include residential units with private bathrooms, food service units with industrial kitchens, offices, and job training facilities. The Plugin House unit types also recognize the importance of not only living spaces but also the wraparound services that are crucial for people transitioning out of homelessness.

TOOF has been approached by practically every kind of innovative building technology in existence and has experienced many of them. However, they are most pleased with how Plugin Houses have worked, and they have collaborated with the Plugin House Company to plan future endeavors.

Plugin House has continued to help promote the use of non-congregate sheltering for homelessness. Plugin House was selected as a handful of innovative housing systems to be showcased at California Governor Gavin Newsom's 2023 State of the State address in Sacramento. Standing in front of a Plugin House he announced a state-wide initiative to fund and expand non-congregate communities throughout California, the state with the largest unhoused population in the country. We have since been contracted to supply the state with Plugin Houses for future communities.

View of the TOOF Flex Unit Model C and a Quonset hut in use for a community event.
Community members congregate around the TOOF Flex Unit Model C.
Side window feature of the TOOF Flex Unit Model C in use.
Interior view of the TOOF Plugin House Flex Unit Model A.
TOOF Flex Unit Models D & E ready for use.
Front view with lighting of the TOOF Flex Unit Model B.

In addition to constructing Plugin Houses to strengthen communities, fostering community through the act of building Plugin Houses has also been an integral part of our work. The experience of being able to transform one's surroundings with your own hands is profoundly empowering, instilling a strong sense of agency. The Plugin House system facilitates this experience by making it easily accessible to all.

The Plugin Houses at Esperanza Community were not only homes but also projects constructed by the residents themselves, in alignment with TOOF's mission to provide job training and employment opportunities to those in need. This collaborative construction process not only underscored the simplicity of building Plugin Houses but also enabled residents to develop a deep understanding of the innovative system, its functionality, and its benefits. By actively participating in the construction process, residents not only acquired valuable skills but also had the opportunity to share their stories and experiences with homelessness. This collaborative effort fostered a stronger sense of community and empathy among all involved, providing insights that enriched the understanding of the challenges faced by individuals experiencing homelessness.

TOOF Esperanza Community members assembling Flex Unit Model C.

Governor Gavin Newsom standing in front of a Plugin House at the 2023 State of the State address in Sacramento.

TOOF Esperanza Community members assembling Flex Unit Model B.

PLUGIN EVERYTHING, EVERYWHERE

by Tau Tavengwa

The UK 2024 election cycle highlighted the challenges many countries face in addressing the global housing shortage. Keir Starmer's winning Labour Party campaign leaned heavily on a pledge to build 1.5 million homes in its first term. Across the Atlantic Ocean, Kamala Harris, in her failed bid to become the first female president in the US, committed to building three million new homes by 2028. Reducing the cost of housing (which rose by 50% across the US from 2019 to 2024) was one of the few things Harris and Trump agreed on as they campaigned around the country. Meanwhile, in India's May 2024 election campaign, Narendra Modi's Bharatiya Janata Party (BJP) pledged to build thirty million new houses in its second term.

Looking out the window of my apartment to the busy construction site next door, where tower after luxury housing tower has been going up as part of the London Dock development, I cannot help but be cynical of these pledges and whether they will amount to anything. London, like many cities globally, is experiencing an awe-inducing affordable housing shortage, while ironically experiencing a boom in luxury apartments like the ones on the site next to mine. The entry level flat at London Dock costs between £750,000 and £850,000 (1 to 1.1 million dollars). The size? Sixty square meters (645 square feet), and they are being snapped up quickly, accelerating the slow transition of Wapping from a sleepy, charming dockside corner of east London into yet another lucrative landing pad for investors from all over the world. The site sales office proudly announces that they have Mandarin, Arabic (and, until a few years ago, Russian) speakers on site to cater for their global clientele. It's a not-so-subtle wink to the pedigree of wealthy buyers they are aiming to attract.

Providing affordable housing in a global environment where investment for that sort of housing is incredibly inadequate is one of the biggest challenges many cities face today. But there are many possibilities, some that buck the trend on how to think about housing in the first place. The conditions in each city differ greatly, and this has been a rolling topic of conversation between James Shen of PAO and myself for a few years.

Dharavi, one of Asia's largest slums, in Mumbai, India.

James and I visited Mumbai a few years ago as part of a group trip. One day, after a day packed with scheduled activities and seemingly endless bus trips through the city, we went rogue. Instead of taking the bus back to our hotel, we chose to walk the ten to fifteen or so kilometers (six to nine miles) instead. We saw the city unfiltered for the few hours it took to walk back.

On that breezy summer afternoon, we walked around the Fort area, passing through some fishing villages, traversing several informal settlements, under the Eastern Freeway, and across a few busy multi-lane roads, passing through leafy, sometimes dusty parks filled with weekend loungers and the occasional loud cricket game in play, as we made our way back to our hotel near the Gateway of India. Mine and James's conversations over the years mostly follow three main strands, and this time was no different. We discussed food (a passion we share) and the books and movies we had recently read or watched. This time, however, as the journey went on, something different happened. Where we had been casually observing everything around us as we went by, I asked him how relevant PAO's plugin projects were in the context and environment we were walking through.

View within Dharavi informal settlement, Mumbai.

The two-billion-dollar Antilia in Mumbai is one of the most expensive houses in India.

Masjid Bandar informal houses built in front of warehouses just 3.2 kilometers (two miles) from Antilia.

That topic started a conversation between us that has lasted almost six years and has colored how I see the role of the designer and architect.

I wasn't taking notes; therefore, I'm taking writerly liberties here. However, as I remember it, his initial response was poignant. First and foremost, he pointed out the environment around us. He went on to tell me how theirs was a practice informed by observing how people undertake day-to-day tasks, how they cannibalize the detritus of the formal world, remaking it to suit their needs in ways that are often unexpected and, while born out of desperation, often surprisingly joyful. Earlier in the day, we had driven past Antilia—the infamously opulent twenty-seven-story, two-billion-dollar single-family tower that is home to the billionaire Adani family, which towers over some informal settlements within view and walking distance. That stark reality was not lost on us as we walked.

He went on to tell me about how, early on in the life of PAO, he and his partners chose to have an office in Dashilar in Beijing, the working-class neighborhood in which they have been located for more than a decade now, and how that has become a laboratory for them—a place where they can observe life in a marginalized community ironically located at the center of a bustling city and not only gain inspiration from it, but find ways to work with and be part of the community. One in which architecture or high design are not daily concerns, but ironically, where lots of innovation and cultural production born out of need is exhibited daily. The formidable outputs—whether in architecture, public art, or product—that PAO has managed to put out into the world over the years would not have been possible without Dashilar, he concluded.

We speculated how the Plugin House that PAO were in the process of trying to introduce to the US market would perform in a neighborhood like the ones we were walking though. How would this product ("Was that how to define it?" I wondered out loudly), with all its built-in flexibilities, do in a tropical climate like Mumbai's; what use could it be in a context where land tenure could be tenuous for the majority of residents; and how could it be integrated into the transitioning of millions from living informally into better, more habitable living

conditions? We posited how a tenure-less Plugin House owner might quickly dismantle their home and move it elsewhere before the wolves at the door could blow it all down to make way for a new real estate development, for example, and wondered whether this would be a desirable way for them to cushion against such shocks in contexts where those sorts of evictions are regular occurrences. We also wondered whether the entry-level Plugin House, coming in at about $10,000, was an accessible price point. To me, coming from more than a decade living in Cape Town, South Africa, a city notorious for its inequality, and in which affordable housing is in short supply, and where a massive number of people live informally, this was not just an intellectual curiosity, but rather, one of real-life consideration.

The next year, I invited James to participate in a gathering of various people with whom my business partner—Edgar Pieterse—and I share interests. Cape Town, South Africa is no Mumbai by any stretch of the imagination, but there are interesting parallels.

In the orientation on the city that Edgar gave to the twenty or so people we had visiting for the gathering, he spoke of the reality of Cape Town being one of the most unequal cities in the world (back then, its Gini coefficient—a measure of wealth inequality—was 0.62; zero being lowest, one being highest). Here you can be in an environment that feels and looks like Monaco on the one hand, and within a fifteen- to twenty-minute drive in any direction transform into informal communities in distressed conditions that could rival any of those found in the Global South.

This nearly five-million-strong city officially has about 1,452,845 households. An additional 16% (about 1.4 million, considered a severe underestimate by some experts) are scattered across the 437 informal settlements that mostly lie on its peripheries. While many of these settlements mushroomed before South Africa's transition from an apartheid to a majority democratic state

◰ An informally built backyard dwelling serves as the homeowner's residence, while the adjacent government-provided house is rented out as a source of income.

◳ Informal backyard dwelling built on right side of photo adjacent to government-provided house in Dunoon township in Cape Town.

in 1994, they are still not recognized as permanent. Their residents exist in these settlements with limited services, and without officially sanctioned occupation rights or tenure security.

Seen as a better-functioning city in comparison to South Africa's seven other metropolitan cities, Cape Town has been experiencing a large influx of the country's middle and upper class, whose increasing numbers have led to a steep increase in the cost of property, making it unaffordable to many. This, however, has not deterred an even larger number of poorer arrivals, most of whom end up in those same peripheral settlements which are the only logical, affordable choice for them to reside in. Cape Town, like most cities in South Africa, has a staggering housing shortage that, at the current construction and investment rate in new affordable housing (a fuzzy, contested term in South Africa) delivery, will take decades to make a meaningful dent that will ease the crisis. Like many informal residents, new arrivals end up in either self-built shacks or pre-fabricated units produced by a new wave of manufacturers specifically catering to this market, sometimes sold off the side of the street, made of corrugated tin roof sheeting. In a city that experiences devastating seasonal fires often concentrated in informal settlements, the pre-fab units offer little in terms of safety. But they are affordable, and a better option than the alternative.

Another solution growing in popularity is the backyard shack—commonly known as Accessible Dwelling Units (ADUs) in the US. But ADUs and backyard shacks, in logic, fabric, condition, and legal status, could not be more different.

According to official South African government statistics, the state has built a substantial number of brick-and-mortar houses in poor communities across the country. In statistics released by the country's Department of Human Settlement (the organ of government tasked with delivering housing) it has provided five million "housing opportunities." This Kafkaesque term refers to a mix of small brick and mortar units commonly known as RDP (Reconstruction and Development) units, typically up to forty square meters (430 square feet) in size, and serviced plots earmarked for formal self-build in poor black and other non-white communities across the country.

A substantial number of these RDP homes now have an appendage/attachment to the back, typically a room or two. Often self-built, the units are by most measures illegal. They are built primarily for rental purposes. In many cases, the occupant of these backyard units is the leaseholder, with a higher-income tenant living in the original unit. South Africa's high unemployment rate and increasing informality mean unemployed homeowners are downgrading their living conditions in order to earn income that enables them to sustain their families. It is a version of the house as an ATM machine.

The *Accessory Dwelling Unit Guidebook* by the City of Boston in Massachusetts makes the clear distinction that whether internal or external, ADUs are officially sanctioned, planned, professionally built units that meet all necessary standards regarding safety, and fit within the aesthetic of the neighborhood they are in. These are not top-of-mind considerations for those building in backyards in the areas of Cape Town mentioned above. Ironically, in conversations with James, he has expressed frustration in how the emphasis on exacting safety standards in places like Boston, while crucial, severely limits the capacity for many homeowners to construct ADUs on their properties due to the bureaucracy involved, as well as the increase in cost that comes with adhering to these standards.

But, as different as the mechanics and contextual social and economic governance dynamics of these two are, they ultimately aim to achieve the same thing. And therein lies the dilemma, and the opportunity for PAO's Plugin House units. The approaches that informal construction presents are mostly lost once you adapt and codify them as the Plugin House seeks to do. The constraints of formalization can make something like the Plugin House unattractive due to the inability of the planning statutes to mirror the speed and adaptability of informal construction. Regulatory oversight is important, but it comes at a cost. The question is, how do you unleash a capacity to self-build and address concerns with safety and standards without compromising either?

I visited James in his hometown of Los Angeles (LA), California in the summer of 2023. After more than a decade living and working in China where he co-founded PAO with his partners Zang Feng and He Zhe, he was back home, and I wanted to see him in his element, so to speak. A year after the COVID-19 pandemic, I was not only eager to catch up but wanted to see in person some of the projects he was working on.

Of particular interest were some developing ideas he had excitedly shared with me that involved working with a few homeless people on LA's infamous Skid Row. In response to witnessing the desperate living conditions among the homeless population in central LA, James was working with some old friends of his who ran an eatery called Nickel Diner on Skid Row, and who have been allies of that community for decades, providing affordable, high-quality food, and a number of food industry jobs. Although not a Plugin House, the approach—a series of interventions aimed at improving the performance of the dwellings they occupied at nighttime—was the same in spirit. Often living in camping tents, many of the city's homeless keep their goods in shopping carts, moving with them wherever they go throughout the day, and making camp in environments they feel safe from harassment by the cops, and from sometimes violent attacks by others within or outside of their immediate communities.

◰ Pre-fabricated buildings systems exhibited and sold along the streets of Cape Town.

This initiative did not come to fruition, but it was the beginning of a process that has seen PAO and its subsidiary partner Plugin House together with our client and partner The Other Ones Foundation (TOOF) build emergency shelters and a skills and job center for people experiencing homelessness in Austin, Texas.

In late 2022, I co-curated an exhibition titled "Multiplicity" with my curatorial partner Vyjayanthi Rao, part of that year's edition of the Lisbon Architecture Triennale. The premise was as simple and as accessible as Vyjayanthi and I thought architecture should be. We set out that the role of the architect had shifted, and what was necessary was an expansion of how we define who makes architecture, what is architecture. We argued that the remit of architecture—and architects—should expand to include thinking not just about how to enable auto-construction, but also issues that range from health to aging on every site and every project. We challenged ourselves to find practices and projects that were providing a view of what this expansion could look like. We identified twenty projects from around the world that we thought lived up to this measure. The Plugin House obviously featured very prominently in the exhibition.

After the project and all the pomp and ceremony around such an undertaking subsided, I was left with the question of where all these wonderful ideas led. This was my state of mind when I arrived in LA, and, in learning about this small, seemingly drop-in-the-ocean project that never materialized, I understood what always drew me to Plugin Houses. Sure, I love the aesthetic, and the spirit of the thing is an idea I can easily plug into, so to speak.

In the many conversations that followed, I realized something that I had not quite appreciated, and that I think many advocates of ADUs in the US and elsewhere do not fully realize. The popularity of ADUs in the US is a realization that the housing development model that produces those towers mushrooming en masse at London Dock will never solve the global affordable housing crisis we face. It's an acknowledgment that there are important lessons to be learnt from some of the innovative solutions that have arisen from informality in the Global South, and in reality, across the world.

Nothing is ever perfect, but the Plugin House is a valiant attempt to bridge these two worlds. It challenges policymakers and built environment professionals to consider how we build, and who gets to build in the first place. It's a battle cry for architects to reconsider who they are there to serve—the London Dock or Antilia-level clientele, or the majority in desperate need of the smartest in the profession to do their bit to solve urgent challenges like affordable housing. The Plugin House offers a window onto what might be and offers a way to think about an architecture that's nimble and adept enough to equally consider the needs of a homeless person on Skid Row, that resident of a decades, perhaps century-old fishing village or city-slicker in Mumbai, a recent arrival in a Cape Town informal settlement and a Bostonian's vision of how they could live better. It proposes an architecture that adjusts to the scale and circumstances of each of their needs from moment to moment. It is a concept of design and architecture as a great leveler, devoid of the scourge of class, geography or permanence. It proposes adaptation, something we are in desperate need of in these times of uncertainty.

Let's imagine a Plugin House in all its scalable parts that we could find and purchase everywhere.

5
HOW DO WE DO HOUSING BETTER?

◰ Bird's-eye view of the Harvard Yard Plugin Demo.
◱ The Boston City Hall Plugin Demo.
◲ The Alamo Plugin Demo at Austin Design Week.

The global demand for better housing is rapidly increasing, while upgrading aging housing stock and adapting to shifting climatic conditions become more challenging. People are desperate for dignified places to live. The need for innovative, adaptable, and affordable solutions has never been more urgent. As we confront these growing challenges, finding new ways to build sustainable and efficient housing is critical. From the inception of the Plugin House initiative in Dashilar, Beijing, we recognized the immense potential of this innovative building system. However, as new opportunities emerged, it became clear that we needed to shift our approach—moving away from our traditional roles as architects to establish the Plugin House as an independent, self-funded venture. Initially supported by individual projects, we soon realized that project funds alone were insufficient to fully explore and unlock the potential of the Plugin House system, especially given its innovative material and structural design.

While we endeavored to develop the system as a product within project constraints, the limited opportunities for trial and error posed significant challenges to our progress. Nevertheless, we managed to explore many aspects of the Plugin House system through a combination of project funding and grants, which afforded us the flexibility to self-initiate projects rather than wait for external opportunities.

Grant funding also supported demonstrations in 2018 at Harvard University and Boston City Hall in Massachusetts, facilitated respectively by collaborations with Harvard's Office for the Arts and the Mayor of Boston's Housing Innovation Lab. These demonstrations served as platforms to introduce the system and its potential applicability in a US context. It was also a way to connect with potential partners.

During this period, James Shen, a Loeb Fellow at Harvard Graduate School of Design, met Anmol Mehra, a fellow in Public Policy at the Harvard Kennedy School. Both shared a strong interest in housing policy and social entrepreneurship, and their backgrounds as mid-career professionals focused on innovative approaches to improving access to housing brought them together. Anmol attended the Plugin House demonstrations and was impressed by the system. Their collaboration emphasized the importance of an entrepreneurial mindset combined with solid business acumen in pursuing the ambitious goal of developing housing as a mass-produced product. In 2019, they partnered to establish the Plugin House Company, a key step in advancing the initiative and expanding its potential impact.

Beyond the development of the Plugin House as a product, the establishment of the company marked an exploration into social entrepreneurship. Together, James and Anmol were captivated by the idea of creating an enterprise with a social agenda that could align with governments and nonprofits. Equally vital was the venture's capacity to sustainably fund itself as a private enterprise, thus circumventing the limitations and bureaucratic processes.

While nonprofit organizations excel when rooted in specific locations and communities, the Plugin House Company aimed for a broader reach across multiple cities and markets. Recognizing that substantial and flexible funding would be necessary for product development, the venture sought to leverage both public and private sector partnerships, a common practice in housing and real estate developments. The aspiration was to combine the strengths of both sectors to achieve the venture's goals.

Anmol is a social impact-oriented housing developer with numerous completed housing projects that benefit underserved groups. He has held positions on the board of several nonprofits and is an active advocate of social entrepreneurship. PAO was founded as a design practice directed by a strong social agenda and was the first architectural office in Asia certified as a B-Corporation, a globally recognized certification for business verifying high social and environmental performance.

With this foundation, the Plugin House Company was founded to make high-quality low-cost housing available to the masses. The company was registered as a benefit corporation, a for-profit corporate entity that can legally balance shareholder interests with those who are affected by and benefit from its work. In contrast to traditional corporations, benefit corporations are not legally bound to maximize shareholder value.

Given the spotty history of pre-fabricated housing companies, the Plugin House Company recognizes the importance of business to the success of a product. A successful commercial product does not have to be well designed, but a well-designed product must exist within a well-run business to succeed [14]. The business model of the Plugin House Company revolves around offering clients a comprehensive, one-stop solution, acknowledging the complexity of every building project. It aims to streamline this process by guiding clients through preliminary planning, permitting, design,

Plugin House Company founders Anmol Mehra and James Shen assemble a Plugin House at TOOF's Esperanza Community.

New Plugin Houses going through a test assembly at the Plugin House Factory in southern China.

MIT

and construction. For larger projects such as the planned expansion of the TOOF headquarters in Austin, Plugin House Company has provided masterplanning services to assist in the earliest conception of the project.

Numerous failed pre-fabricated building ventures of the past made the mistake of focusing on the product itself with insufficient attention paid to the business marketing and production processes. Many such systems were developed by architects who are not generally knowledgeable in industrial manufacturing [14]. However, since our inception we have always incorporated industrial design in our practice with product designers on staff. With degrees and experience in both product design and architecture, James has helped the practice bridge across disciplines.

To increase the capabilities of the Plugin House Company, in 2023 the company became the largest shareholder in the Plugin House manufacturing facility. This strategic investment bolsters the cost advantage of Plugin House by mitigating third-party vendor expenses and ensuring greater control over the supply chain. By integrating manufacturing with design and engineering, we are able to accelerate product development and innovate. Through continuous experimentation with new materials, processes, and product integration, we will continue to make strides in making homes more accessible to those who need them most.

The initial Plugin House products consisted of low-cost Accessible Dwelling Units (ADUs) and emergency shelters. However, extensive research revealed that the cost of constructing ADUs, despite their potential to expand housing stock, often remains prohibitively high for many individuals. Such projects are typically highly customized and stick-built, resulting in elevated costs. Additionally, the small scale of these projects often makes the utilization of architectural

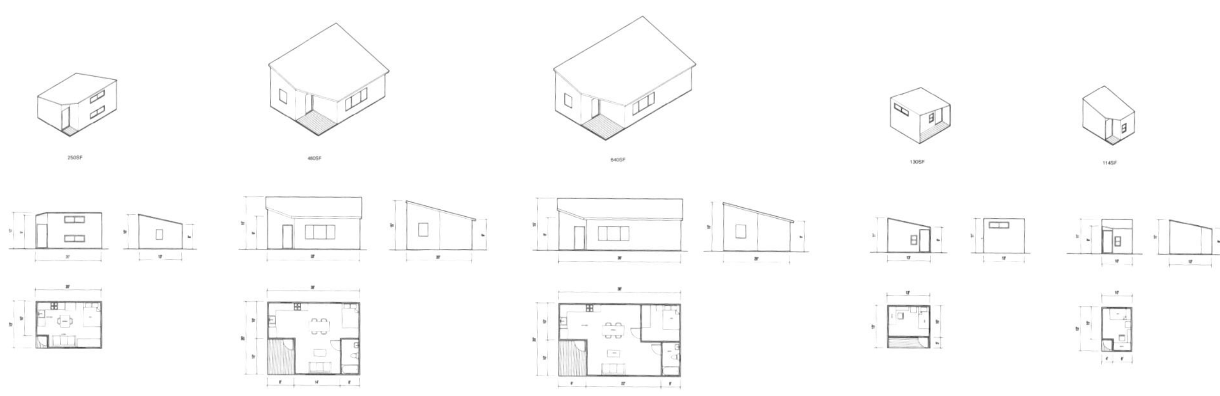

services inefficient, as these services tend to be more cost-effective for larger projects. For these reasons, growth in the construction of ADUs has been modest. Plugin House sought to address these challenges by offering ADUs at significantly lower costs and completing them within shorter timelines.

Emergency shelter units, typically constructed of tent-like materials, often suffer from water and air leaks and poor insulation. In contrast, Plugin House builds emergency shelters with quality equivalent to that of a typical single-family home, and at a competitive cost relative to other companies. This approach reflects the belief that individuals experiencing homelessness deserve dignified living conditions.

From the standpoint of the architectural profession, the spinning off of the Plugin House Company as a separate entity from PAO signifies a departure from traditional architectural practice and the launch of an entrepreneurial endeavor. Architectural firms typically operate as consultancies, wherein architects move from one commissioned project to another, guided by predetermined needs and requirements. Architects are usually brought onboard when many aspects of a project are already well defined and funding is allocated accordingly. Consequently, the scope of architects' involvement is limited. Architects may identify potential opportunities to address underlying issues more comprehensively, but to pursue them would most often necessitate additional investment in time and resources beyond the scope of an individual project. In the case of Plugin House, no project, even when it involved many Plugin Houses, could sufficiently fund the development of the Plugin House into a mass market product.

This consultancy model inherently restricts scalability as each commission is unique, with design concepts rarely extending beyond the confines of a single project and its associated fees. Architects primarily accumulate experience and knowledge from one project to the next, hindering the leveraging of previous designs. Consequently, the economics of design consultancies tend to push architects toward large-scale projects, such as towers, where similar floorplans are replicated vertically, achieving economies of scale.

The time required to design a small project may not significantly differ from that of a larger one, and negotiating with clients remains a time-consuming process regardless of project size. Consequently, architects gravitate toward large-scale projects where limited design work yields a substantial quantity of design content. Architectural fees reflect this dynamic, with design services being more affordable for larger projects and prohibitively expensive for smaller ones.

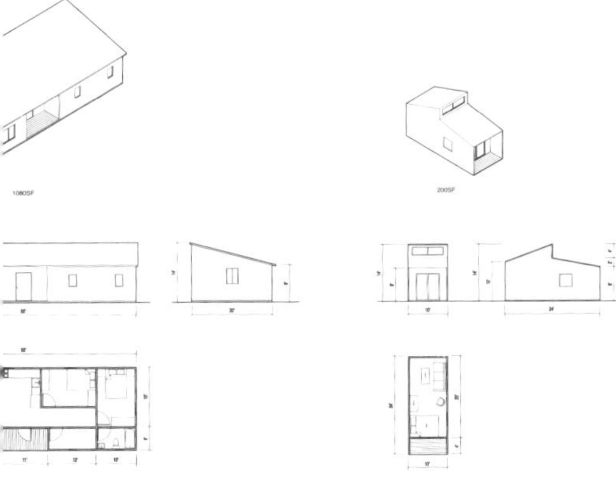

The different Plugin House models offered by the Plugin House Company.

Due to these factors, it can be exceedingly challenging for architects to engage in a diverse range of projects that could greatly benefit from their design expertise.

In a product company, scale is achieved through the volume of replicated units, rather than the size of an individual project. The Plugin House Company envisions housing as a replicable object akin to other consumer goods. We can raise the investment capital needed for the research and development of an innovative product [3]. Such capital is usually not available to consulting practices and is crucial for product development.

And revenue generated from growth provides designers with greater agency, enabling them to actively seek out new avenues and purpose-driven projects. This departure from the traditional service provider–client model empowers us to more fully address societal needs. Just as well-designed mass-produced products make quality goods accessible to a wider audience, architecture as a product has the potential to make well-designed homes attainable for everyone.

The key isn't that Plugin House stands as the ultimate housing solution or that pre-fab housing is the optimal answer. Instead, more companies that offer alternatives to the Plugin House should be cultivated, thereby diversifying building systems, and creating more opportunities to engage communities in tackling housing affordability. By broadening the spectrum of options, we increase the likelihood of addressing contemporary challenges, not only for the benefit of society but also to preserve the relevance of the architectural profession.

Ole Bouman has appealed to architects to rethink their roles and consider pursuing unsolicited architecture:

> "Why is unsolicited architecture undeniably superior to any other? Because it keeps architecture autonomous. The autonomy of architecture once meant hermetic seclusion from reality, but now we know that it is a matter of becoming inclusive beyond any client expectation. Autonomy is in the drive, not the territory...Because it ultimately preserves architecture's long-term relevance and legitimacy. Unsolicited architecture is acquisition for the long-term and finding new objects for the application of architectural intelligence." [12]

View of the People's Canopy appendage of the People's Station, Yantai, Shandong province as a mobile unit and as an attached expansion to the main building.

Bouman advocates for a departure from the conventional service provider–client model to enable architects to pursue social ideals more effectively. Currently, architects primarily serve a limited number of clients, who often belong to a small segment of the social elite. Consequently, architects may not fully represent the needs of the general public. Bouman suggests that unsolicited architecture encourages exploration and agency within the field.

To maintain the architect's relevance in tackling today's most pressing challenges, designers must transcend traditional boundaries and apply design thinking across various professions in ways that directly engage with society. Engaging in urban prototyping in collaboration with city officials towards policy innovation, developing new materials and building systems, and creating new ways to engage communities are only some examples of alternative design practice that can better address complex societal issues beyond simply form making.

The work of architects takes them to different cities, different countries, private and public sectors, and fields from public art and humanitarian aid to institutional housing. An architect does not specialize but rather is a jack-of-all-trades or a bricoleur. They are particularly well positioned to innovate because the profession lies at the intersection of different fields and interests. They are exposed to and practiced in navigating multiple incongruent viewpoints. It is at this intersection where opportunities arise, and where architects can offer possibilities and alternatives where those in specialized fields cannot.

Since the inception of the first Plugin House projects, we at PAO have been committed to exploring alternative uses and pushing the boundaries of the pre-fabricated system. While most Plugin House projects have been single-story structures, with a few featuring interior mezzanines, the focus has primarily been on horizontal flexibility at ground level. However, acknowledging the need for vertical density, we have built a number of experimental multistory buildings to investigate possibilities for extending flexibility in both vertical and horizontal dimensions.

◰ View of the People's Canopy appendage of the People's Station as a mobile unit and as an attached expansion to the main building.
◳ View of the Plugin Tower on display in Shenzhen.
◲ Bird's-eye view of the People's Station in Yantai.
⇥ Night view of the People's Station in Yantai.

SPA

Projects such as the Plugin Towers and the People's Station were conceptualized as two to three-story steel superstructures, with each floor supporting spaces built using Plugin panels. By utilizing pre-fabricated steel node and strut members, these Plugin projects facilitated flexible assembly and continuous expansion in all directions. These initiatives were influenced by experimental architectural movements of the 1960s, notably the work of Archigram, a British architectural group that envisioned futuristic, modular, and flexible buildings, and the Metabolists, a group of Japanese architects who explored biomimetic designs and megastructures capable of continuous growth and transformation. The concept of the megastructure was central to both movements, emphasizing large, adaptable frameworks for urban living, which directly inspired the Plugin House approach. A megastructure can be defined as followed:

> "Not only a structure of great size, but...also a structure which is frequently:
>
> 1. Constructed of modular units;
> 2. Capable of great or even 'unlimited' extension;
> 3. A structural framework into which smaller structural units (for example, rooms, houses, or small buildings of other sorts) can be built – or even 'plugged-in' or 'clipped-on' after having been pre-fabricated elsewhere;
> 4. A structural framework expected to have a useful life much longer than that of the smaller units which it might support." [8]

◳ Construction of Kisho Kurokawa's Takara Beautilion at the Expo '70 in Osaka.

◲ Plug-In City, Peter Cook (Archigram), 1964.

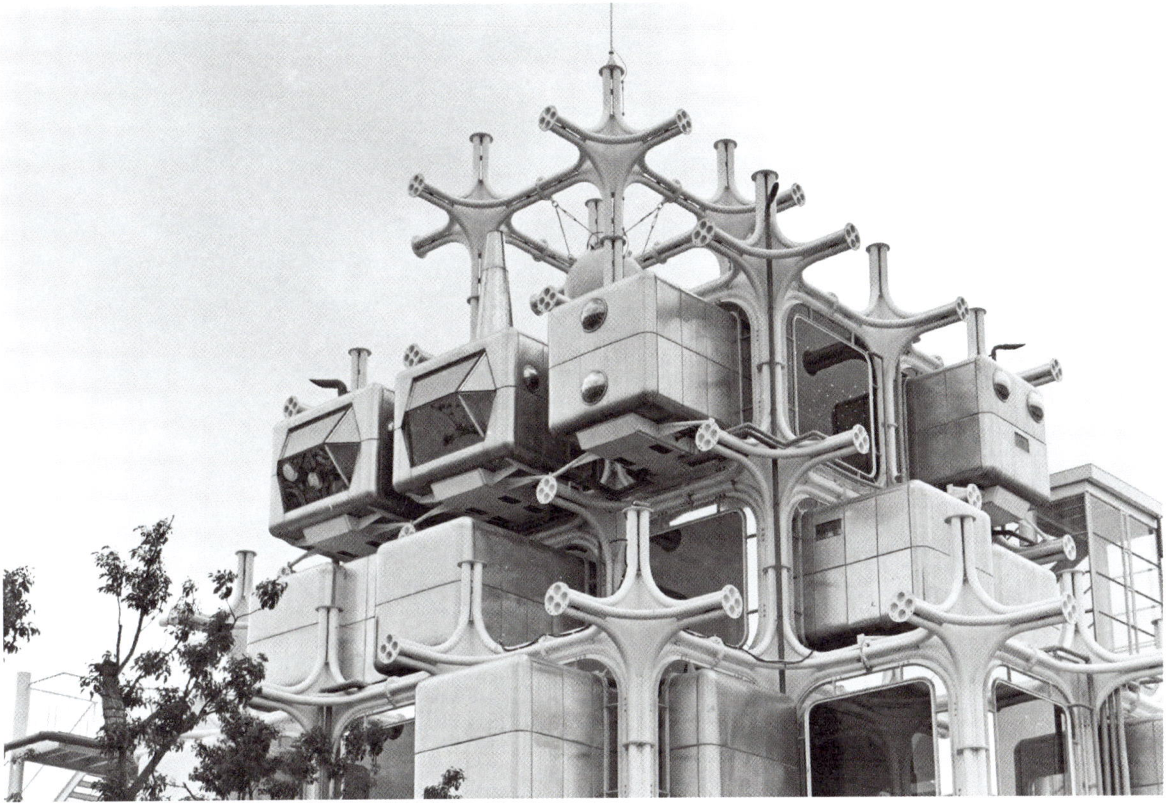

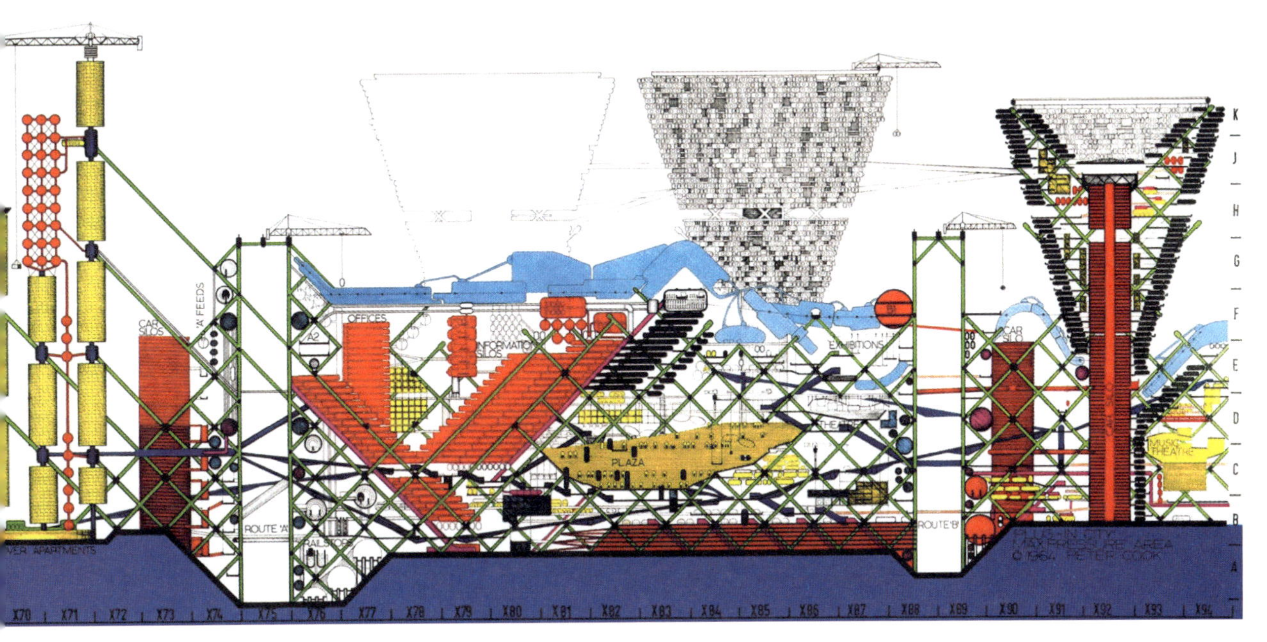

CAR SILOS
'A' FEEDS
OFFICES
A2
INFORMATION SILOS
EXHIBITIONS
PLAZA
ROUTE 'A'
RAILSTOP
ROUTE 'B'
CAR SILO
MUSIC THEATRE
K
J
H
G
F
E
D
C
B
A
X70
X71
X72
X73
X74
X75
X76
X77
X78
X79
X80
X81
X82
X83
X84
X85
X86
X87
X88
X89
X90
X91
X92
X93
X94

The many incarnations of the megastructure concept had focused on developing the flexibility of the structural components of the building. However the enclosed spaces within were constrained to modules of limited size. The Metabolist Nakagin Capsule Tower in Tokyo serves as a prominent built example, with a vertical spine conceived as an expandable structure on which individual capsule-like modules were hung. Although the tower potentially allowed for adjustability in terms of housing module arrangement, the modules themselves were restricted in shape and size.

Construction of Kisho Kurokawa's Nakagin Capsule Tower in Tokyo in 1970.

View of Expo '67 in Montreal with the "Man the Producer" pavilion by Affleck, Desbarats, Dimakopoulos, Lebensold, Sise in the foreground.

View of the Lakeside Plugin Tower and its red service tower containing vertical circulation and an off-grid sewage system.

View at dusk of the Lakeside Plugin Tower in the Changping district of Beijing.

Interior view of the Lakeside Plugin Tower.

Incorporating Plugin panels on each level of a superstructure provided newfound freedom to expand, contract, and modify the enclosure as necessary. The superstructure supported both floor and ceiling panels, facilitating uninterrupted spaces with continuous spans. Additionally, cores containing vertical circulation and utilities connected each level, a concept initially explored in a Plugin House project in Yantian, Shenzhen, and further refined in the Lakeside Plugin Tower in Beijing.

The Lakeside Plugin Tower exemplified these advancements, integrating sustainable technologies and featuring a design lifted from the ground to reduce runoff and minimize impact on the natural landscape. The incorporation of large, operable openings facilitated ample natural ventilation, while the well-sealed and insulated interiors ensured efficient climate control within the building. Covered with solar panels, the tower achieved net-zero status by generating its own electricity.

While these projects remain speculative, each iteration of the vertical Plugin Tower system is an advancement on the previous one. The future of our Plugin Tower in real-world applications remains uncertain, yet without its existence, it would be even more challenging to envision better alternatives to today's conditions. Similarly, applications for the house-in-house within the Plugin House system have been limited to specialized uses. However, this exploratory work ultimately led to the establishment of the Plugin House Company and the development of ADU and emergency shelter models with ample practical applications.

Incorporated into the Plugin Tower projects are the failures and criticism of the megastructure proposals of the 1960s and 1970s. These concepts continued to increase in scale throughout the megastructure movement which ended with critics calling out elements of hubris in the designs. Often megastructure proposals either existed outside of any context or required the complete replacement of existing urban fabric. Other proposals such as those from architect Yona Friedman incorporated existing urban fabric but did so with a megastructure floating above. In doing so, the megastructure approach could be seen as a way to avoid the complexities of the existing city. Megastructure proposals were also criticized for creating an illusion of flexibility, offering adjustability only within a set range of options determined by the designer and no other [13].

By the time megastructures were losing favor, their earliest proponents, including Archigram, had already started moving on from the megastructure itself to focus on other aspects, such as the flexibility of the modular living spaces themselves [13].

PAO's plugin architecture proposes the existing city as the original megastructure. Plugin Tower designs incorporate a large superstructure that provides vertical flexibility but does so at the scale of buildings, not cities. The superstructure is made of pre-fabricated modular parts that provide flexibility, but in its application it would be woven into pre-existing urban fabric. The system is open, distributed, and adaptable, capable of combining with other systems and methods to suit different and changing conditions.

Imagining plugin architecture applied across a city, we created the Megacity Plugin proposal for the recently published *Archigram Ten*, the first issue since 1974. Megacity Plugin presents a city in constant flux, teeming with social activity activated by a mixture of programmatic uses that include temporary activations and events. The city is reimagined so that housing is "plugged into" industrial sites, dilapidated buildings, and most importantly transportation infrastructure. repurposed for living. One third of city land, from highways to parking lots, are freed up for living. Swaths of land reserved not for people but the temporary storage of cars—empty private spaces—are no longer necessary. The density of the city makes public transportation practical, convenient, and efficient. Moving about with the use of cycles or simply walking makes sense.

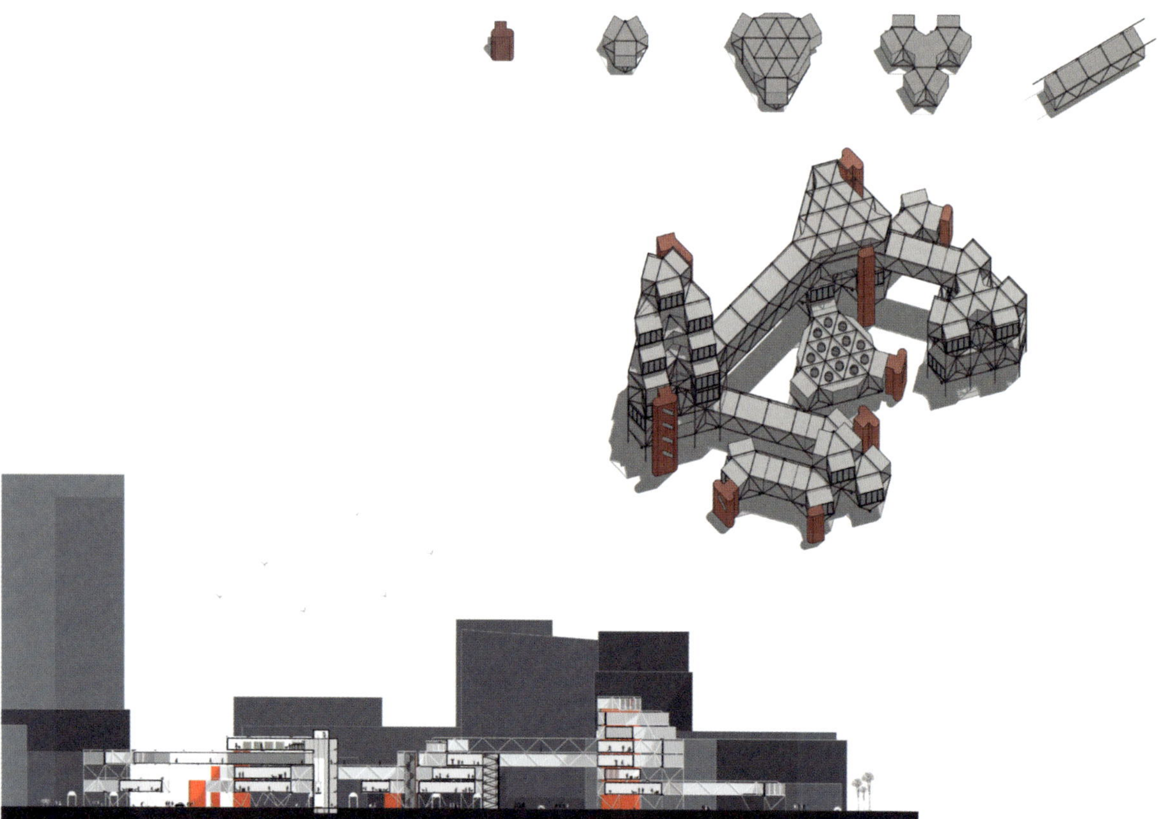

◱ Individual Plugin Tower modules and assembly methods with a section drawing of an assembled and interconnected Plugin Tower in an existing city context.
◳ Artist's impression of a larger interconnected Plugin Tower structure.
⇥ The Megacity Plugin, conceptual drawing.

CONCLUSION

The inception of Plugin House is rooted in visionary ideas aimed at addressing social problems and explored through drawing and built form. In our practice at PAO, there is a parallel process of sustaining a culture of invention while making incredible efforts to bridge the gap between concept and real-world application. The Plugin House story is one of the persistent pursuit of possibilities, guided by needs verified through observation and testing. Along the way, we have innovated with not only architectural designs but also ways of practice, funding, and operating a business to sustain the work of turning a design concept into a mass-produced product. The founding of the Plugin House Company is a culmination of the pragmatic pursuit of plugin concepts.

The Plugin House journey has taken us to opposite sides of the world, observing how people confront uncertainty and develop ways of adapting to change through economical means. Communities from Dashilar in Beijing to Esperanza in Austin, Texas grapple with the challenges of rapid urbanization and increasing income disparities. It is important to learn how communities have converted properties—often through informal interventions—to confront changing conditions. Addressing housing needs with similar flexibility is vital, especially in densely built and challenging urban areas where affordable housing is in greatest demand.

With one office in historic Dashilar and another in the urban village Nanshan in Shenzhen, we greatly value the ability to investigate, design, and build within the communities where it is located. And through this experience, we continue to work on projects in locations where people live in precarious conditions.

Our design approach embraces uncertainty. By observing and learning from residents who understand challenges firsthand, we imagine possibilities through their efforts and initiate opportunities for community feedback through physical and spatial prototypes and demonstrations. These efforts of trial and error rely on close collaboration with stakeholders such as policymakers, public institutions, nonprofits, and individual residents.

In addition, Plugin House facilitates new possibilities through temporary installations and public events that engage communities to shift perspectives and aid in the acceptance of new policy changes. The ease of assembly enables participation in construction even for those inexperienced, creating learning experiences and job opportunities. Temporary applications of the Plugin House can facilitate new uses for vacant sites, as exemplified by The Blue House, an artist residency space in Austin.

Plugin architecture represents new possibilities for densification in pre-existing communities. Building a house within a house brings new life to unused or dilapidated buildings. A dwelling that can be effortlessly transported, assembled, disassembled, and reconstructed enables the activation of spaces and community engagement in novel ways. Customizable and affordable, the Plugin House opens up new avenues for housing in unconventional locations, allowing for expansion, contraction, or relocation without starting from scratch.

Projects in Dashilar, Shenzhen and Jingdezhen demonstrate the house-in-house approach, repurposing dilapidated buildings with minimal disruption and cost. These initiatives show how Plugin Houses can be customized on a community scale to fit diverse property shapes and sizes. Mrs. Fan's House in Beijing and the Alamo

Plugin Demo in Austin illustrate seamless integration into different sites as ADUs, achievable economically through our factory-produced panelized system. At The Other Ones Foundation (TOOF) in Austin, the Plugin House emergency shelter units show how an industrial site can be quickly transformed into a housing community that meets urgent needs.

Through working across sectors with policymakers, innovating with building technology, and engaging communities, we at PAO aim to design without barriers to improve access to housing, and advocate for change. Through plugin architecture, we will continue to aspire to make housing more accessible for those in greatest need in the most desirable locations.

PLUGIN

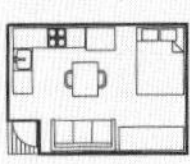
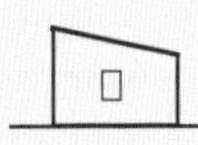
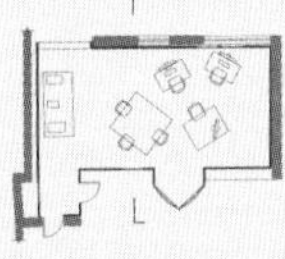
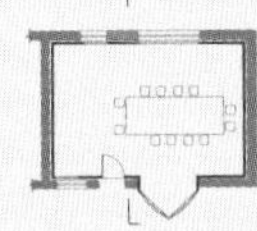
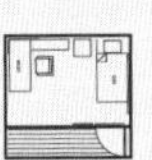
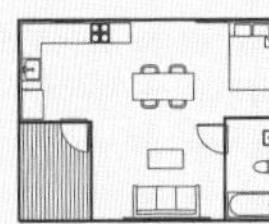
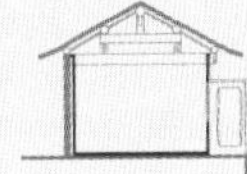

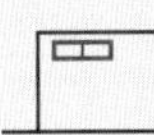
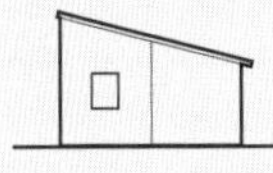
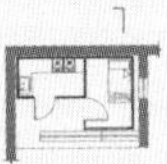
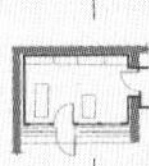
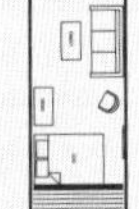
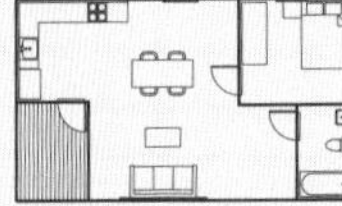

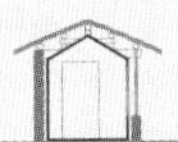
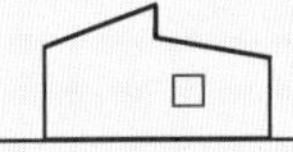
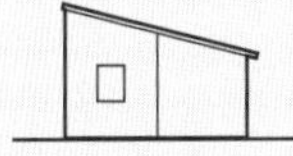
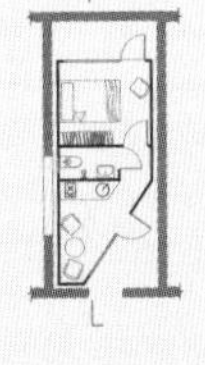
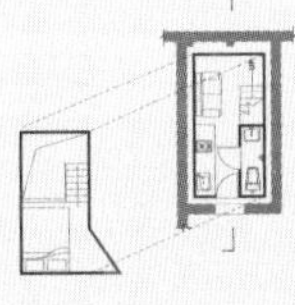
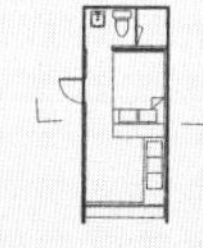
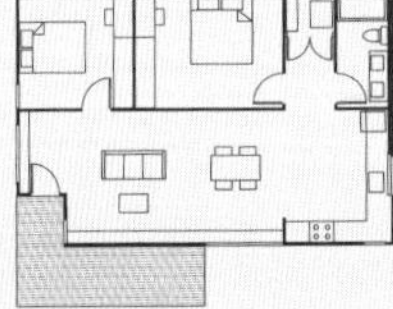
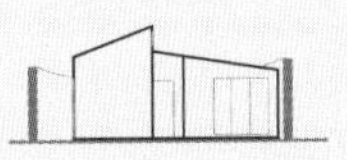
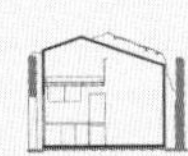
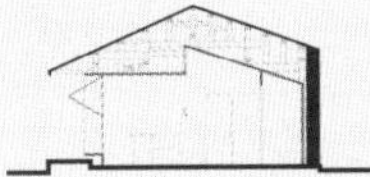
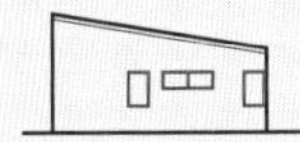
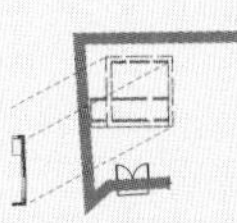
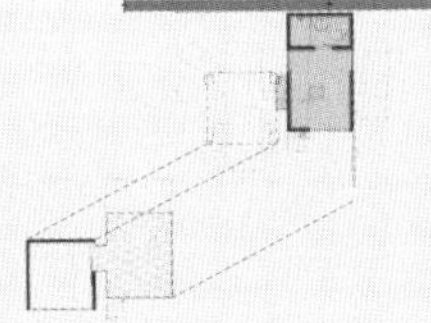
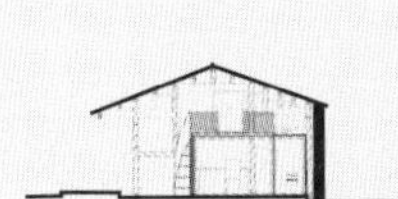

ATLAS

The Plugin Atlas is a comprehensive collection of all Plugin Houses designed and constructed by PAO from 2013 to the present. This compendium offers detailed documentation of each Plugin House, providing insights into their design, construction, and implementation, and serves as an extensive reference.

COURTYARD 72 OFFICE

LOCATION:
Dashilar, Beijing

RESIDENTS/CLIENTS:
Dashilar Platform

PROGRAM:
Office

SIZE: 43.7m^2 (470.4ft^2)
COMPLETED: 2014

0 4m 8m

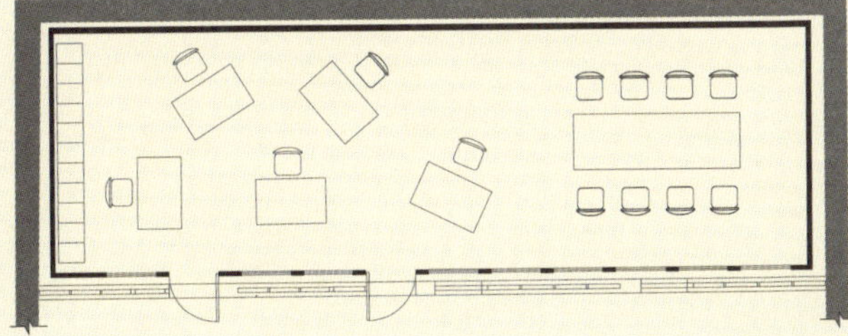

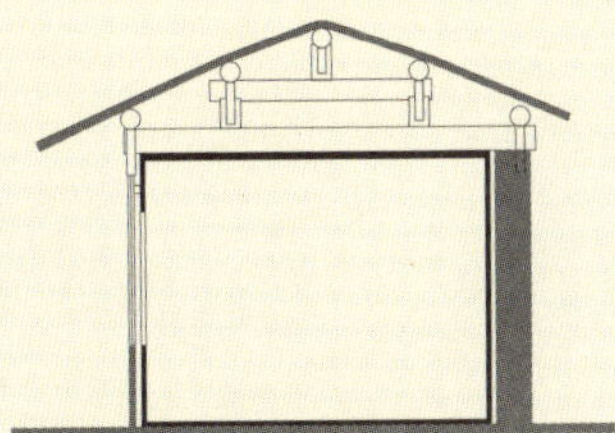

The Courtyard 72 Office is one of the first Plugin Houses, developed as an office space for the Dashilar Platform, the project team of the state-owned developer focused on revitalizing the Dashilar district. The Dashilar Platform used the Yangmeizhu Street office space from 2014 until around 2017.

The space is designed to maximize insulation for the cold Beijing winters and hot summers by creating a well-insulated interior. A mini-split HVAC system provides efficient heating and cooling. It also incorporates windows in the ceiling panels that provide views of the original roof and beam structure, preserving a sense of place and the courtyard's history. The office is furnished with tables, chairs, and a custom-made bookshelf, all designed by PAO.

COURTYARD 72 PLUGIN DEMO

LOCATION:
Dashilar, Beijing

RESIDENTS/CLIENTS:
Dashilar Platform

PROGRAM:
Rental housing

SIZE: 20.3m² (218.5ft²)
COMPLETED: 2014

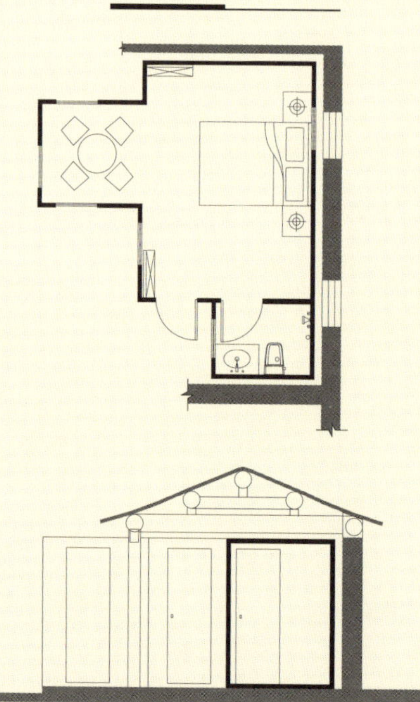

The Courtyard 72 Demonstration Residence was also created in collaboration with the Dashilar Platform to test the system in a home environment. This government-led initiative aimed to provide Dashilar residents with a cost-effective option for upgrading and renovating their living spaces. Additionally, it explored the potential of addressing vacant properties by converting them into rental units with modern amenities using the Plugin House system.

The Demonstration Residence features a bedroom, a combined work and dining area, and a fully equipped bathroom. This setup incorporated an independent septic system with the Plugins. The home was showcased at the 2014 Beijing Design Week, giving local residents and visitors the opportunity to understand and experience the concept firsthand.

MRS. DONG'S PLUGIN HOUSE

LOCATION:
Dashilar, Beijing

RESIDENTS/CLIENTS:
Mrs. Dong

PROGRAM:
Private home

SIZE: 14.1m^2 (150.7ft^2)
COMPLETED: 2014

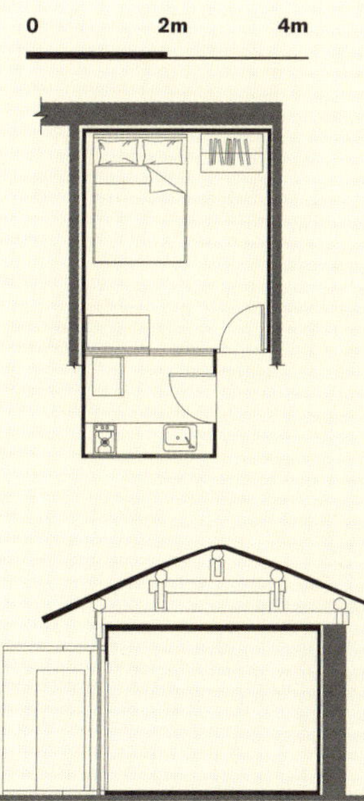

Mrs. Dong lived in the same courtyard opposite the Dashilar Platform office and observed the renovations using the Plugin House system, which sparked her curiosity. Her house was in disrepair and space in the fourteen-meter-square (150-foot-square) apartment, shared with her adult son, was extremely limited. Mrs. Dong was particularly interested in the benefits of better insulation. Although her family owned an apartment on the city's outskirts, Mrs. Dong's son preferred inner-city life. He also required constant medical attention and staying in the neighborhood meant he could access excellent care in the nation's best hospitals. With a minimal budget and support from the Dashilar Platform, she commissioned PAO to create a custom Plugin House.

For Mrs. Dong's home, PAO integrated the kitchen, originally an informal addition, into the living area and added a new shower feature. Mrs. Dong previously showered outdoors in the common courtyard by creating a private enclosure with two wooden doors. The Plugin House includes a retractable accordion space that replaces her improvised shower area, providing a more functional and private solution. She had previously covered her ceiling and walls with fabric and left a distance between her furniture and the walls to reduce dust from the centuries-old structure. Although the Plugin panels take up interior space, the renovation provided more usable space because she could place all of her furniture against the walls.

PAO OFFICE

LOCATION:
Dashilar, Beijing

RESIDENTS/CLIENTS:
People's Architecture Office

PROGRAM:
Office

SIZE: 48.7m² (524.4ft²)
COMPLETED: 2015

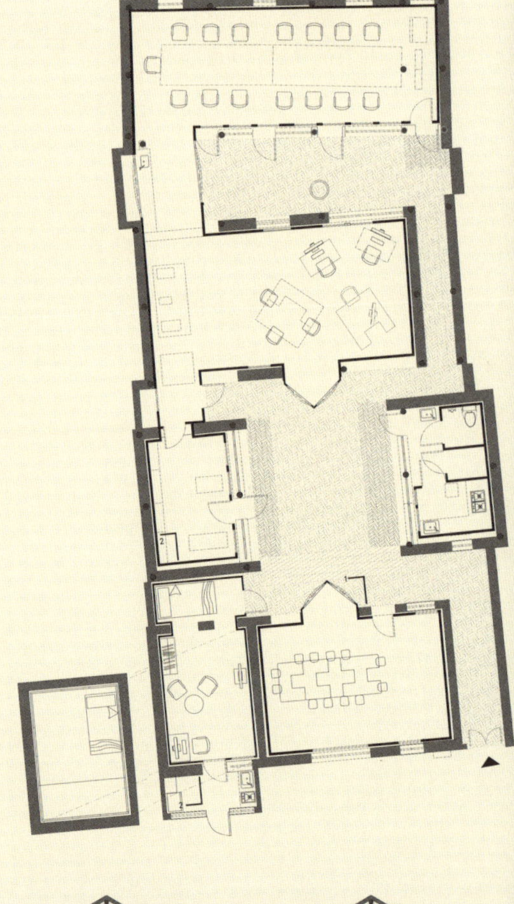

Located in the historic Dashilar area of Beijing, near the Forbidden City palace complex, PAO's office occupies the north-east portion of a traditional courtyard house. This space includes two main office areas and a kitchenette, enclosing a narrow courtyard. The office renovation involved exposing the original wood beam structure, as PAO was not permitted to make structural changes to the courtyard house and was limited by the small spaces.

The forty-meter-square (432.7-foot-square) office space, twenty-meter-square (215.2-foot-square) guest room, and kitchenette are part of a small courtyard. By applying the Plugin House module, we introduced modern concepts and facilities while highlighting the contrast between modernity and heritage. A convertible solarium, inspired by DIY additions in Chinese courtyard houses, serves as a space that can open upwards to become a semi-outdoor extension connecting the interior to the yard.

Additionally, the design features a fully equipped kitchen and bathroom, a workshop, and two separate courtyards connected by a walkway that also serves as a material storage space. The design approach and furniture design reflect the constraints of the space. The truss bookshelf spans the entire six-meter (twenty-foot) length of the north office, while the wooden truss table spans eight meters (twenty-six feet) with only four legs.

Being located in a hutong neighborhood allows the architectural practice to better understand the context of hutong living, which was essential to the early development of the Plugin House. This project served as one of the first prototypes of the Plugin House and continues to function as the PAO headquarters.

DASHILAR PLATFORM COMMUNITY SPACE

LOCATION:
Dashilar, Beijing

RESIDENTS/CLIENTS:
Dashilar Platform

PROGRAM:
Office

SIZE: 28.7 m^2 (308.9 ft^2)
COMPLETED: 2015

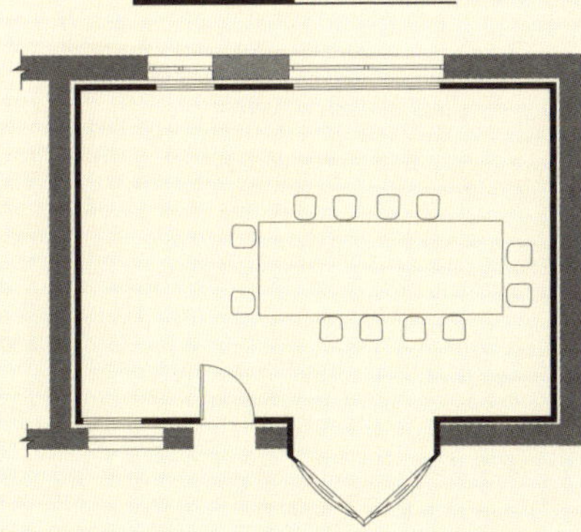

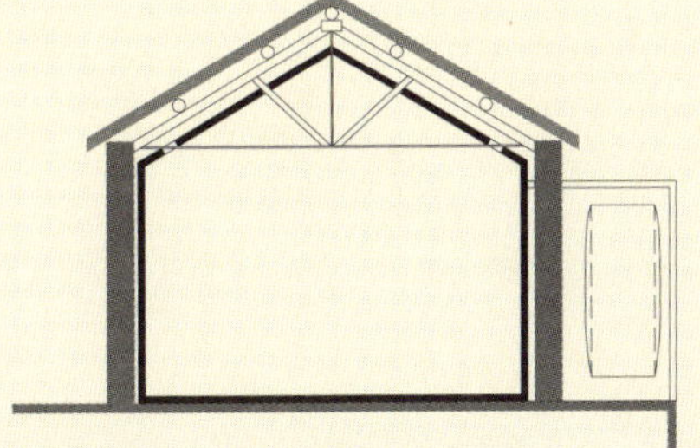

As part of the same courtyard as the PAO office, the Dashilar Platform tasked PAO with renovating the south house into a community meeting space.

The original beam ceiling structure, a unique combination of metal and wooden elements, is left exposed as a special feature of the space. Additionally, PAO experimented with a gold finish on the Plugin panel seams, allowing visitors to better understand the renovation structure and appreciate the panelized construction system. The main window faces the hutong alley and provides passersby with a view into the interior of the courtyard, a rare feature in this neighborhood.

MR. SUN'S PLUGIN HOUSE

LOCATION:
Dashilar, Beijing

RESIDENTS/CLIENTS:
Mr. Sun

PROGRAM:
Private home

SIZE: 27.1m² (291.7ft²)
COMPLETED: 2015

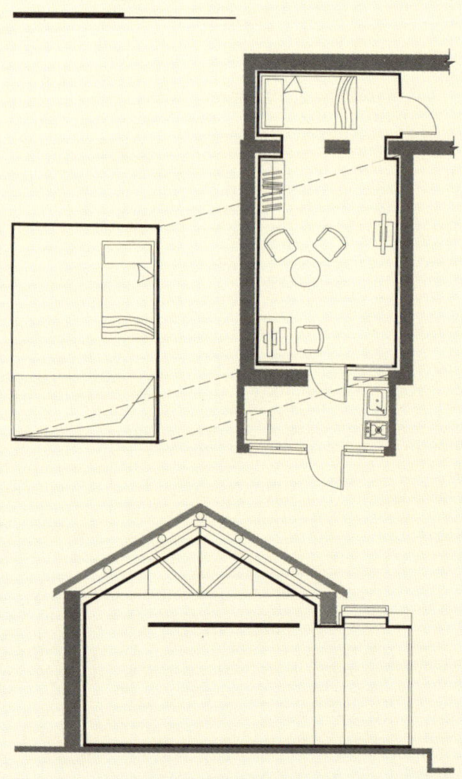

Also located in the same courtyard as the PAO office is Mr. Sun's residence, where he lives with his adult daughter in a very small space. To upgrade the house, PAO added skylights to bring in more natural light and a new mezzanine level to serve as a separate sleeping area for his daughter. This addition not only maximizes the limited space but also provides a sense of privacy and comfort for Mr. Sun's family.

Mr. Sun continues to live happily in his upgraded home, which now better accommodates his family's needs and enhances their quality of life. He also shares the renovated courtyard with PAO where he does his gardening. The improvements have transformed the small, cramped space into a more functional and pleasant living environment, demonstrating the big impact on everyday living.

COURTYARD 30 NORTH HOUSE

LOCATION:
Dashilar, Beijing

RESIDENTS/CLIENTS:
Dashilar Platform

PROGRAM:
Office

SIZE: 8.4m² (90.4ft²)
COMPLETED: 2015

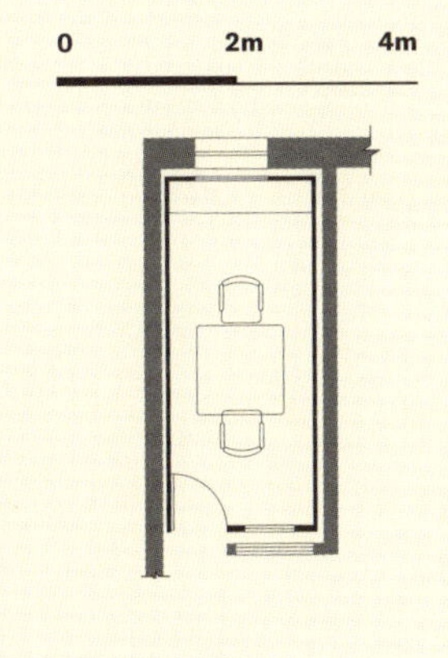

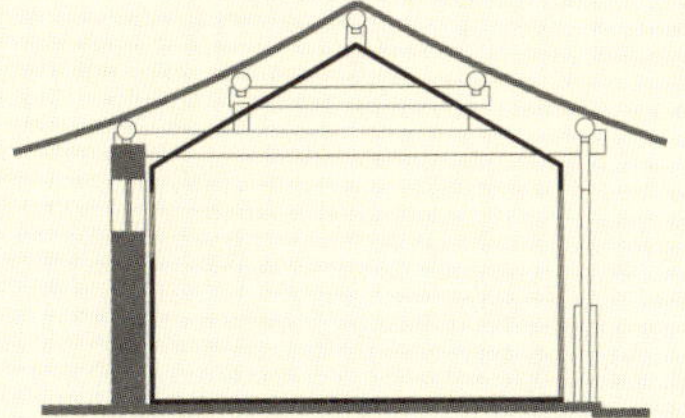

The Courtyard 30 North House in Dashilar was created in 2015 to upgrade a small space in a shared hutong courtyard, serving as an office and meeting room. From 2013 onward, fifteen Plugin Houses were completed in Dashilar as part of the Dashilar district's urban regeneration program, with the North House being one of these projects.

In 2022, due to a new renovation plan for the courtyard, the North House Plugin was dismantled and removed. Later that year, it was selected to participate in a design exhibition at the Chuanyechang Culture and Art Center in Beijing. The house was transported to the exhibition space and rebuilt on the spot within an afternoon. The aim of the exhibit was to demonstrate the benefits of more flexible strategies in architecture, highlighting how modular and easily transportable designs can adapt to changing urban environments and needs.

COURTYARD 30 EAST HOUSE

LOCATION:
Dashilar, Beijing

RESIDENTS/CLIENTS:
Dashilar Platform

PROGRAM:
Rental housing

SIZE: 14.6m² (157.2ft²)
COMPLETED: 2015

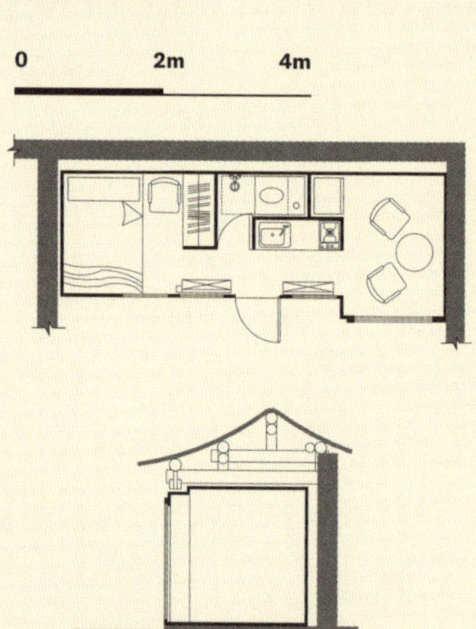

The Courtyard 30 East House was part of the 2015 hutong courtyard upgrades organized by the Dashilar Platform. Designed to function as a residence or B&B, the unit includes a separate bedroom, a living room, a kitchen, and a bathroom.

The living-room facade is designed to slide open, allowing for courtyard access during temperate weather and effectively expanding the living space outward. This design enhances the connection between indoor and outdoor areas, making the most of the courtyard setting. The Plugin House exterior features a distinctive gold finish, marking the beginning of a new phase of experimentation with color and outer cladding for the Plugin Houses.

COURTYARD 32 NORTH HOUSE

LOCATION:
Dashilar, Beijing

RESIDENTS/CLIENTS:
Dashilar Platform

PROGRAM:
Live/work rental unit

SIZE: 24.5m² (263.7ft²)
COMPLETED: 2015

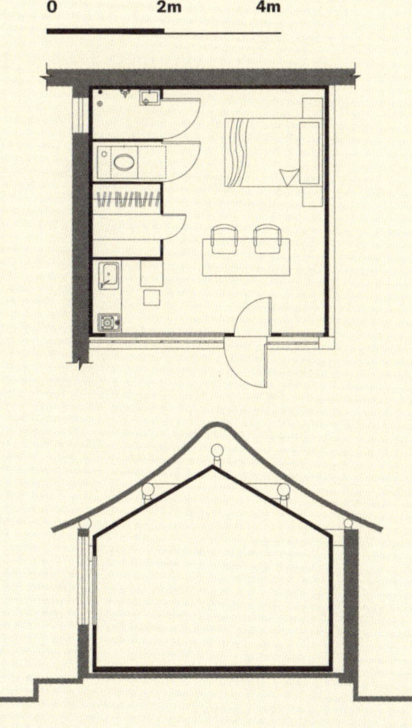

The Courtyard 32 North House was designed as a live/work studio space, incorporating a kitchen and bathroom. The Plugin House was custom-designed to retain the original structural beam that intersects the space, thereby creating both a link to the past and an interesting visual contrast within the overall space. To harmonize with the wooden beam, wood-colored finishes were chosen for the window and door frames, enhancing the aesthetic coherence and warmth of the interior.

For a period, the space was utilized as an office by a literary translation agency. This usage highlighted the flexibility of the design, demonstrating how the studio could seamlessly transition between residential and professional functions.

COURTYARD 32 SOUTH HOUSE

LOCATION:
Dashilar, Beijing

RESIDENTS/CLIENTS:
Dashilar Platform

PROGRAM:
Rental housing

SIZE: 22.8m² (245.4ft²)
COMPLETED: 2015

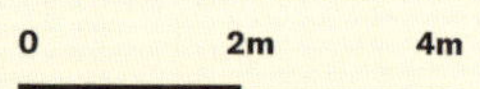

This Courtyard 32 South House was designed as a residence with optimal space utilization, integrating a mezzanine level for the sleeping area and a living room on the ground floor, along with a private bathroom. The addition of a mezzanine level maximizes vertical space, creating a cozy and efficient sleeping area while leaving ample room for daily activities below.

A distinctive feature of this residence is the front facade, which is designed to swing outward on warmer days. This innovative design element not only adds space but also creates a fluid transition between indoor and outdoor living areas, enhancing the sense of openness and connectivity with the surrounding environment. The design expands the functional living space but also fosters a stronger connection to the outdoors, making the residence feel larger and more inviting.

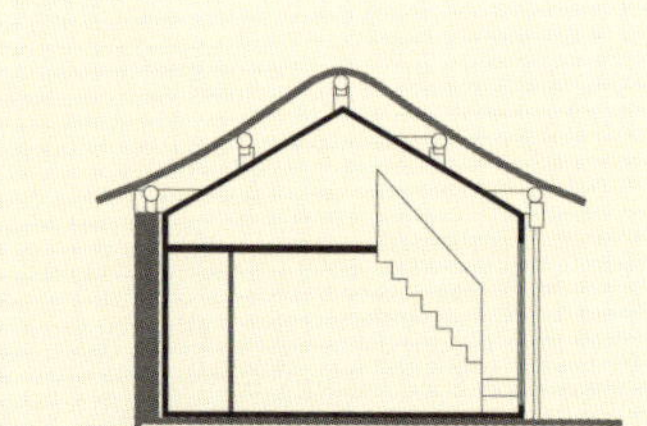

MRS. FAN'S PLUGIN HOUSE

LOCATION: Beijing

RESIDENTS/CLIENTS: Mrs. Fan

PROGRAM: Private home

SIZE: 15.5m² (166.8ft²)
COMPLETED: 2016

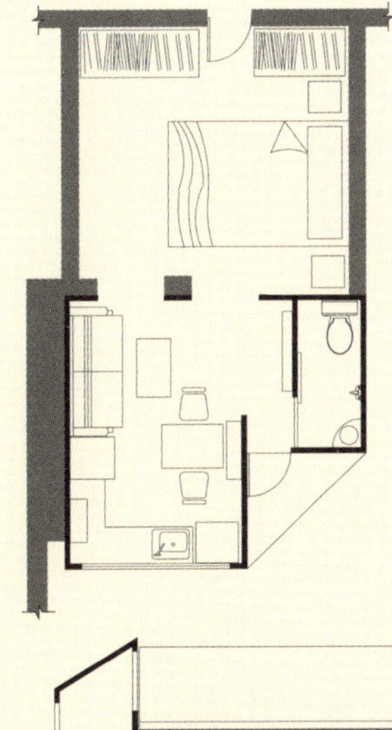

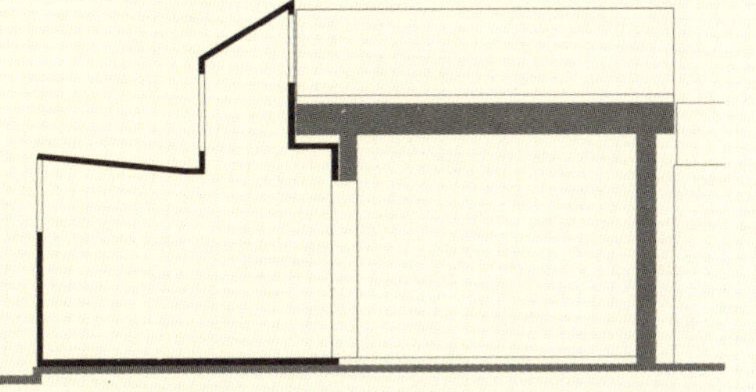

Mrs. Fan's Plugin House is custom-designed for her and her family. The living-room ceiling extends upwards to create a double-height space with skylights on either side, channeling sunlight from above to flood the previously dark interior with natural light. To alleviate Mrs. Fan's claustrophobia, the small bathroom also features a skylight that receives reflected sunlight from a blue privacy screen, bathing the bathroom in a soothing blue tint even on gloomy days. Additionally, a roof deck provides much-needed breathing room from the dense surroundings and offers a private social space.

The architectural form of the Plugin House is shaped not by regulatory limitations but by the negotiated demands of surrounding neighbors. On all sides, the structure is designed to avoid blocking sunlight, air circulation, and views for the adjacent properties. Even during construction, new demands emerged, and the Plugin panel material made accommodating these changes practical, allowing entire sections of the building to be modified on-site.

This design optimizes the use of the small floor space by incorporating a bedroom, living area, bathroom, and kitchen with a view of the street. A roof deck was installed to provide coveted leisure space in the dense neighborhood. The inclusion of a composting toilet adds both convenience and environmental benefits. By meeting these diverse needs, Mrs. Fan's Plugin House strategically enhances her family's quality of life.

MR. ZHAO'S PLUGIN HOUSE

LOCATION:
Beijing

RESIDENTS/CLIENTS:
Mr. Zhao

PROGRAM:
Private home

SIZE: 5.6m^2 (60.3ft^2)
COMPLETED: 2016

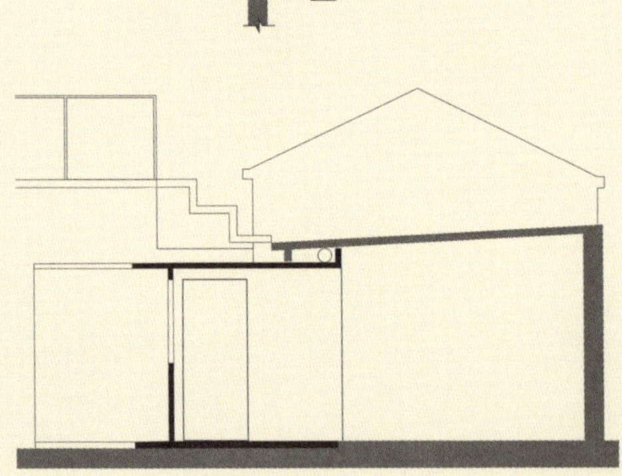

Mr. Zhao initiated the construction of a Plugin House with a dual objective: to upgrade the living conditions of his home and to positively impact his mental wellbeing.

A retired English professor, Mr. Zhao lives with his adult daughter in a courtyard house passed down from the previous generation. The house, like all houses in this old neighborhood, has experienced a complex history including parts taken over by strangers and unsolicited demolitions. Being of advanced age, Mr. Zhao suffers from depression and a number of physical ailments. For him, the decision to undertake this renovation project is both bold and transformative.

With the incorporation of the Plugin House, a once-lost direct pathway from his bedroom to the kitchen has been restored. This vital modification negates the need to either traverse his daughter's living space or walk outside in the cold. Beyond the practicality it offers, this change has had dramatic effects on his relationship with his daughter, who remains steadfast in her decision to cohabit with him. In essence, the Plugin has streamlined Mr. Zhao's daily routine.

Additionally, Mr. Zhao desperately wanted a private space to escape to. The Plugin House supports a connection across the roof of his house to a new terrace. Mr. Zhao has said that the view of his neighborhood has been essential for improving his mental health.

MR. YANG'S PLUGIN HOUSE

LOCATION:
Yantian, Shenzhen

RESIDENTS/CLIENTS:
Mr. Yang/Yantian District Government

PROGRAM:
Rental housing

SIZE: 45m^2 (484.4ft^2)
COMPLETED: 2017

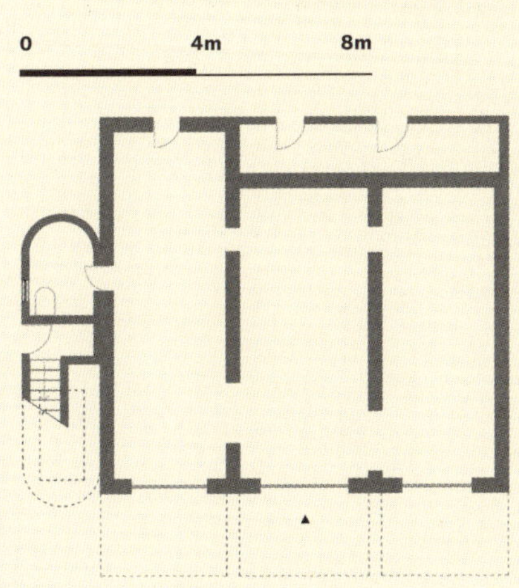

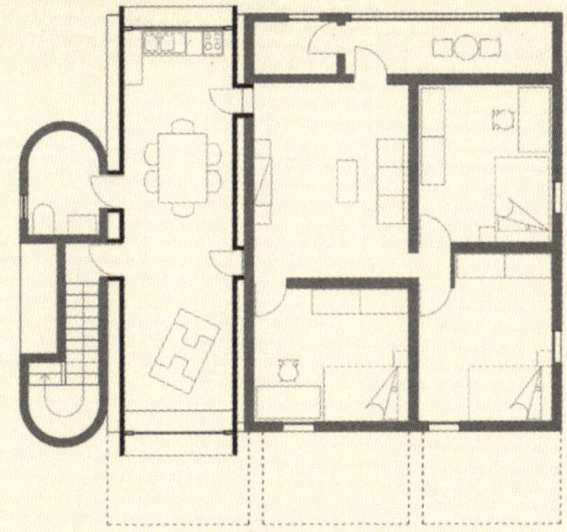

Mr. Yang's Plugin House was designed as an add-on rental unit to an existing two-story building in the Yantian district of Shenzhen. Mr. Yang wanted to create an independent studio on the second floor with its own entrance on the ground floor. The Plugin House fits neatly into a previously open rooftop and features a vertical core that houses a stairwell bathroom, a precursor to the core modules used in the Lakeside Plugin Tower.

On the first floor, the building houses three shop spaces. PAO enhanced these spaces by adding sunscreens in front of each shop entrance, extending the shop areas into the street and providing additional shading from the sun. The design overall aims to not only maximize the utility of the existing structure, but also enhance the functionality and comfort of both the rental unit and the retail spaces.

MR. LI'S PLUGIN HOUSE

LOCATION: Beijing

RESIDENTS/CLIENTS: Mr. Li

PROGRAM: ADU

SIZE: 35m^2 (376.7ft^2)
COMPLETED: 2017

Mr. Li's Plugin House was created with the support of a grant from the Leping Social Entrepreneur Foundation, which co-funded the construction of two Plugin Houses resulting from an open call for applicants. Mr. Li responded to the call, expressing his interest in building a Plugin House in the backyard of his house located in the outskirts of Beijing. While ADUs are not often permitted in China, Mr. Li's property was one where such construction was possible.

The house is fully equipped and features a living room, dining area, bedroom, separate storage room, kitchen, and bathroom. The design includes clerestory windows to enhance the natural brightness of the indoor space. The layout ensures a comfortable and functional living environment that maximizes the use of Mr. Li's backyard.

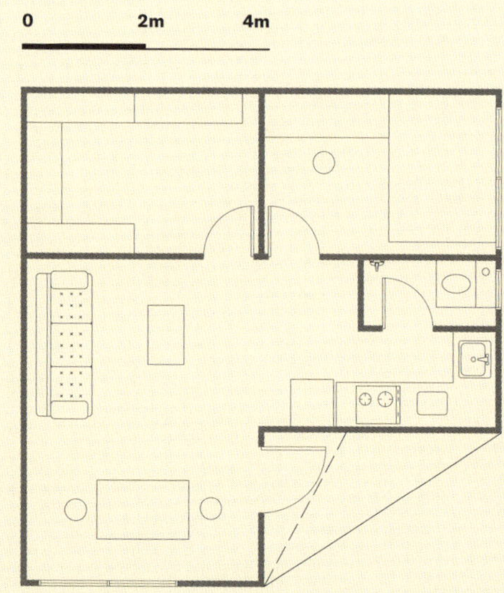

HUANG FAMILY PLUGIN HOUSE

LOCATION:
Shangwei, Shenzhen

RESIDENTS/CLIENTS:
Guanhu Subdistrict/
FuturePlus Academy

PROGRAM:
Artist studio

SIZE: 18.8m² (202.4ft²)
COMPLETED: 2018

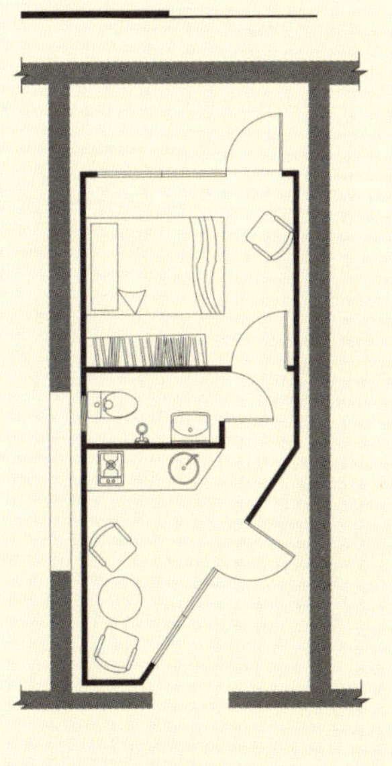

The Huang Family Plugin House is part of the Shangwei Plugin Houses project, aimed at rehabilitating old, abandoned homes in the village of Shangwei. With the rapid urban expansion of nearby Shenzhen, Shangwei turned into an urban village with many properties left vacant. The local government, along with the Shangwei Village Cooperative, sought to support a budding community of local artists and craftsmen through creative rehabilitation efforts. With backing from the Leping Social Entrepreneur Foundation and FuturePlus Academy (a nonprofit organization focused on urban planning and design), and in partnership with PAO, a pilot project was initiated to renovate these uninhabitable properties without affecting adjacent structures.

The Huang Family Plugin House occupies a compact eighteen-square-meter (202.4-square-foot) space. The Plugin House insertion reinforces the remaining parts of the original roof and protects against structural issues. To maximize space, the bedroom is placed on a mezzanine level with a corner window that cantilevers over a collapsed wall, offering panoramic views of the village roofline. A skylight, placed where the original roof had collapsed, floods the deep lot with natural light. The Plugin House system improves living standards by incorporating efficient mini-split units for heating and cooling, a modern kitchen, and an off-the-grid composting toilet system, transforming the once-ruined house into a functional, comfortable home.

FANG FAMILY PLUGIN HOUSE

LOCATION:
Shangwei, Shenzhen

RESIDENTS/CLIENTS:
Guanhu Subdistrict/
FuturePlus Academy

PROGRAM:
Artist studio

SIZE: 25.8m^2 (277.7ft^2)
COMPLETED: 2018

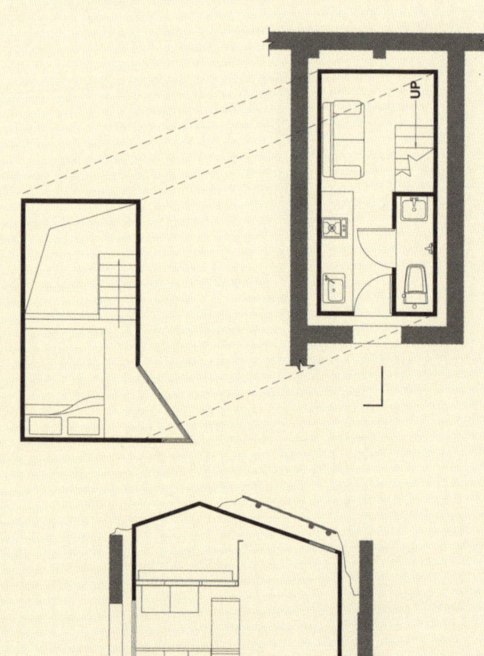

The Fang Family Plugin House, slightly larger at twenty-five square meters (277 square feet), is another example of the Shangwei Plugin Houses project. The project aimed to address the fact that the village government is legally bound to renovate uninhabitable properties where the roofs have collapsed. However, such properties are difficult to renovate because any work would affect adjacent structures. To circumvent this problem, the Plugin House leaves the original structure untouched while a new structure is built inside the existing house.

The Fang Family Plugin House features a clerestory window that brings southern light into the bedroom area at the rear of the house, enhancing the space with natural light. The house also includes efficient mini-split units for heating and cooling, a modern kitchen, and an off-the-grid composting toilet system. The overall design of the house also ensures it does not block sunlight, air circulation, or views for adjacent properties.

MR. WANG'S PLUGIN HOUSE

LOCATION:
Baiyun, Guangzhou

RESIDENTS/CLIENTS:
Mr. Wang

PROGRAM:
Private home

SIZE: 27m² (290.6ft²)
COMPLETED: 2018

0 2m 4m

Similar to Mr. Li's Plugin House, this project was also funded through a grant from the Leping Social Entrepreneur Foundation. Mr. Wang, a former engineer disillusioned with urban life, wanted to live and raise his family in the countryside. Building and purchasing a house in rural China is complex and prohibitive, but the Plugin House offers a flexible solution that remains within regulatory guidelines.

Mr. Wang is one of millions of people in China who originally moved to urban centers for work opportunities, and who are returning to their hometowns in rural areas. Many are faced with the challenge of finding adequate housing. Now an organic farmer, he is dedicated to developing natural farming methods, running his own farm, and ensuring his newborn child is exposed to nature.

The Plugin House brings modern amenities to the rural living environment while minimizing environmental impact. It is equipped with efficient heating and cooling systems and includes independent bathroom facilities. In rural areas where labor is increasingly scarce, the Plugin House can be easily and quickly built. The panelized design of the Plugin House makes it convenient to transport to remote areas, ensuring that houses can be constructed even in hard-to-reach locations. Mr. Wang's Plugin House thus serves as a viable model for others seeking rural living.

HARVARD YARD PLUGIN DEMO

LOCATION:
Cambridge, Massachusetts

RESIDENTS/CLIENTS:
Harvard University

PROGRAM:
Prototype home

SIZE: 35m^2 (376.7ft^2)
PRESENTATION: 2019

The Plugin House was brought to Harvard University in Massachusetts as a demonstration model to showcase its innovative features, sponsored by Harvard's Office of the Arts and the Loeb Fellowship at Harvard Graduate School of Design. Students, many of whom were new to design and construction, built the Plugin House in the heart of Harvard Yard in only six hours. On temporary display during Harvard's ARTS FIRST festival, the Plugin House served as an animating force through art and cultural programming, bringing activity, vibrancy, and audiences to the center of Harvard Yard.

In collaboration with Loeb Fellow Eric Williams and Chicago's art and culture curators Silver Room, the Plugin House hosted site-specific installations and events, including video installations, DJ sets, art exhibitions, and dance performances. This initiative not only demonstrated the Plugin House's practicality and ease of assembly but also highlighted its potential as a dynamic space for community engagement and cultural expression. This iteration of the Plugin House underscores its versatility and its ability to transform and enliven public spaces through design and creative programming, using the house as a hub.

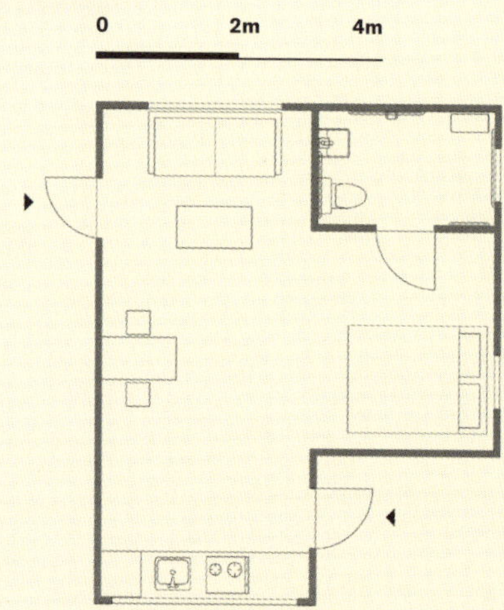

BOSTON CITY HALL PLUGIN DEMO

LOCATION:
Boston, Massachusetts

RESIDENTS/CLIENTS:
People's Architecture Office

PROGRAM:
Prototype home

SIZE: 35m² (376.7ft²)

PRESENTATION: 2019

Partnering with the Mayor of Boston's Housing Innovation Lab (iLab), volunteers erected the Plugin House in front of Boston City Hall, Massachusetts. Artists for Humanity, a local nonprofit, created drawings on the walls and floor to help visitors envision how the Plugin House interior could be furnished and organized. The iLab organized open events with community leaders, policymakers, and housing advocates to discuss how solutions like the Plugin House can help alleviate the city's housing crisis. A public exhibition showcased PAO's plugin work, provided information on ADUs, and detailed the city's current ADU policy pilot.

The Plugin House hosted over 1,000 visitors and gathered valuable feedback for policymakers during the two-week display period. Initially exhibited at Harvard Yard, the house was disassembled and rebuilt at Boston City Hall. The entire relocation process was completed in one day and demonstrated the Plugin House's ease of assembly and flexibility.

This collaboration highlighted the Plugin House's potential as a viable solution for urban housing challenges. The project emphasized the importance of innovative, scalable designs in addressing the housing crisis and showcased the Plugin House's adaptability and practicality. By engaging the community and policymakers, the exhibition at Boston City Hall sparked public imagination and helped bring future possibilities for urban living closer to reality.

RURAL STUDIO PLUGIN

LOCATION:
Newbern, Alabama

RESIDENTS/CLIENTS:
Rural Studio

PROGRAM:
Prototype/
Educational space

SIZE: 35m^2 (376.7ft^2)
PRESENTATION: 2020

Rural Studio is a design-build architecture program run by Auburn University in Newbern, Alabama. It educates students about the social responsibilities of the architecture profession while providing quality housing and buildings for disadvantaged communities in rural west Alabama.

PAO collaborated with Rural Studio to explore ways of reducing housing costs through design innovation alongside students. Before its relocation to Newbern, the same Plugin House was showcased as a demonstration unit at Harvard University and Boston City Hall. Now permanently housed at Rural Studio, the Plugin House serves as an example of innovative pre-fabrication technology and rapid manual construction.

Built by Rural Studio students, the Plugin House serves as an instructional space and a practical tool for students to provide additional feedback to PAO. It contributes to an educational program renowned for fostering collaboration and advancing sustainable and affordable housing solutions. Through this partnership, both PAO and Rural Studio aim to drive meaningful improvements in rural housing while helping equip future architects with the skills and knowledge to make a positive impact.

JINGDEZHEN C-34 PLUGIN HOUSES

LOCATION:
Jingdezhen

RESIDENTS/CLIENTS:
Jingdezhen Ceramic Culture Tourism Group

PROGRAM:
Live/work artist studios

SIZE: 59.6m² (641.5ft²)
COMPLETED: 2021

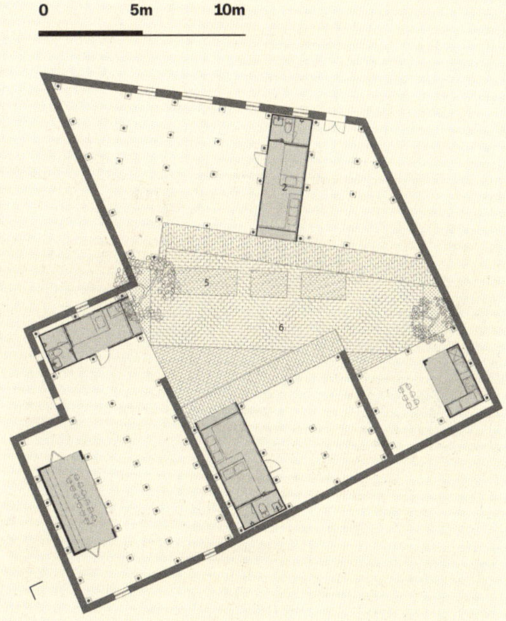

The C-34 unit was the first experimental renovation utilizing Plugin units in historic Jingdezhen courtyards. Known as China's 'Porcelain Capital', Jingdezhen has been producing ceramics for at least 1,000 years. As part of the city center's revitalization, this courtyard was designated by the government for use as an artist studio.

Located in the preserved part of the historic district, this former greenware ceramics courtyard lay vacant for a long period. To upgrade it for contemporary use while preserving its historic structure, PAO used the Plugin House system to transform the space into a living and working studio for artists. The irregular shape and structure of the drying partition frames posed a challenge, but the flexible Plugin House system adapted easily, showcasing its advantages.

The Plugin Houses in this courtyard combine the bedroom and bathroom into one integrated space and include a separate, actively used kitchen plugin. The upgraded space serves primarily as a workspace, with some using the bedroom as a tea room, keeping the courtyard functional and well-maintained.

The Plugin units, placed within the wooden frame structure, create a space within a space, providing a comfortable living environment. The remaining semi-outdoor space between the Plugins has been transformed into various working areas. By preserving the original structure, the heritage building has been revitalized for contemporary use, becoming a flexible and sustainable crafts center.

JINGDEZHEN H-20 PLUGIN HOUSES

LOCATION:
Jingdezhen

RESIDENTS/CLIENTS:
Jingdezhen Ceramic Culture Tourism Group

PROGRAM:
Live/work artist studios

SIZE: 22.1m^2 (237.9ft^2)
COMPLETED: 2021

The H-20 courtyard renovation was one of the early Plugin House projects in Jingdezhen. Given the courtyard's relatively small size, the possibilities for renovation were limited. To optimize the use of space, PAO decided to install four separate Plugin units, each serving a different function. These units include a workspace, a mezzanine bedroom space, a kitchen, and a bathroom. This arrangement transforms the spaces between the units into small working areas, allowing the central yard to remain a larger, open space for work and relaxation.

The design of H-20 reflects PAO's innovative approach to maximizing utility within confined spaces. By incorporating a mezzanine level for the bedroom, the vertical space is effectively utilized, creating a cozy yet efficient sleeping area without encroaching on the ground-level workspace. The kitchen and bathroom units are strategically placed to provide easy access while maintaining the flow of the courtyard.

The design of the H-20 courtyard balances practicality with creativity, making it a versatile space that caters to the needs of contemporary artists while preserving the historical essence of Jingdezhen.

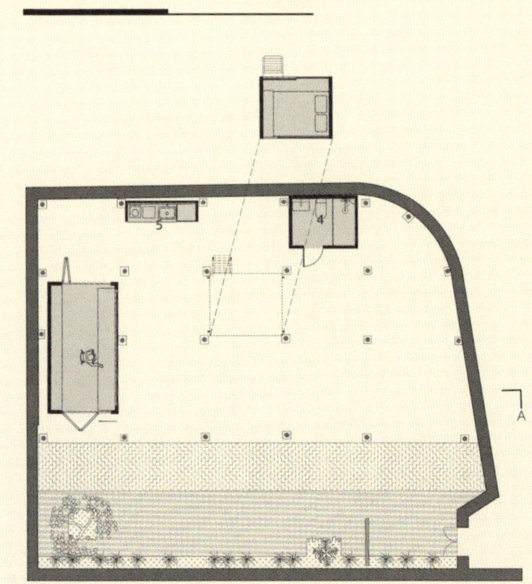

JINGDEZHEN YANGHUA NONG PLUGIN HOUSES

LOCATION:
Jingdezhen

RESIDENTS/CLIENTS:
Jingdezhen Ceramic Culture Tourism Group

PROGRAM:
Live/work artist studios

SIZE: 65.5m² (705ft²)
COMPLETED: 2022

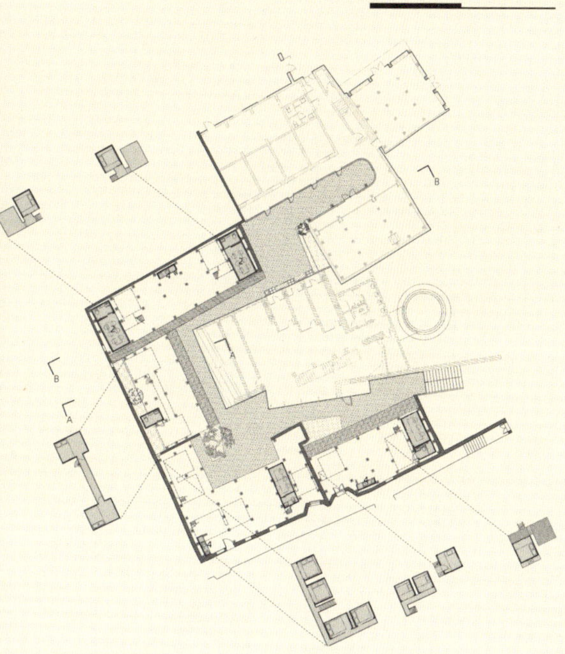

Yanghua Nong is a cluster of buildings that were previously used for ceramic production. The renovation of this cluster includes a cafe that connects to the courtyard space, creating an integrated complex. Initially, the courtyard was renovated to provide short-term residencies for artists, but it is now primarily used as long-term studio spaces.

The Plugin units in this courtyard are divided into first and second-floor units. The first floor features plugins with a workspace and a bathroom, while the second-floor plugins serve as bedroom units with open platforms above the first-floor units. Additionally, there are three separate kitchen modules distributed throughout the space. This layout provides a functional and versatile environment for the artists, enhancing the courtyard's usability and maintaining its historical essence.

JINGDEZHEN P-58 PLUGIN HOUSES

LOCATION:
Jingdezhen

RESIDENTS/CLIENTS:
Jingdezhen Ceramic Culture Tourism Group

PROGRAM:
Live/work artist studios

SIZE: 46.3m² (498.4ft²)
COMPLETED: 2022

P-58 is a long courtyard featuring three distinct functional plugin modules: a ground-floor workspace with an integrated bathroom, a second-floor bedroom, and a small platform on top of the workspace. Additionally, there is a communal kitchen module designed to serve the needs of multiple users. This layout ensures that each functional area is optimally utilized, creating a balance between work and living spaces.

The courtyard also includes an untouched three-walled house that serves as an exhibition space, accessible directly from the street side. This preserved structure provides a dedicated area for artists to showcase their work, enhancing the cultural and creative value of the courtyard. As part of the overall Jingdezhen project, the Plugin House offers a reversible renovation method, allowing easy assembly and disassembly. This feature is crucial for preserving the historic value of these properties, as it ensures that any modifications can be undone without damaging the original structures, making it an ideal solution for heritage sites.

The Plugin House also addresses the Jingdezhen climate by providing better insulation for both hot summers and cold winters. The pre-fabricated panels used in the construction offer superior thermal performance, ensuring that the interior spaces remain comfortable year-round. Despite the enhanced insulation, the design maintains a strong connection to the outdoors, allowing most work to be carried out in open-air spaces.

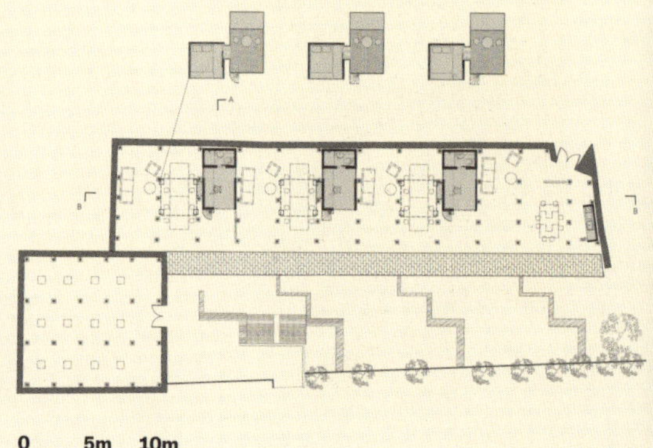

ALAMO PLUGIN DEMO

LOCATION:
Austin, Texas

CLIENT:
AusBos Social Housing

PROGRAM:
House

SIZE: 18.6m^2 (200.2ft^2)
COMPLETED: 2021

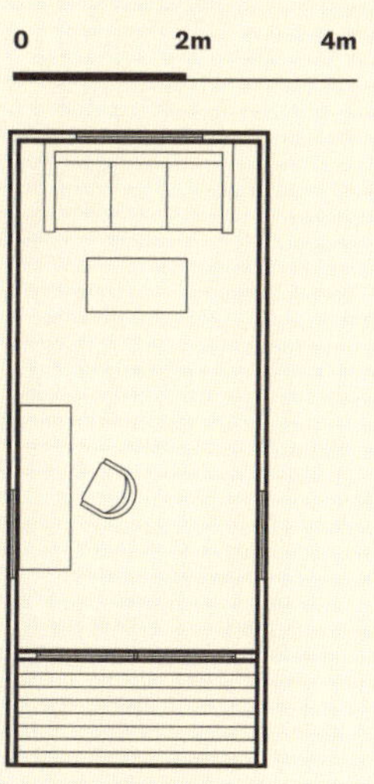

A Plugin House demonstration in the Blackland neighborhood for Austin Design Week in Texas was the debut for the newly formed Plugin House Company. It showcased how easily and quickly a Plugin House can be assembled for use as a backyard ADU.

The demonstration unit is built on a lot owned by the affordable housing initiative, Blackland Community Development Corporation. The lot was split into two, with the vacant portion purchased by AusBos Social Housing, a socially conscious housing developer owned by Plugin House co-founder Anmol Mehra. The proceeds were used to fund affordable housing efforts for the nonprofit. The setup hosted various events with the Plugin House in its bare state to present its appearance during construction to the public. The finished unit is painted a vibrant blue and features an elevated porch, perfect for outdoor relaxation and enjoying the surrounding environment. Inside, the Alamo Plugin Demo is designed with both functionality and comfort in mind. Clerestory windows were incorporated to ensure a bright and airy indoor space, enhancing the natural light throughout the house.

The Alamo Plugin Demo exemplifies what is possible with the Plugin House system, both inside and out. Its design and efficient use of space demonstrate how the Plugin House can be adapted to meet various needs and preferences.

THE BLUE HOUSE PROJECT

LOCATION:
Austin, Texas

RESIDENTS/CLIENTS:
Raasin in the Sun/
AusBos Social Housing

PROGRAM:
Artist studio

SIZE: 18.5m^2 (200.2ft^2)
COMPLETED: 2023

The Blue House Project is an artist residency space in Austin, Texas designed to support and nurture the city's vibrant creative community. The Alamo Plugin Demo was moved to make way for a new larger Plugin House. It was transported as a complete unit by truck to a location in an adjacent neighborhood where the nonprofit art organization, Raasin in the Sun, runs The Blue House Project artist residency.

The Blue House Project is a collaboration between community organizations Raasin in the Sun and Franklin Common. This partnership aimed to address the scarcity and expense of space for artists in Austin. The space now serves as an art residency for short-term periods, offering artists a dedicated environment to focus, create, and showcase their work, addressing the need for affordable and accessible creative spaces in Austin.

The lot will eventually host a large multi-family housing development where the artist residency will be permanently housed. The Plugin House allows for the site to be utilized while the housing development awaits approval.

TOOF FLEX UNIT MODEL A

LOCATION:
Austin, Texas

RESIDENTS/CLIENTS:
The Other Ones Foundation

PROGRAM:
Residence

SIZE: 22m² (236.8ft²)
COMPLETED: 2022

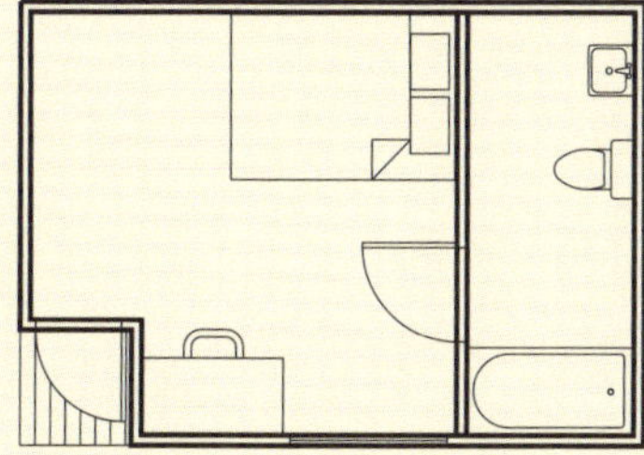

The Plugin House Company provided numerous Plugin Houses for community services and residences for people experiencing homelessness at the Esperanza Community, a non-congregate emergency shelter complex in Austin. Managed by The Other Ones Foundation (TOOF), a nonprofit organization, the Esperanza Community has helped approximately 150 people transition into an engaged community through humanitarian aid, case management, and employment opportunities. The Plugin Houses are part of the first phase of an upgraded complex that will eventually serve 200 to 300 community members on the seven-acre (2.8-hectare) site.

TOOF Flex Unit Model A serves as a residential unit within the community, allowing residents to personalize and make the unit their home. Currently, there are two Model A units. One is built with a full private bathroom as an example of a new type of unit for the community. Additionally, one of the Model A units was borrowed from TOOF and shipped flat to Sacramento for a one-day event organized by the California governor to address homelessness and the state's upcoming initiatives. The speed of assembly and disassembly was demonstrated at the event before it was shipped back to TOOF. The work at TOOF highlights the flexibility and impact of the Plugin House system in providing innovative housing solutions for vulnerable populations.

TOOF FLEX UNIT MODEL B

LOCATION:
Austin, Texas

RESIDENTS/CLIENTS:
The Other Ones Foundation

PROGRAM:
Flex space

SIZE: 21.3m² (229.3ft²)
COMPLETED: 2022

TOOF Flex Unit Model B is a versatile unit that can function either as a single space or as a duplex. Currently, there are two of these units within the compound; they are intended to be used for shared facilities such as libraries and offices for case workers, providing essential services to the community.

Model B, along with other Plugin Houses, adds a vibrant touch of color to the site. These units were constructed by individuals experiencing homelessness from the Esperanza Community and civic association Springdale Park Neighbors. The construction process not only provided much-needed housing but also offered job training and employment opportunities for those who typically lack access to such resources. This initiative highlights the dual benefits of the Plugin House system, addressing both housing and employment needs within the community.

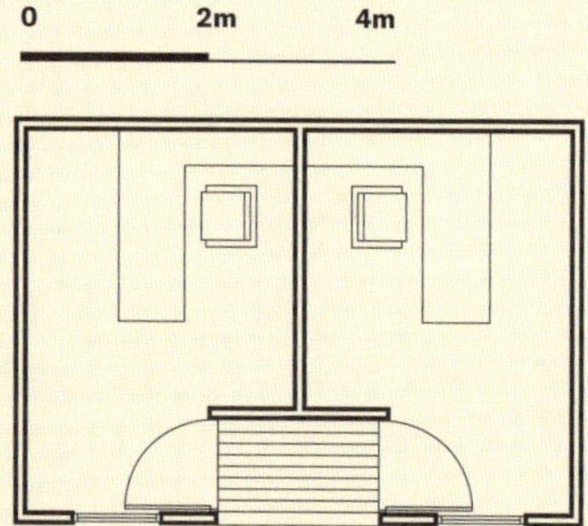

TOOF FLEX UNIT MODEL C

LOCATION:
Austin, Texas

RESIDENTS/CLIENTS:
The Other Ones Foundation

PROGRAM:
Flex space

SIZE: 17.6m² (189.4ft²)
COMPLETED: 2022

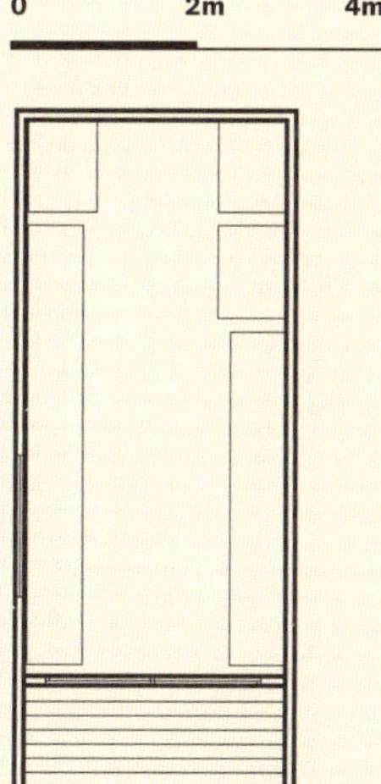

TOOF Flex Unit Model C serves as a vital food distribution hub for the community. There are two of these units located on the TOOF site. The design features a large window on the side that functions as a food counter, making it easy to distribute meals to community members efficiently.

Each Model C unit is situated underneath a large arched structure known as a Quonset Hut, also designed by PAO. These huts provide ample space for community gatherings and events, enhancing the overall utility of the site. The combination of the Quonset Huts and the Model C units creates a dynamic environment that fosters community interaction and support.

TOOF FLEX UNIT MODEL D

LOCATION:
Austin, Texas

RESIDENTS/CLIENTS:
The Other Ones Foundation

PROGRAM:
Flex space

SIZE: 10.4m^2 (112ft^2)
COMPLETED: 2022

TOOF Flex Unit Model D is the smallest Plugin unit designed for the TOOF community, serving as a flexible space for various community services. These compact units are highly efficient, taking one hour to erect and can be quickly completed to meet immediate needs.

The flexibility of Model D allows it to be utilized for a range of purposes, from meeting rooms and counseling spaces to small workshops and storage areas. Its rapid assembly process ensures that the community can adapt and respond swiftly to changing needs and circumstances. Despite its small size, it plays a significant role in supporting the community by providing essential services and space for activities that foster social interaction and support. The design of Model D, along with the other Plugin units, demonstrates a commitment to creating efficient, functional, and adaptable solutions that enhance the quality of life for residents in the TOOF community.

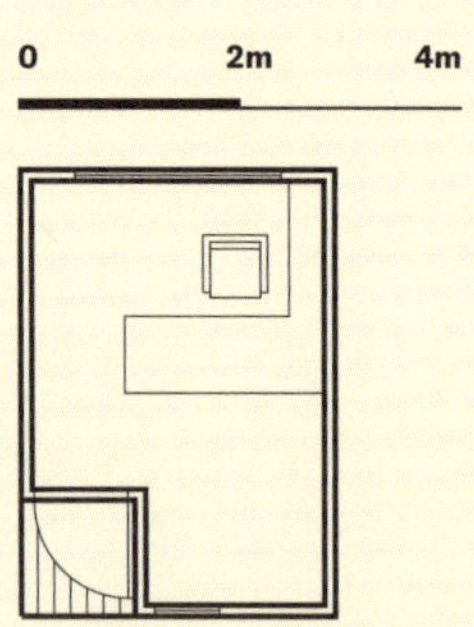

TOOF FLEX UNIT MODEL E

LOCATION:
Austin, Texas

RESIDENTS/CLIENTS:
The Other Ones Foundation

PROGRAM:
Flex space

SIZE: 12.5m² (134.5ft²)
COMPLETED: 2022

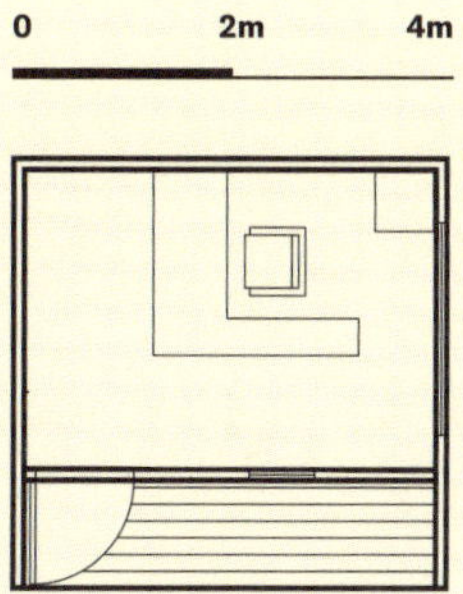

The TOOF Flex Unit Model E is designed as a versatile unit, featuring a shaded porch area that provides shelter from both sun and rain for users and visitors. Its straightforward layout allows for multiple use possibilities, making it adaptable to various community needs.

By offering similar yet distinct spaces, the design fosters a sense of belonging and avoids the uniformity that can make an area feel camp-like and uninviting. Each unit's unique features and configurations encourage individuality while maintaining a cohesive aesthetic across the community.

The shaded porch area of Model E not only provides practical benefits but also serves as a welcoming space for social interaction and community engagement. Residents can gather, relax, and connect with one another, enhancing the overall sense of community.

TOOF PLUGIN SKILLS CENTER

LOCATION:
Austin, Texas

OPERATOR/CLIENTS:
Austin Community College, The Other Ones Foundation

PROGRAM:
Skills center

SIZE: 74m² (796.5ft²)
COMPLETED: 2024

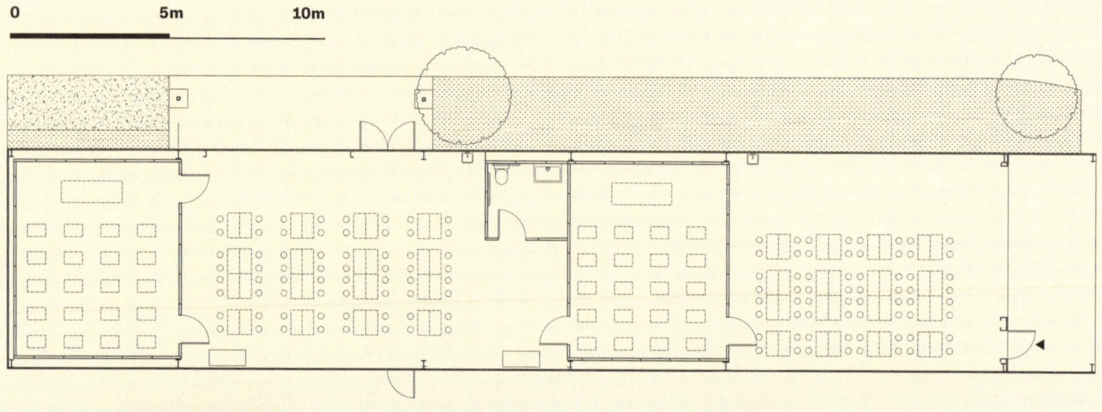

The TOOF Plugin Skills Center is a job training facility that supports residents at TOOF as well as the greater community of Austin, Texas. The facility is run by Austin Community College and is being used to train electricians and future HVAC technicians. Job training is a crucial part of the process of recovering from homelessness.

To keep costs low, the main structure was built as a pre-fabricated metal building with an open interior that is minimally insulated and left without climate control. Given the constantly evolving nature of TOOF's work, it was important to maintain significant flexibility within the space. To accommodate this, two classrooms and a restroom were inserted into the metal structure using the Plugin House system, occupying the interior much like PAO's house-in-house projects. The classrooms are air-conditioned and benefit from excellent insulation, while the rest of the building is used as workshop space.

Having this facility as part of the TOOF community is a significant aid to one of TOOF's core agendas.

PLUGIN TOWER

LOCATION:
Shenzhen

RESIDENTS/CLIENTS:
China Vanke Co., Ltd./LDG Narrative Design

PROGRAM:
Prototype

SIZE: 35m² (377ft²)
COMPLETED: 2016

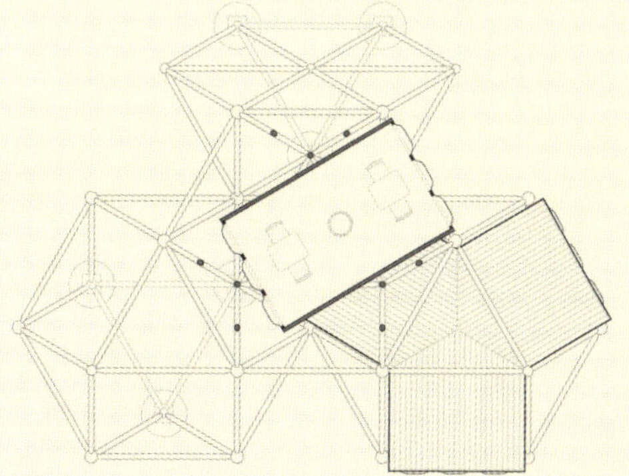

For the real estate developer China Vanke Co., Ltd.'s inaugural design event, which explores a pressing architectural theme each year, PAO was invited to tackle the "future of housing" through an experimental built work. Installed at Vanke's headquarters in Shenzhen, the Plugin Tower addresses the insecurity of private homeownership in China, where land is held exclusively by the government and private homes are typically reserved for the wealthy.

Classified as a temporary structure, the Plugin Tower does not require an underground foundation, thus circumventing the strict planning approval needed for permanent structures and easing the requirements for building a private house. The Plugin Tower also reduces the investment necessary for building a home by mitigating the risk of losing one's property: residents can pack up the structure and relocate it if needed.

A multistory pre-fab system inspired by Metabolist principles, the Plugin Tower comprises a steel space frame and a kit of parts that can be assembled in various configurations. Empty bays within the frame are plugged with living units that can be altered and unplugged as necessary. These units are made with the Plugin panel system. Unlike shipping containers or larger capsule-like units, Plugin panels allow living spaces to be added without heavy machinery and do not confine layouts to a box shape.

The "future of housing" proposed by PAO is essentially a flexible design that adapts to changing needs and fluctuating conditions, suggesting a dynamic solution to the instability of housing in China.

PEOPLE'S STATION

LOCATION:
Yantai

RESIDENTS/CLIENTS:
Yantai Chuangyuan Cultural Media, Ltd.

PROGRAM:
Cultural center

SIZE: 363m² (3,907ft²)
COMPLETED: 2017

The People's Station is a cultural center designed to reinvigorate the Kwan-Yen district of Yantai. Situated just beyond the edge of the business district, the building features large open entryways, semi-outdoor areas, and sections elevated above the ground. This design invites visitors to explore the historic core of the city, creating a nexus of activity and engagement.

The project followed an unusually tight schedule. With the use of the Plugin House system, the People's Station was conceived and built in a total of three months. The building is sited on a space previously used as a parking lot.

The interior of the People's Station boasts a large events hall flooded with natural light from pyramidal clerestory windows. The exhibition space extends upwards and diagonally towards the staggered second and third floors, where visitors can enjoy a lounge, a bookstore, and a cinema. Outdoor terraces on each level offer elevated views of the surrounding historic buildings and the ocean beyond.

On the ground floor, portable appendages can be attached to increase the building's footprint in an accordion-like manner, extending the range of uses for the facility. This flexible design makes the People's Station a vibrant addition to the social fabric of Yantai, actively engaging with its citizens and offering a dynamic space for cultural activities. The building now functions as a restaurant.

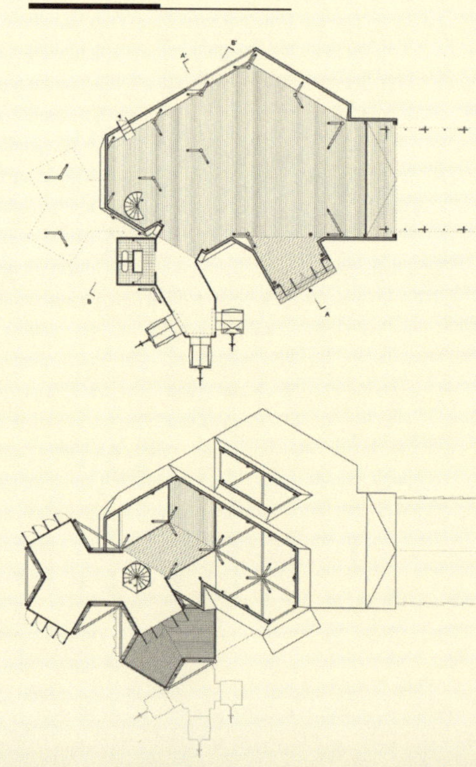

LAKESIDE PLUGIN TOWER

LOCATION:
Changping,
Beijing

RESIDENTS/CLIENTS:
Shenzhen Institute
of Building Research
Co., Ltd.

PROGRAM:
Live/work

SIZE: 480m^2 (5,167ft^2)
COMPLETED: 2017

The Lakeside Plugin Tower is a 480-square-meter (5,167-square-foot) live/work housing prototype developed in partnership with the Shenzhen Institute of Building Research. It is designed for the Xiong'an New Area, a model city being developed by the Chinese government one hundred kilometers (sixty-two miles) south-west of Beijing. Xiong'an aims to be a clean, affordable, and congestion-free alternative to the capital, with all housing subsidized to keep it affordable. The city will use 100% clean electricity, and 10% of the area is protected as permanent farmland.

To minimize its environmental impact, the Lakeside Plugin Tower is built on distributed concrete piers and raised one story above ground to allow stormwater absorption, aligning with China's sponge city concept (a new urban planning model that centers on effective flood management). This elevation also ensures ample sunlight for vegetation across the site. The building is pre-fabricated, reducing costs and construction time. The Plugin panel system used for the building envelope is built separately from the steel structure, allowing for maximum flexibility. Sections of each level can be extended or removed as needed without affecting the rest of the building, enhancing usability and reducing future renovation needs.

Designed using net zero building principles, the tower's roof is covered with solar panels. Full-height operable windows allow for natural ventilation. Each floor is connected to service towers containing vertical circulation and an off-the-grid sewage system for sustainable wastewater treatment.

The Lakeside Plugin Tower envisions housing development where buildings integrate seamlessly into the natural environment with minimal impact, offering a sustainable model for new cities.

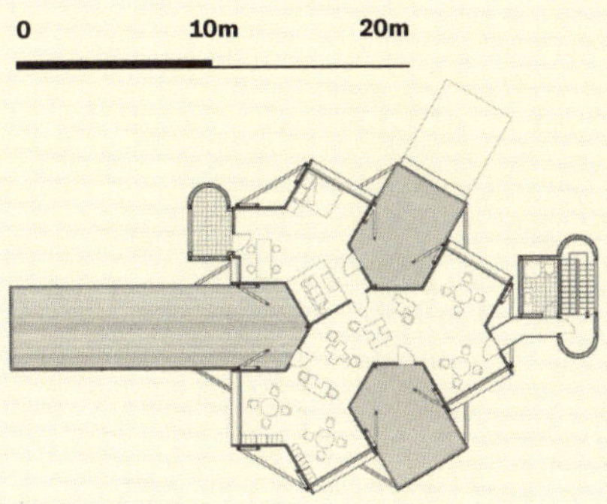

ABOUT THE WRITERS

James Shen is Principal of PAO and Co-founder of the Plugin House Company. He holds a Master of Architecture from the Massachusetts Institute of Technology and a Bachelor of Science in Product Design from California State University, Long Beach. Shen has been a Loeb Fellow at the Harvard Graduate School of Design, a Senior Research Fellow at the Harvard Joint Center for Housing Studies and an Innovation Fellow at MIT's China Future City Lab. He has taught at MIT's School of Architecture and Planning and Harvard's Graduate School of Design.

Zang Feng is Principal of PAO and Co-founder of the Plugin House Company. Originally from Lanzhou, Gansu province, Zang Feng is a registered architect in China. He received his Master of Architecture from the Graduate Center of Architecture, Peking University. He received the Professional Achievement Award for Xicheng District, Beijing, and is a Visiting Professor at the School of Architecture, Tsinghua University.

He Zhe is Principal of PAO and Co-founder of the Plugin House Company. Originally from Jinhua, Zhejiang province, He Zhe is a registered architect in China. He received his Master of Urbanism from the Xi'an University of Architecture and Technology, and is a Visiting Professor at the School of Architecture, Tsinghua University.

People's Architecture Office (PAO)

PAO is an international practice with offices in Los Angeles, Beijing and Shenzhen. Founded in 2010 by James Shen, He Zhe, and Zang Feng, the firm is a multi-disciplinary art and design practice focused on work that fosters social interaction and diverse perspectives. Domus named PAO as one of the world's best architecture firms of 2019 and Fast Company listed PAO as one of the world's ten most innovative architecture companies in 2018. The studio's award-winning works have been exhibited at the Venice Biennale of Architecture, The Milan Triennale, Design Society and the Design Museum, London. In 2020, PAO spun off the Plugin House Company in partnership with Anmol Mehra to develop low-cost pre-fabricated housing as a way to address the housing crises affecting many cities and to support communities experiencing homelessness or displacement.

EDITORS

Anouchka van Driel, Smile Leung

EDITORIAL CONSULTANT

Jennifer Sigler

DESIGN TEAM MEMBERS FOR PLUGIN HOUSE PROJECTS

Smile Leung, Lin Mingkai, Li Zhenghua, Anouchka van Driel, Feng Ziqing, Kong Ming, Sha Jinghai, Chen Yihuai, Sun Liming, Zhang Xiao, Cui Gangjian, Xiang Weixing, Xie Jun, Xu Xi, Jiang Hao, Zhang Minghui, Gao Tianxia, Yuan Yingzi, Zhang Meng, Qi Ji, Yue Wenbo, Yang Quanyue, Hou Yingqi, Wan Yuexiao, Luo Qinming, Yang Qian, Liu Ziwen

ABOUT THE ESSAYISTS

Peter Cook, a founder member of the visionary group Archigram in the early 1960s, revolutionized architectural possibilities with his radical ideas. Although these visions took time to manifest, they culminated in the 2003 opening of the Kunsthaus in Graz, designed with Colin Fournier. Cook became a leading architectural educator in the UK, ran the Institute of Contemporary Arts, and directed Art Net, all while redefining architectural drawing. His influence extended to prominent architects like Zaha Hadid and Rem Koolhaas. As professor at the Bartlett School, UCL, since 1990, he transformed it into a leading center for creative design.

Cao Fei is an internationally renowned Chinese contemporary artist living in Beijing, known for her films and installations that blend social commentary, popular aesthetics, Surrealism, and documentary conventions to reflect the rapid changes in Chinese society. Her works have been featured in numerous international biennales and triennales, including Venice, Shanghai, Moscow, Taipei, Sydney, Istanbul, and Yokohama. Recent major projects include exhibitions at MoMA PS1, Guggenheim Museum, Tai Kwun Contemporary, K21 Düsseldorf, Centre Pompidou, Serpentine Galleries, UCCA Beijing, MAXXI Rome, and Pinacoteca Contemporânea. She is a professor at the Central Academy of Fine Arts in Beijing and has served on various prestigious juries, including the Berlin Biennale and Hugo Boss Asia Art Award, and won the Deutsche Börse Photography Foundation Prize in 2021.

Andrew Freear, from Yorkshire, UK, is the Wiatt Professor and director of Auburn University's Rural Studio in Hale County, west Alabama. For nearly two decades, he has led architecture students in designing and building community structures for under-resourced towns and nonprofits. Notable projects include the forty-acre Lions Park, Akron Boys & Girls Club, and the Newbern Library. Freear has also overseen the creation of the Rural Studio Farm to combat food deserts and severe health issues in rural areas. His students have built over twenty prototypes of the 20K rural house as an affordable housing alternative. Freear has lectured globally and exhibited at prominent venues such as the Whitney Biennial and MoMA in New York. He has received several awards, including The Ralph Erskine Award and the American Academy of Arts and Letters Award in Architecture.

Marina Tabassum, a Bangladeshi architect and educator, founded Marina Tabassum Architects in Dhaka in 2005. Her work emphasizes a contemporary architectural language rooted in climate, context, culture, and history. Notable projects include the Bait Ur Rouf Jame Mosque, known for its minimalist design and multifunctional space. Tabassum is a Professor at Delft University of Technology and has taught at several prestigious institutions. She has received numerous accolades, including the Aga Khan Award for Architecture and the Soane Medal. She chairs the Foundation for Architecture and Community Equity (F.A.C.E) and is a fellow of the Royal Society of Arts (RSA).

Tau Tavengwa is the founder and co-editor of *Cityscapes Magazine*, which explores urban life in Africa, Latin America, and South Asia. He is a 2018 Loeb Fellow at Harvard Graduate School of Design, an LSE Cities Associate at the London School of Economics, and curator-at-large at the African Center for Cities at the University of Cape Town. With a background in architecture and museum design, Tavengwa has spent the last decade focusing on urban issues in the Global South through exhibitions, publications, and events. Notable projects include the 2014 "City Desired" exhibition at the African Center for Cities and contributions to the Rotterdam and Chicago Architecture Biennales. He is also exploring the establishment of a collaboration platform for policymakers, activists, and academics to tackle urban challenges in the Global South.

WORKS CITED

[1] Balakrishnan Rajagopal, "Adequate housing as a component of the right to an adequate standard of living, and on the right to non-discrimination in this context," United Nations, 2023: https://reliefweb.int/attachments/803f6555-7ff5-4cd2-a9e8-4401fb6b1b4e/EN.pdf, accessed 31 Jan. 2025.

[2] Barry Bergdoll, *Home Delivery*, New York, 2008.

[3] C. Theodore Koebel, "Innovation in Homebuilding and the Future of Housing," *Journal of the American Planning Association*, 74 (2008), 45–58.

[4] Camille Viros, Jaebeum Cho, Andrew Lombardi, Nadiam Ahmad, "Confronting the cost-of-living and housing crisis in cities," OECD, 2023: https://www.oecd.org/content/dam/oecd/en/publications/reports/2023/06/confronting-the-cost-of-living-and-housing-crisis-in-cities_b5fa23ba/7a6008af-en.pdf, accessed 31 Jan. 2025.

[5] Casey J. Dawkins, C. Theodore Koebel, Marilyn Cavell, Steve Hullibarger, David B. Hattis, Howard Weissman, "Regulatory Barriers to Manufactured Housing Placement in Urban Communities," United States Department of Housing and Urban Development, 2011: https://papers.ssrn.com/sol3/papers.cfm?abstract_id=1808904, accessed 31 Jan. 2025.

[6] Christopher Herbert, Chadwick Reed, James Shen, "Comparison of the Costs of Manufactured and Site-Built Housing," Harvard Joint Center for Housing Studies, 2023: https://www.jchs.harvard.edu/sites/default/files/research/files/harvard_jchs_pew_report_1_updated_0.pdf, accessed 31 Jan. 2025.

[7] Emmanuel Saez, "Striking it Richer: The Evolution of Top Incomes in the United States (Updated with 2022 estimates)," University of California, Department of Economics, 2024: https://eml.berkeley.edu/~saez/saez-UStopincomes-2022.pdf, accessed 31 Jan. 2025.

[8] Fumihiko Maki, *Investigations in Collective Form,* Washington, 1964: 8.

[9] Jake Wegman, "Research Notes: The Hidden Cityscapes of Informal Housing in Suburban Los Angeles and the Paradox of Horizontal Density," *Buildings & Landscapes*, 22: 2, (2014), 89–110.

[10] Li Shi, "Recent changes in income inequality in China," *World Science Report 2016*, UNESCO, 2016: https://en.unesco.org/inclusivepolicylab/sites/default/files/analytics/document/2019/4/wssr_2016_chap_15.pdf, accessed 31 Jan. 2025.

[11] NAHB Research Center, "Factory and Site Building Housing—A Comparison for the 21st Century," US Department of Housing and Urban Development, Office of Policy Development and Research, Washington, DC, 1998.

[12] Ole Bouman, "Unsolicited, or: The New Autonomy of Architecture," *Volume* (Apr. 2007): https://archis.org/volume/unsolicited-or-the-new-autonomy-of-architecture/, accessed 25 Mar. 2025.

[13] Reyner Banham, *Megastructure: Urban Futures of the Recent Past*, London, 1976.

[14] Ryan E. Smith, *Prefab Architecture: A Guide to Modular Design and Construction*, Hoboken, 2011.

[15] Sam LaTronica, "Smaller, Faster, and Creative: Innovations in Affordable Single-Family Home Construction," Joint Center for Housing Studies of Harvard University, Nov. 2016: https://www.jchs.harvard.edu/sites/default/files/media/imp/harvard_jchs_smaller_faster_creative_latronica_2016.pdf, accessed 18 Mar. 2025.

[16] Scott Hassell, Anny Wong, Ari Houser, Debra Knopman, Mark Bernstein, *Building Better Homes: Government Strategies for Promoting Innovation in Housing*, RAND Corporation, 2003: https://www.rand.org/content/dam/rand/pubs/monograph_reports/2005/MR1658.pdf, accessed 31 Jan. 2025.

[17] Steven Winter Associates, Inc., "A Community Guide to Factory-Built Housing," US Department of Housing and Urban Development, 2001: https://www.huduser.gov/publications/pdf/factbuilt.pdf, accessed 31 Jan. 2025.

[18] Thomas Piketty, Li Yang, Gabriel Zucman, "The Rise of Wealth, Private Property, and Income Inequality in China," Stanford Center on China's Economy and Institutions, 2019, updated 2023: https://fsi9-prod.s3.us-west-1.amazonaws.com/s3fs-public/2023-08/rising_inequality_1978-2015_8.1.23.pdf, accessed 31 Jan. 2025.

PICTURE CREDITS

t = top; b = bottom; c = center; l = left; r = right

pp. 1, 2, 10–13, 14b, 16 PAO; 17 © Edward Burtynsky, courtesy Flowers Gallery, London/Nicholas Metivier Gallery, Toronto; 18, 19 Sun Haiting; 20–36, 37r PAO; 37l, 38–43, 44l First published in the 50th Venice Art Biennale exhibition publication by Ou Ning and Cao Fei in association with U-thèque members (eds.), The San Yuan Li Project (Guangzhou: U-thèque Organization, 2003); 44r, 45–61 PAO; 64t © CORBIS/Corbis via Getty Images; 64b E+/Getty Images; 65 *Audels Carpenters And Builders Guide #3; A Practical Illustrated Trade Assistant on Modern Construction*, by Graham, Frank D. and Thomas J. Emery, 1923; 66 Thomas Edison National Historical Park; 67t Sears Modern Homes; 67b The Image Bank Unreleased/Getty Images; 68–9 Médiathèque Terra - Ministère de l'Aménagement du territoire et de la Décentralisation; 69–71 Photo President and Fellows of Harvard College; 71 Photo President and Fellows of Harvard College © DACS 2026; 72–89 PAO; 90–91 © Jorge Taboada; 94, 95, 96t, 96bl Timothy Hursley; 96br Rural Studio; 97 Timothy Hursley; 98t Keith Isaacs; 98b Danny Wicke; 103 PAO; 104 JiaRong presentation; 105 PAO; 106 Beijing Design Week; 107 Sans Practice; 108–129 PAO; 130–131, 132b Maggie Janik; 132a PAO; 133, 280t Christopher Abrams; 134–136 PAO; 137t Asif Salman; 138b City Syntax; 138t Afsary Islam Toma; 138b, 140b Asif Salman; 140l, 140r, 142r City Syntax; 142l Asif Salman; 143 Marina Tabussam; 144l, 144b Asif Salman; 144r City Syntax; 145–181 PAO; 182, 183t Archigram; 183b, 184 PAO; 185–188 Peter Cook; 192–210 PAO; 211 Jake Wegmann; 212t Flickr/Daniel Lobo; 212b PAO; 214 Raasin in the Sun; 215, 216t, 216br Plugin House Company; 216c, 216bl Raaisin in the Sun; 218–226 Plugin House Company; 227 Shutterstock/MDV Edwards; 228, 229, 230r PAO; 230l Alexia Webster, courtesy of *Cityscapes* magazine; 232, 236t, 236bl PAO; 236br, 239t Plugin House Company; 239b PAO; 240 Plugin House Company; 242–247 PAO; 249t yoneyan/PIXTA; 249b Archigram; 250 © Tomio Ohashi; 250–1 Keystone Press/Alamy Stock Photo; 252–297 PAO

ACKNOWLEDGMENTS

We'd like to thank the early supporters of our Plugin House work, including Beatrice Leanza, Jia Rong, Huang Weiwen, Chen Xue, Ouning, Liu Kecheng, Xu Yijing, Neil Geddes, Ole Bauman, Smile Leung, Jaff Shen, John Peterson, Marcy Osberg, Anmol Mehra, Chris Baker, Matt Arnold, Lauren Welker, Lung Chi Chang, and James Pekele. We are especially grateful to Huang Danhua, Zhu Minjie, and Sherrie Qin, who have been our partners in manufacturing Plugin Houses over a decade. We also thank our earliest Plugin House residents: Wang Pengcheng, Li Zhe, Zhao Zhongyuan, Fan Ke, Dong Da Ma, and Sun Shifu.

With heartfelt thanks to Jennifer Tran, Cao Lu, and Zhu Mufeng, whose presence and support have sustained us through every step of this work. We are deeply grateful to our families, whose love, patience, and encouragement made this work possible.

Special thanks to Anouchka van Driel and Jennifer Sigler, who were there from the very beginning and instrumental in conceiving this book, and to our publishing team—Augusta Pownall, Frank Gallaugher, Helen Fanthorpe, Anna Watson, Lucas Dietrich and Kate Thomas—for their guidance and care in bringing it to life.

INDEX

Page numbers in *italics* refer to illustrations

On the front cover: Fang Family Plugin House in Shangwei, Shenzhen, China. Photo and drawing by PAO. On the back cover: Top: Huang Family Plugin House in Shangwei, Shenzhen, China by PAO; Center: Plugin House demonstration built by students at Harvard University. Photo by Maggie Janik; Bottom: Drawing by PAO.

First published in the United Kingdom in 2026 by Thames & Hudson Ltd, 6–24 Britannia Street, London WC1X 9JD

First published in the United States of America in 2026 by Thames & Hudson Inc., 500 Fifth Avenue, New York, New York 10110

For full picture credits, see page 301

Interior design by LMNOP
Cover design by Steve O Connell

EU Authorized Representative: Interart S.A.R.L.
19 rue Charles Auray, 93500 Pantin, Paris, France
productsafety@thameshudson.co.uk
interart.fr

A CIP catalogue record for this book is available from the British Library

Library of Congress Control Number 2025940307

ISBN 978-0-500-02758-5
01

Printed in China by RR Donnelley